מסורה

ArtScroll Halachah Series®

Rabbi Nosson Scherman / Rabbi Meir Zlotowitz

General Editors

Business
Published by
Mesorah Publications, ltd

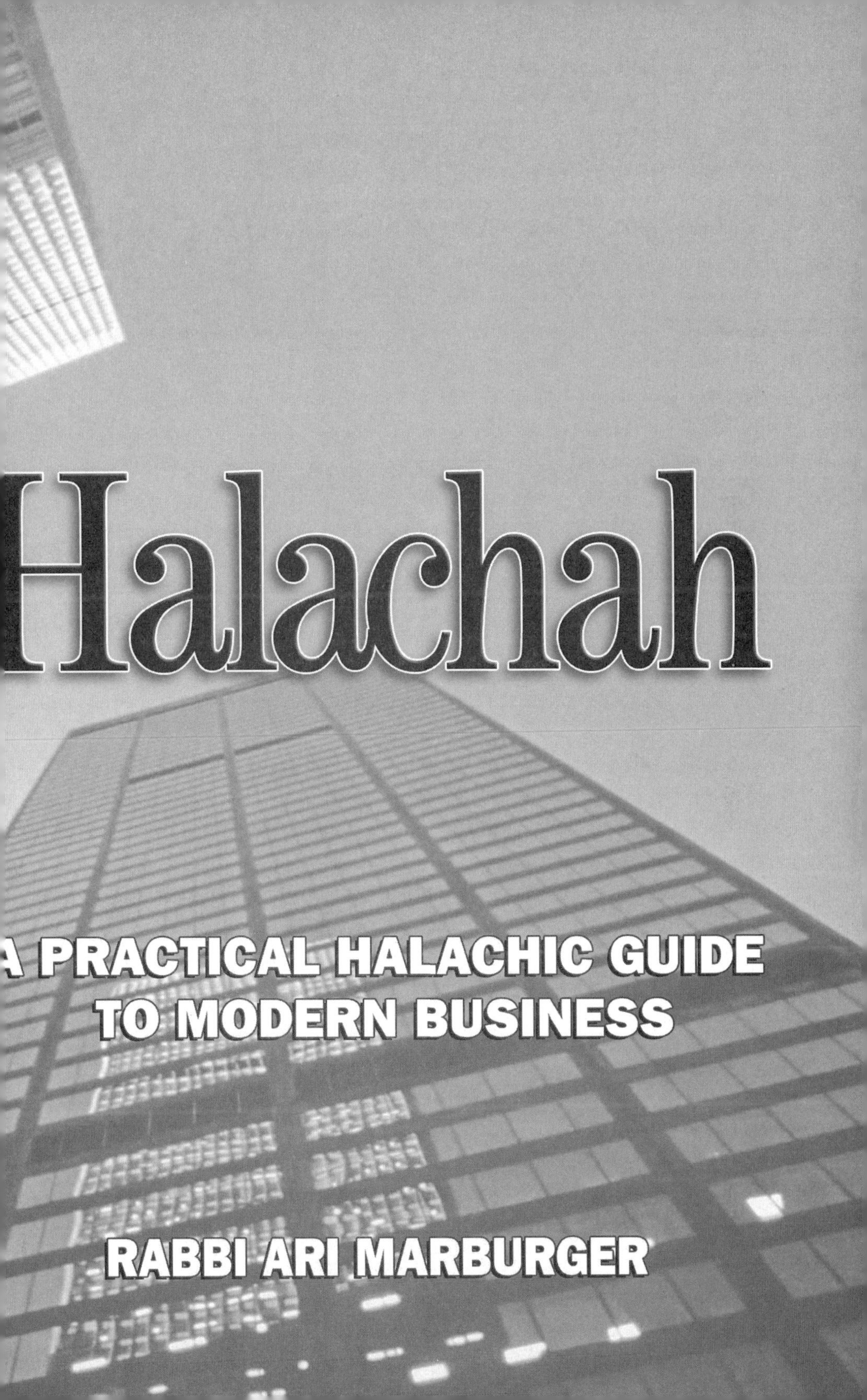
Halachah
A PRACTICAL HALACHIC GUIDE
TO MODERN BUSINESS
RABBI ARI MARBURGER

FIRST EDITION
First Impression ... January 2008

Published and Distributed by
MESORAH PUBLICATIONS, LTD.
4401 Second Avenue / Brooklyn, N.Y 11232

Distributed in Europe by
LEHMANNS
Unit E, Viking Business Park
Rolling Mill Road
Jarow, Tyne & Wear, NE32 3DP
England

Distributed in Australia and New Zealand by
GOLDS WORLDS OF JUDAICA
3-13 William Street
Balaclava, Melbourne 3183
Victoria, Australia

Distributed in Israel by
SIFRIATI / A. GITLER — BOOKS
6 Hayarkon Street
Bnei Brak 51127

Distributed in South Africa by
KOLLEL BOOKSHOP
Ivy Common
105 William Road
Norwood 2192, Johannesburg, South Africa

ARTSCROLL HALACHAH SERIES®
BUSINESS HALACHAH

ISBN:
ISBN 10: 1-4226-0547-7 / ISBN 13: 978-1-4226-0547-9

Typography by CompuScribe at ArtScroll Studios, Ltd.

Printed in the United States of America by Noble Book Press Corp.
Bound by Sefercraft, Quality Bookbinders, Ltd., Brooklyn N.Y. 11232

לזכר נשמת איש המעש והישר

שלמה בן משה ע״ה

In Memoriam

Bert Marburger ע״ה

His unassuming manner in performing Chesed
and commitment to Emes in a world of compromise
truly exemplify the words of the prophet —

ומה ה׳ דורש ממך כי אם עשות משפט ואהבת חסד והצנע לכת עם אלוקיך:
(מיכה ו:ח)

ולזכר נשמת אשתו החשובה בעלת החסד

געלא בת מנחם הכהן ע״ה

Gerta Marburger ע״ה

Who was a true partner to her husband in their
life-long dedication to Torah and Tzedakah

Dedicated in Honor of
Our Dear Parents

Arthur and Alice Stern שיחיו

עוסקים בצרכי ציבור באמונה

Paragons of

חסד, ערליכקייט, ישרות, וצדקה

Role models for our family and all of כלל ישראל

״הולך תמים ופעל צדק ודובר אמת בלבבו״

לזכר נשמת

ר׳ חיים צבי וויינבערגער ז״ל

ויבלח״ט לכבוד ריעתו

מרת רויזא בת ר׳ גדלי׳ תחיי

לזכר נשמת

ר׳ יחזקאל צבי ב״ר יצחק שווארצבוים ז״ל

ורעיתו

מרת אלטא זלאטא פערל בת ר׳ יעקב ע״ה

They lost their families in the Holocaust.
With siyata d'Shemaya, emunah and a total dedication
to the values of the generations that preceded them,
they were zoche to build true Torah homes and
raise families that are a credit to Klal Yisrael.

יוסף שלו׳ אלישיב

ירושלים

בס״ד, ו׳ מרחשון תשס״ח

הובא קמיה מרן עט״ר הגרי״ש אלישיב שליט״א ספרו של הרה״ג רא״ש מארבורגר שליט״א מליקוואוד שרחש לבו ללמד את אחב״י לעשות צדקה ומשפט ולבן ליבן את ההלכות השכיחות בעניני מסחר (רבית וחו״מ) ואף הוסיף תירגום הדברים לשפה המדוברת במקומם.

כבר באו בשבח הספר הרבנים הגאונים יושבי על מדין — כי הכל עשת בטוטו״ד ביגיעת וחכמת התורה.

ובירכו מרן שליט״א, כי חפץ השי״ת בידו יצלח לשקוד באהלי תורה ולאפוקי שמעתתא להתחיל ספרים אחרים ולסיימם להגדיל תורה ולהאדירה.

הכו״ח בהוראת מרן עט״ר שליט״א

יוסף י. א. אפרתי

בע״ה

RABBI ARYEH MALKIEL KOTLER
BETH MEDRASH GOVOHA
LAKEWOOD, N.J. 08701

ארי׳ מלכיאל קוטלר
בית מדרש גבוה
לייקוואוד, נ. דז.

כ״ט תשרי תשס״ב

באורח צדקה אהלך בתוך נתיבות משפט (משלי ח׳ כ׳) ופי׳ הגר״א צדקה יותר משפט וגם משפט אין צדקה (עי׳ סנהדרין ו׳) וז״ל הגמ׳ פ׳ השוכר (ב״מ פ״ג ע״א) רבה בר בר חנה תברו ליה הנהו שקולאי חביתא דחמרא, שקל לגלימייהו אתו אמרו ליה לרב אמר ליה הב להו גלימייהו אמר ליה דינא הכי אמר ליה אין למען תלך בדרך טובים (משלי ב׳) יהב להו גלימייהו אמרו ליה עניי אנן וטרחינן כולה יומא וכפינן ולית לן מידי אמר ליה זיל הב אגרייהו אמר ליה דינא הכי אמר ליה אין וארחות צדיקים תשמור (שם) ע״כ הרי דנתיבות ודרך המשפט מוסיף כולל בתוכו אורח של צדקה ומשפטי התורה הם חוקים ומשפטים צדיקים ואורח של צדיקים, וכן מבואר בדברי חז״ל שכל הלימוד חי של הדין הוא אורח הדרך ונתיב שצריך לעסוק בהם להטות ימין ושמאל ועל משפטי צדקים להיות מודיע ונזהרים על מאזני המשפט עד שנעשה דרך החיים, ושולחן ערוך של הלימוד רצון התורה,

אשרינו נמצא, לראות ידידי הרב הגאון ר׳ אריה מרבורגר שליט״א מחשובי הלומדים והאחד פה בבית מדרש גבוה אשר שם לילות כימים בלימוד התורה בעיון הסוגיות לעומקם והיקפם. ולהוסיף שמעתא אליבא דהלכתא, ומשנתו מופיע לאור ספר יקר ונחמד בספר המלוכנת בעניני חושן משפט מורה דרך באורחותיה במשפט בחיי יום יום ובפרט לאנשי עסקים שיש עלבן בארח זו בלא לימוד ההלכות והרחבה והתמדת הדרך הרי הוא כמו יטה מן הנתיב ויפלו כסומא באפלה. על כן דברי יה״ט. ספר זה תועלת מרובה ללומדים ומעיינים ויהי שיתקבלו דבריו ויהנו ממנו רבים יפוצו מעיינותיו עוד יזכה לחבר ולהוציא כהנה וכהנה להגדיל תורה ולהאדירה

אריה מלכיאל קוטלר
בית מדרש גבוה לייקוואוד

LETTERS OF APPROBATION • הסכמות ומכתבי ברכה

מכון לחושן משפט

MACHON
L'choshen Mishpat

MACHON L'CHOSHEN MISHPAT

Tel: 877-MISHPAT (647-4728) • Fax: 206-337-0730
1937 Ocean Avenue, Brooklyn, NY, 11230 • info@choshenmishpat.org

בס"ד

ב"ה

יום ל' אדר תשס"ז

בחפץ לב הנני בא בשבחו של הרה"ג הנעלה, ברוך הכשרון, אברך כפשוטו וכמדרשו, הרב ר' ארי מרבורגר שליט"א מחשובי הלומדים בעי"ת לייקווד יע"א ודיין מצויין בבית דין מישרים דשם, וספרו שחיבר על עניני חושן משפט.

להגיד נחיצות ספרו היקר על עניני חושן משפט למעשה, הוא אך למותר, אכן ייחודיות הספר הוא שמדריך את הלומד להתנהג על פי דין תורה בסוגי המסחר הנהוגים היום. כדי להקל הקורא כתב הרב הנ"ל את ספרו בלשון המדוברת בסדר נפלא וכדי שלא יהיה כספר החתום, כתב בהערות המקורות לכל דין בקיצור נמרץ ומדוייק.

וכדי שלא יחסר המזג, דרוש דרש במקומות הנחוצים, את חוקי ומנהג המדינה, לדוגמא בדינים הנוגעים לכתיבת חוזים (קאנטראקט) כתב את הדברים הצריכים תיקון שיהיה נעשה כדין תורה. ובזה בודאי עשה מצוה גדולה, כי מלבד שיש בספר תועלת בלימוד המביא לידי מעשה, עוד יותר נעשה בזה מצות השבת אבדה למנוע הפסד ממון ועגמת נפש.

ואינני בא בזה כשר המסכים, כאשר משרה זו ממני והלאה, אלא הנני נמנה להיות שותף לדבר מצוה, לחזק את ידי הרב הנ"ל שיצליח בפעלו להרבות הלימוד והידיעה במקצוע שאדם אוכל פירותיהם בעולם הזה והקרן קיימת לו לעולם הבא.

המברך מקרב הלב
חיים קאהן

מנחם מנדל הכהן שפרן

בס"ד

ער"ח שבט תשס"ז

משה רבנו באר התורה בשבעים לשון ובמשך כל הדורות חיברו ספרים בלשון המדוברת בפי העם ומי לנו גדול מהרמב"ם שחיבר פי' המשניות וספר המצות ומורה נבוכים בלשון ערבי וכן רבנו בחיי את ספר חובת הלבבות וכן גדולי ישראל באשכנז חיברו עבור ההמונים ספרים ופירשו חומש ורש"י, משניות ועין יעקב בלשון אשכנז אידיש המדוברת. דבר חשוב עשה הרה"ג ארי' מארבורגר שליט"א מלייקווד שחיבר בלשון אנגלית ספר הבא לבאר ולהזהיר עניני הזהירות בממון שאינם ידועים להמון ולסוחרים כמו עני המהפך בחררה, מחוסר אמנה, בר מצרא, אונאה ומק"ט, רבית והיתר עיסקא, עובד ומעביד, שוכר ומשכיר, פרשאות ודין תורה ופשרה, ראשי הפרקים גדולים של הספר והוא בא במדה ומשקל נכון לעורר על הנקודות שיש בהם שאלה [ולא הוי כעורכי הדיינין שמלמדין איך לרמות]. הספר בודאי יוסיף הזהרת הזהירות בה"י במצוות ה' וירבה הדעת וקיום ההלכה למעשה בחיי היום יום.

אשר זעליג וייס
כגן 8
פעיה"ק ירושלם ת"ו

בס"ד

תאריך י"ג כסלו ס"ט

הן ראיתי את ספרו הנפלא של הרב הגאון המצוי"ן דיין מומחה הורה נאמנה של בלננו, הרב צבי מארבורגר שליט"א. הנני, ושמחתי אל נכון, שהרי זה הספר צורך השעה הוא, לבאר בלשונו שפוקתו סוגיות עמוקות ולהציגן מוכן בשפה ברורה ונעימה בשפת האנגלית המדוברת. ניכר עמל המחבר שליט"א בעומק העיון, בבהירות, בסדר נכון וברור טעם ודעת.

ניכר שהמחבר עמל בזה ונזכיתי להכיר את גדלו בתורה בהיותו יושב לפני בבית הדין בהוראה עיה"ק, וראיתי עיקר הרב נאמן לו בכל באמת בתורה אשר באנר.

ברכתי למהר"ג שליט"א שיתקבלו דבריו ברצון באהלי של היכלי התורה, ויזכה להגדיל תורה ולהאדירה בשמחה שלוה ונחת.

בברכה רבה
ומוקירו בהוראתו

אשר זעליג וייס
ריש מתיבתא להוראה "מנחת אשר"
אב"ד "דרכי הוראה" ירושלים

בס"ד

BETH MEDRASH GOVOHA — בית • מדרש • גבוה

LAKEWOOD

כאשר ידידי הרב הגאון ר' ארי' מרברגר שליט"א נשא לבו לזכות את הרבים ועוד מתוך עמל יגיעה שלחן מלא טוב בעניני מקח וממכר ללמד דרכי תורה והנהגות הלכות אלו אשר הנוגעות לרבים. ואשר מצוי לרוב בימינו העוסקים במו"מ ויורד לעומקה של הלכה. ובכשרון רב זכה להבהיר ולסדר את הדברים מסודרים וערוכים. אשר נתלבנו מתוך פלפול ובדוק הדברים. ואם כי דברים עמוקים כים וקצת שנוי קל ישתנה הדין אמנם בכללי ההלכות והמסתעף ימצאו המעיינים הדרך מוכן לפניהם.

הכו"ח לכבוד התורה
לומדי' ועמלי'
והושע קרופע

RABBI AARON KOTLER INSTITUTE FOR ADVANCED LEARNING • בית מדרשו של רבנו הגאון רבי אהרן קוטלר זצוק"ל

617 SIXTH STREET, LAKEWOOD, NJ 08701 TEL (732) 367-1060 FAX (732) 367-7487

Letters of Approbation • הסכמות ומכתבי ברכה

RABBINICAL COURT
MAYSHARIM
GUIDED BY RABBI NISSIM KARELITZ
BAIS DIN TZEDEK OF BNEI BRAK

בית דין צדק
מישרים
בהכוונת בית דין צדק - בני ברק
בראשות מרן הגאון **רבי נסים קרליץ** שליט"א

בס"ד

כ"ז יום לחדש שבט תשס"ז לפ"ק

ענוותו של ידידי היקר והנכבד הרב הגאון מוה"ר ארי שמעון מארבורגר שליט"א תרבני, בדרישתו כי אבוא בדברי הסכמה על ספרו הנוכחי "ביזנס הלכה" הערוך בשפה האנגלית, השגורה יותר בפי קהל הקוראים שלמענו נתחבר במחשבה תחילה.

ובכן, לא אמנע הטוב מבעליו, ומקצת שבחו ייאמר בפניו, כי ביודעי ומכירי קאמינא, אשר במשך השנים שעשינו יחד בלימוד מילי דנזיקין, וביותר בתקופה הנכבדה מאז, כד הוי יתיבנא בצוותא במותב תלתא זימנין טובא, אנא סהדא דאיתמחי גברא עד מאוד במשנתו הסדורה בהאי הילכתא רבתא, ונפלאתי לחזות מקרוב במומחיותו המיוחדת לרדת לעומקא דדינא, לאסוקי שמעתתא ולהגיע לחקר דין אמת לאמיתו מתוך כשרון של התמצאות מושלמת בפרטי הדו"ד המובאים בפני הבי"ד.

ואכן, מתוך עסקו התדיר בדיני דממונא שבנ"א דשים עליהם בעקבם באין-יודעין, נתעורר הרב הנ"ל שליט"א בכוונה טהורה לחבר ספר כללי בשפה המדוברת, על-מנת להעיר תשומת לב הרבים להילכתא גבירתא והררי-הררים של מכשולות חמורות התלויים לפעמים אף בשערה אחת של עסקי משא-ומתן. ואם בכל דבר הלכה תמיד יש להעיר לעורר, לפקוח עין ולהזהיר הגדולים על הקטנים – וכפי שנהגו גדולי עולם זצ"ל לעמוד על המשמר ולהודיע לעם חוקי האלוקים ותורותיו – כמה יותר נחוץ כן בכל הנוגע לחלק חו"מ שבשו"ע, שבו אין ביד כל אדם "מסורת-אבות" של מנהג והנהגה, דרך ואורח-מישרים, ושלא כבהלכות שבחלקי או"ח ויו"ד שהרבה מהם כבר מושרשים בקרב הציבור ע"פ מה שראו בקודמיהם.

ואנא סהדא גם אהא דאיתמחי קמיעא, באשר בעוברי על חלק נכבד מהספר הנוכחי נוכחתי על עריכתו בטוטו"ד, כי מיד ה' על המחבר השכיל לפרוס ביריעתו המצומצמת מערכה נכבדה של ידיעות נרחבות בתחומים הנוגעים ביותר לחיי המעשה, באופן שהקורא ילמד להבחין ולדקדק בשאלות ובספיקות ההלכתיות השונות הכרוכות במצבים ועסקים שונים – מה שלא עלה על דעתו עד האידנא. וא"כ מה נשגב פעלו של המחבר הדגול לסקל המסילה ולהרים מכשול מדרך הרבים אשר ייאותו לאורו, ואשר בזכותם לא יבוא חטא על ידו, כמאמרם ז"ל (יומא פז.).

ועל כגון דא שנינו (תנחומא משפטים ה וכעי"ז במ"ר): "רבי אליעזר אומר, אם יש דין למטן אין דין למעלן, אם אין דין למטן יש דין למעלן. כיצד, אם יעשו התחתונים את הדין מלמטה, אין הדין נעשה מלמעלן. לפיכך אמר הקב"ה, שמרו את המשפט, שלא תגרמו לי לעשות משפט מלמעלן, שנאמר ואלה המשפטים". ובכן נוחיל נא למרום, כי חלקו של הספר דנן יהא שמור בהפיכת מידת הדין לרחמים, עד כי יגולו רחמיו ית' עלינו לגאלנו בדבר ישועה ורחמים, בב"א.

בברכה אהבה ואחווה למחבר הדגול שליט"א, שיזכה להוסיף אומץ ולהרבות חיל באסוקי שמעתתא אליבא דהלכתא, להקים עדות ביעקב ולהשים תורה בישראל, מתוך בריות גופא ונהורא מעליא, הנני ידידו השמח בגדולתו באמת ובתמים,

יששכר דוב הכהן כהנא

יששכר דוב הכהן כהנא
אב"ד בי"ד מישרים, ליקוואוד יצ"ו

Office & Mailing Address: 625 Forest Avenue, Lakewood, N.J. 08701 • **Telephone:** 732.905.3388 • **Fax:** 732.905.5880

Rabbinical Courtrooms: 625 Forest Avenue, Lakewood, N.J. (Rear Entrance) **:לשכות הבד"צ**
2913 Avenue L, Brooklyn, N.Y. (Lower Level)

Contents

Management

Real Estate

Appendices

Business
Halachah

Introduction

Over the past years, there has been an explosion of knowledge of practical halachah. Topics and their applicable halachos that were virtually unheard of years ago are today widely known and discussed. Yet, one vital area of halachah has been largely neglected. The laws of halachically-appropriate behavior in the marketplace remain a mystery to most people.

There are numerous reasons for this phenomenon. People often view these laws as just a matter of business ethics, believing that the halachos reflect simple concepts of honesty, respecting other people's rights, and not stealing. As long as a person acts honorably, the assumption is that he should have no concern about halachah, and no need to question his actions. This perception reduces *Devar Hashem,* a complex system of Divine halachah, to a simplistic collection of self-evident clichés.

People would never dream that they could rely on their intuition to decide what should be kosher without learning the appropriate laws in *Yoreh Deah*. No one would have the audacity to presume that he could guess what Hashem would consider kosher. Yet, we are often completely uninhibited in our business decisions. We unilaterally decide what the appropriate behavior is for a Torah-true Jew, and we do not even feel the need to inquire about or confirm our decisions. This is because we do not view it as a matter of Halachah; we tend to view it simply as a matter of doing what is ethical. We all believe that we have a strong sense of integrity. We believe that we can trust our intuition to do what is right, and that we have a strong sense of *yashrus* (fairness) even without a background in halachah.

This is a fundamental mistake.

In reality, *Choshen Mishpat* and *hilchos ribbis* are among the most complex areas of halachah. They are just as detailed, just as specific, and just as vital as other sections of *Shulchan Aruch.* And these laws are not intuitive to modern man. The Torah's concept of honest business practices is often at odds with the values reflected in today's business environment. *Ehrlichkeit,* integrity, and honesty are characteristics that have defined the Jew for generations, but are today under constant attack. This makes learning these concepts all the more important. Yet, these areas of halachah are not accessible to most people. The laws are numerous and complex. Even after one masters the halachos, applying them to modern scenarios is difficult, since many situations that are common today are simply not specifically discussed in earlier *teshuvos* (responsa).

The purpose of this work is to make these halachos accessible, to explain their underlying concepts and their application to modern-day scenarios. This is not intended to be an exhaustive work, nor is it intended to serve as a collection of *piskei halachah.* Rather it is intended to serve as a guide — to introduce the basic concepts of halachah and to offer practical guidance on how to keep one's business dealings kosher.

Accordingly, the work is divided into two sections. The main text is a compilation of various halachos that commonly occur in business situations. In general, I have concentrated on areas of halachah that relate to *issur v'hetter,* how to avoid violating the many mitzvos and prohibitions regarding financial matters. Issues related to *t'oein v'nitan,* how to resolve financial disputes, are not included in this work.

The footnotes contain sources for the main text, along with comments, additional sources, and references. In order to make it easier for those who wish to research the halachos, I have quoted primarily from *Shulchan Aruch,* rather than from earlier sources. The footnotes include additional halachos that are cited for their *chiddushim* (novellae), even if they are not applicable in practice.

Unlike the laws of Shabbos, kashrus or other topics in *Orach Chaim* and *Yoreh Deah,* business law is one area of halachah in which even one who is knowledgable may not unilaterally make his own decisions. Regardless of how knowledgable, fair, and honest a person may be, he does not have the right to unilaterally impose his view or understanding of business halachah on others. In the event of any dispute, the matter must be brought to an impartial halachic authority acceptable to all parties for a decision.

Accordingly, this work is intended to raise awareness of halachah rather than to serve as a source definitive *psak.* Every actual dispute must be brought to a mutually acceptable Rav, and one should never attempt to *pasken* (issue a verdict) based on this book.

Acknowledgments

This work is a part of **Machon L'Choshen Mishpat's** efforts to raise awareness of *Choshen Mishpat* issues and to help people apply these halachos to their daily lives. I have had the privilege of working with Harav Chaim Kohn on this project. His dedication to the ideals of the Machon, his tireless efforts in disseminating halachah through his network of Etz Chaim Kollelim, and his involvement in the seminars, *shiurim*, and business reviews of the Machon, has been a true inspiration. I am truly grateful for the opportunity to have a close relationship with such an outstanding *dayan*. May he be *zocheh* to continue his work of *harbatzas haTorah*.

A special thank you to the board of Machon L'Choshen Mishpat: **Leibel Burger**, **Zvi Feiner**, **Shimon Glick**, **Moshe Hartstein**, **Yossi Kazarnovsky**, **Shmuel Reider**, **David Retter**, and **Gedalia Weinberger**, and for their support and encouragement for our projects.

This work is a reflection of our entire *chaburah*. My role was simply to be the scribe, to record the wisdom of others. Our *chaburah* has been privileged to be graced by the leadership of **Hagoan Harav Yehoshua Krupenia**, Rosh Kollel of Bais Medrash

Govoha. The breadth and depth of his learning, and his ongoing leadership, is greatly appreciated by the entire group .

I have been privileged to be part of Beis Din Maysharim of Lakewood, led by **Harav Dov Kahan**. Many of the concepts reflected in the book were derived from the *pilpul chaveirim* — the ongoing discourse — between the *dayanim*. Rav Kahan's knowledge and talent are indispensable, and his wisdom and insight are reflected in virtually every page of this work.

A special thank you to **Rabbi Yitzchok Grossman** who invested the time to review the entire manuscript. His insightful comments and vast knowledge enhanced this publication.

A special thank you to my *chavrusos*, **Rav Chaim Mayer Roth**, **Rav Hillel Fried**, and **Rav Mendy Weinberger** for their help reviewing parts of this book, and for their insights on the many halachos that were discussed by the *chaburah*.

The *ribbis* sections of this work were reviewed by **Harav Moshe Silberberg**, **Rav Avraham Moshe Lewanoni**, and **Rav Ahron Weider**.

Many people provided valuable feedback that helped shape this work. **Yossi Kazarnovsky**, **Morty Minchenberg**, **Moshe Smith**, **Nesanel Mordowitz**, and my brother **Eliezer**, graciously reviewed portions of the book, and provided helpful insights to make it more understandable to the public.

The inspiration to write this *sefer* came from an esteemed member of our *chaburah*, **Reb Yakov Frommer**. He, along with the other members of our *chaburah* and *beis din,* **Rabbis Yoel Amoyelle**, **Ephraim Birnbaum**, **Meir Bloch**, **Avi Bookman**, **David Cohen**, **Avraham Gutman**, **Daniel Harris**, **Reuvain Lefton**, **Reuvain Millet**, **Chaim Nachmad**, **Rachamim Neham**, **Ari Robowski**, **Yechiel Rothschild**, **Dovid Mordechei Rottenberg**. **Moshe Peretz Schwartz**, **Rav Michoel Yardley**, **Shlomo Zafrani**, and **Rabbi Dovid Grossman** of Kollel Zichron Gershon, have been an integral part of our journey through *Choshen Mishpat*. May we *be zocheh* to continue learning together and to complete the entire *Shulchan Aruch.*

A special thank you to **ArtScroll/Mesorah** for their superb job creating a professional work out of my drafts. I am indebted to **Rabbi Eliyahu Meir Klugman** and **Rabbi Shmuel Munk** for their comments and insights. **Mrs. Judi Dick** was masterful in her editing. **Mendy Herzberg** coordinated the many phases and stages of the manuscript, and I greatly appreciate **Eli Kroen's** magnificent cover and his creative page design. I thank **Mrs. Faigie Weinbaum** and **Mrs. Mindy Stern** for their proofreading, **Mrs. Nechama Nafisi** for laying out the book, and **Mrs. Esther Feierstein** and **Suri Reinhold** for entering the many editorial corrections.

I have been privileged to have wonderful role models who are particularly outstanding in the areas of integrity and honesty. I am deeply grateful to my dear parents, **Steven and Barbara Marburger**, and my parents-in-law, **Gedalia and Rachael Weinberger**, and to my wonderful grandparents, **Bert and Gerta Marburger**, *a"h,* and, *yblch"t,* **Arthur and Nana Stern**. Each of them is truly a paragon of a Torah approach to interpersonal relationship and a walking *kiddush Hashem.* Their self-sacrifice, devotion, and encouragement have inspired me in all my endeavors. It is impossible to thank them enough for their constant support and guidance. May Hashem grant them many more healthy years to derive *nachas* from their families. May all of their children, grandchildren, and great-grandchildren be inspired by their ways and continue in their footsteps.

This entire book bears witness to the tremendous dedication and support of my wife. Her encouragement, wisdom, and *mesiras nefesh* enabled me to have the time and *menuchas hanefesh* required to produce this work. May Hashem grant us strength and *Siyata Dishmaya* to raise our children with the values of *Torah U'mitzvos.*

It is with tremendous gratitude to the *Ribono Shel Olam* that I present this *sefer*. May it be His will that it succeed in being *marbeh kevod Shamayim*.

Foreword

Justice

Scripture states that one may glorify himself only for "*Haskel Vyado'a Osi,*" contemplating and knowing Me (*Yirmiyah* 9:23).

How does one know and understand an infinite Hashem?

The *pasuk* continues: *ki Ani Hashem oseh chesed u'mishpat u'tzedakah baaretz,* for I am Hashem Who does kindness, justice, and righteousness in the Land.

While we are unable to see Hashem, we are able to recognize His footprint. Kindness, **Justice,** and Righteousness are His hallmarks, and they are attributes that we must strive to emulate. By understanding and appreciating them, we bring ourselves closer to His service.

These verses teach us an important message. Being fair and honest in our business dealings is not only an obligation of *bein adam lechaveiro*, a responsibility that we have to our fellows. It is an integral part of *bein adam laMakom*, of our service to Hashem. To bring ourselves closer to Hashem, we must emulate His ways.

Mishpat — The Beginning of a Journey

Kabbalas HaTorah, which is described in *Parashas Yisro*, is immediately followed by *Parashas Mishpatim*, which contains the laws of damages and guidelines for *Beis Din*. One would imagine that the first priority of the people of a nation that had just been charged with its epic mission would be to immerse themselves in prayer and offerings. Yet this was not the case. The Torah's first priority is to teach the laws of *financial dealings*. The first step in the Jewish nation's journey toward *avodas Hashem* was to ensure that their interpersonal dealings measure up to Judaism's standards. Only after they mastered the appropriate behavior between fellow Jews could they advance to the next stage of service to Hashem.

Mishpat —

The Great Sanhedrin, high court, was situated near the Altar. Through offerings and prayer, we elevate the mundane. Through the Altar, a mere animal becomes a vehicle of service to Hashem. When we pray, our everyday needs serve as catalysts to bring us closer to Hashem.

Mishpat too, transforms our business dealings into a powerful declaration of our faith in Hashem. Observing the Torah's laws of *business* infuses our workday with an element of service to Hashem. We are not simply earning a living; we are demonstrating to the world our unwavering commitment to the ideals of the Torah, and our absolute belief that success can be achieved only through uncompromising adherence to His word.

Mishpat — The End of a Journey

The *Smag* writes that in today's times, after we have already suffered through a long and bitter *galus*, we need to be especially careful that our dealings with both Jews and non-Jews meet the highest standards of honesty.

Shearis Yisrael lo ya'asu avlah v'lo yedaberu chazav, The remnants of Israel will not commit corruption, they will not speak falsehood (*Tzephania* 3:13).

When Hashem brings the Final Redemption, the nations of the world will acknowledge that the Jews are a nation of truthfulness, and therefore deserve to be redeemed. For if we act in a shrewd and underhanded manner, the nations of the world would note that Hashem has chosen for Himself a group of thieves and dishonest people.

This message was delivered by the *Smag* some 800 years ago to a group of Jews who had been exiled from Jerusalem. Today, the message is even more potent.

Tziyon bemishpat tipadeh, Zion will be redeemed through justice (*Yeshayah* 1:27).

Sales
and
Marketing

1 Pricing / Ona'ah

Introduction

When Bilaam was commissioned to curse Klal Yisrael, he claimed that his services were worth Balak's entire palace full of gold and silver. He justified the exorbitant fee by arguing that Balak's sole alternative would be to enlist an entire army to fight Klal Yisrael. Yet, the Midrash labels Bilaam as a "nefesh rechavah, v'chomed mamon acheirim," an especially greedy person who covets another's money.

Interestingly, our pricing decisions often reflect similar values. We often observe a client and assess how much he stands to gain from our services and what his alternatives are before we determine how much we can charge for our services. However, this approach is rooted in greed. Pricing should reflect the true value of an item or service. How desperate the client is,[1] or what his alterna-

1. Clearly, the value provided by a service will be reflected in its market price. The problem with *Bilaam's* demand was that it reflected a specific client's desperation, and not a true market value. See *Ketzos* 227:1 for further discussion of this issue.

tives are, does not change the true value of our service, and is not a legitimate reason to raise prices.

In modern capitalist economies, the laws of supply and demand determine market prices. Vendors are free to charge whatever they please for their wares and markets are expected to regulate themselves. Governments intervene only in times of crises or to prevent criminal activity. In such scenarios, price-gouging laws limit the amount that sellers can charge, and prevent them from taking advantage of temporary disruptions. However, under normal circumstances, as long as a seller does not mislead an unsuspecting buyer, there are few legal restrictions on the prices that a vendor may charge.

Halachah has a very different outlook on pricing. The laws and guidelines defining appropriate pricing are called *ona'ah*.

Ona'ah

The Torah prohibits both overcharging a buyer and underpaying a seller.[2] Prices must reflect the true market value of an item. Taking advantage of an unsuspecting customer or an unaware seller is an illegitimate business practice and is comparable to stealing.[3]

These laws apply regardless of how high or low the seller's profit margin may be. Halachah does not define what a fair profit margin should be or set market prices.[4] Rather, it insists that prices adhere to the prevailing market price.

---

2. *Choshen Mishpat* 227:1. וכי תמכרו ממכר לעמיתך או קנה מיד עמיתך אל תונו איש את אחיו (ויקרא כה:יד).

The examples given in this chapter generally involve overcharging a buyer as opposed to underpaying a seller, as the former is the more common scenario. The halachos apply in both instances.

3. *Tur, Choshen Mishpat* 227.

Intentionally misleading a buyer or a seller about the value of an item is *geneivas daas* as well (see *Sma* 227 (51) and *Choshen Mishpat* 228:6).

4. There are a few cases where *Chazal* imposed limits on the amount of profits that one may earn. These laws are limited to basic staples and apply only in areas that are predominantly inhabited by Jews. See *Choshen Mishpat* 230 for these halachos.

These halachos likewise apply to merchants.[5] If an item in a store is underpriced, one is obligated to inform the storeowner.[6] Buying the item without notifying the owner of the item's true value is *ona'ah*, even though the merchant made the mistake on his own. Although the customer merely paid what the merchant was asking for the item and did not mislead him in any way, if the price does not reflect the item's true value, the prohibition of *ona'ah* has been violated.

Level of Ona'ah

The recourse available to the cheated party will vary based on the size of the cost discrepancy, and the type of item purchased. Most transactions (unless they involve real estate, labor, or debt[7]) may be divided into three categories:

1. Discrepancies of greater than one-sixth:

If the item was overpriced by more than ⅙ or $16.\overline{66}$ percent, the sale may be voided.[8] The buyer[9] has the right to return the item and demand a full refund.

For example, if one buys a camera for $250 and then realizes

---

5. Ibid. 227:14.

This halachah is subject to a dispute between the *Tanna Kamma* and R' Yehudah (*Bava Metzia* 51). R' Yehudah maintains that a merchant is presumed to be aware of the true market value of his wares. If he agrees to accept a lower price, he is making a conscious decision to waive *ona'ah*, and will have no recourse. The *Tanna Kamma* argues that we do not have the right to make such assumptions. Even experienced merchants make mistakes, and we cannot strip them of their rights to claim *ona'ah*. The halachah follows the ruling of the *Tanna Kamma*.

6. *Shulchan Aruch HaRav, Ona'ah* 3.

7. These transactions are discussed in "Real Estate and Debt" and "Labor."

8. *Choshen Mishpat* 227:4.

9. *Rama* 227:4 writes that the seller (who perpetrated the *ona'ah*) may also void the sale, (unless the buyer specifically agreed to waive his claim of *ona'ah*) provided that he acts within the appropriate time frame (see "Time Frame").

Shulchan Aruch argues that the party who perpetrated the *ona'ah* may not void the sale.

See also *Yerushalmi Bava Metzia,* Chapter Four, halachah three, which supports the position of *Rama* (quoted by *Aruch HaShulchan* 227:3).

that its market value is only $200, he may return the camera. The seller is obligated to accept the return and refund the complete purchase price. Even if the seller offers to refund the $50 that was overcharged, the buyer may return the item and is entitled to a full refund. Similarly, the buyer may not compel the seller to refund the $50 overcharged. His sole right is to void the sale and return the item.

The seller is obligated to refund the buyer's money regardless of the store's return policy.[10] This applies even if the buyer used the item before realizing that he was overcharged.[11]

2. Discrepancies of precisely one-sixth:

If the price charged was incorrect by exactly ⅙,[12] the sale is valid but the amount overcharged must be refunded to the buyer. Neither party may void the sale.[13] For example, if someone paid $360 for a suit worth $300, the buyer is entitled to a refund of the $60 that he overpaid. He may not, however, void the sale and return the suit.

3. Discrepancies of less than one-sixth:

If the sale price was within ⅙ of the item's true value, the sale remains in force at the agreed-upon price.[14] The buyer may not return the item and is not entitled to any refund. It must be noted

---

10. To override the laws of *ona'ah*, a formal *tenai* (see Appendix II) is required. See *Choshen Mishpat* 227:21.

11. See "Using the Item."

12. There are two ways to calculate ⅙.

a) ⅙ of the total sale price. For example if the purchase price was $360, ⅙ of the purchase price is $60 (360 divided by 6). Therefore, if the true value was only $300, the *ona'ah* is exactly ⅙ and must be refunded.

b) ⅙ of the item's true value. For example, if the item is really worth $300, and one pays $350, he has overpaid by exactly ⅙ of the item's true value. ($300 value divided by six is $50. $300+ $50= $350.)

In halachah, either way is considered *ona'ah* of ⅙ (*Choshen Mishpat* 227:2). Therefore, whether one pays $350 or $360 for an item worth $300, the sale is valid and one may demand a refund of the amount overcharged.

13. Ibid. 227:2.

14. Ibid. 227:3.

that although there are no financial penalties for overcharging a customer by less than ⅙, the *Rosh*[15] suggests that the Biblical prohibition of *ona'ah* may be violated.[16] Accordingly, one should not overcharge a customer by any amount.[17] If one realizes that he

15. *Ramban, Vayikra* 25:16, *Taz* 227:6, *Imrei Baruch, Chochmas Shlomo* 227:27 write that the prohibition applies to price discrepancies of less than ⅙.

See *Sefer Chassidim* 532, *Chinuch* 337, *Bal HaMaor, Bava Kamma* 4 that the prohibition does not apply to price discrepancies of under ⅙.

16. *Choshen Mishpat* 227:6.

The *Rosh, Bava Metzia, Perek HaZahav Siman* 20 suggests two possible reasons why a price discrepancy of less than ⅙ is not actionable in *beis din*.

a. A cheated party will not claim *ona'ah* because of the difficulty in proving his case. To successfully claim *ona'ah*, one needs to establish the item's exact value in order to prove that he actually overpaid. Because assessments are never exact, if the price discrepancy is less than ⅙, the buyer will not be able to prove the item's true value with enough precision to win the case. As such, he is *mochel* and waives his right to claim *ona'ah*.

According to this explanation, if one knows the exact value of an item, it is a violation of *ona'ah* to overcharge by any amount, even less than ⅙. However, the claim will not be actionable in *beis din* because there is a presumed waiver of the claim.

b. Small price discrepancies are tolerated because it is normal for buyers and sellers to deviate somewhat from standard market prices for any number of legitimate reasons. A seller may be willing to accept a lower price in order to move merchandise. A buyer may be willing to overpay in order to quickly close a deal. Accordingly, halachah accepts minor price fluctuations as legitimate pricing.

According to this interpretation, deviating by less than ⅙ is permitted and is not a violation of *ona'ah*.

The *Rosh* does not render a definitive conclusion, but writes that a *yerei Shamayim*, one who fears heaven, should avoid such practices.

Chofetz Chaim, Hilchos Rechilus, Klal 9:10 discusses a fascinating ramification of this law. If a merchant is about to overcharge someone by ⅙ or more, one is obligated to warn the unsuspecting customer (provided one follows the laws of *rechilus*. See *Chofetz Chaim, Rechilus, Klal* 9:12). What happens if the merchant is trying to overcharge a customer by less than ⅙?

If we assume that the prohibition of *ona'ah* applies to even minor price discrepancies, one would be obligated to warn the parties to prevent the transgression. Informing the customer would be permitted, and would not be *rechilus*.

If, however, there is nothing wrong with overcharging by less than ⅙, one may not interfere with the sale. Because the sale price is legitimate, informing the customer that he could get a better deal elsewhere would be inappropriately hurting the seller and is *rechilus*.

Because the *Rosh* does not render a clear verdict, the seller must refrain from overcharging by any amount. However, if the seller ignores his responsibility and overcharges a customer by less than ⅙, it is unclear if a bystander may interfere with such a sale since if *ona'ah* does not apply, informing the buyer that the item is overpriced would be *rechilus*.

17. *Choshen Mishpat* 227:6 .

overcharged a customer, a *yerei shamayim*, one who fears heaven, should refund the discrepancy, even if it is less than ⅙.[18] However, the buyer has no recourse in *beis din*.

Discrepancies in Volume, Weight, or Count of Items

Ona'ah applies to discrepancies in the price of an item. If there is a discrepancy in the volume, weight, or count of the sale, the parties are entitled to redress the issue regardless of the amount of the discrepancy.[19] For example, if a customer orders 50 chairs and receives only 49, he is entitled to the missing chair.[20] The limitations of the laws of *ona'ah*, such as the time frame in which the buyer must make his claim (see "Time Frame"), do not apply.[21]

Sales and Markdowns

When it is clear that both parties understand the true value of the item and are willing to waive their rights and either overpay or undercharge, there is no prohibition of *ona'ah*. For example, if the price is so absurd that it is clear that both parties

18. *Sma* 227:6 (14).

However the buyer should not accept the money, since he may not be entitled to the refund. It is appropriate for the seller to insist on returning the money, and to offer it as a gift (*Taz* (6)).

Chasam Sofer (6) adds that whenever one purchases an item and suspects that he is being slightly overcharged, one should be *mochel* (waive his rights to) the discrepancy. The buyer has nothing to lose; regardless, he has no recourse in *beis din*. He should be *mochel* the seller to save him from a possible transgression.

19. *Choshen Mishpat* 232:1. The leeway given in the laws of *ona'ah* reflect both the difficulty in establishing precise values, and normal market fluctuations. The count, size, and weight of goods can be measured easily and precisely.

20. If the seller cannot deliver the agreed-upon amount, the buyer **may** be entitled to void the entire sale. See *Sma* 232:2, *R' Akiva Eiger* 232, *Aruch HaShulchan* 232:9, *Shevus Yaakov* 3:169, *Nesivos* 182:8, and *Mishpat Shalom* 182 for parameters of this halachah.

21. *Choshen Mishpat* 232:1; *Sma* (3).

are aware that it does not reflect the market value of the item, there would be no claim of *ona'ah*.[22]

By definition, a sale or markdown is also permitted. By advertising 30 percent off, the merchant is agreeing to sell an item at a discount. He is making it clear that he understands the true price and there is an implicit agreement to waive any claim of *ona'ah*.

If the Buyer Was Aware that He Was Being Overcharged

If the buyer was aware that he was being overcharged, and purchased the item with the intention of subsequently demanding a refund, he may claim *ona'ah*.[23] There is a disagreement among the *poskim* whether this applies to all categories of *ona'ah*,[24] or if it is limited to *ona'ah* of exactly ⅙.[25]

22. *Choshen Mishpat* 220:8, *Ketzos* 227:5.

23. *Rama, Choshen Mishpat* 227:7; *Sma* (18); *Ketzos* (5); *Nesivos* (4).

See *Bach* (9) who disallows the claim unless the buyer notified witnesses in advance that he intended to pursue his claim.

Contrast to the above-mentioned halachah that when it is clear to both parties that the price is inappropriate, *ona'ah* will not apply. If the price discrepancy is clear to both parties, and they nevertheless finalize the deal, there is an implied agreement to accept the price and to waive all rights of *ona'ah* (*Ketzos* (5); *Aruch HaShulchan* 227(9); cf. *Nesivos* (4)). This is true only when it is clear to each party that the other party is aware of the discrepancy, and is nevertheless willing to proceed with the transaction. However, if it is not obvious to all of the parties that there is a price discrepancy, and the seller believes he is fooling the buyer, there is no implied agreement to waive *ona'ah*. The buyer may therefore proceed with the deal and claim *ona'ah* afterward, even if he happened to have recognized the price discrepancy at the time of the sale.

24. *Chavos Yair* 187, *Sma* (18).

Nesivos 264 (8) agrees under certain limited circumstances.

25. *Nesivos* (4); *Hagahos HaSma* (18); *Machaneh Ephraim, Ona'ah* 19. When the *ona'ah* is exactly ⅙, the sale remains in force and the discrepancy must be refunded. Therefore, the buyer may claim *ona'ah* by explaining that he bought it with the intention to keep the item and to force the seller to refund the *ona'ah*. However, when the *ona'ah* is greater than ⅙ the entire sale is void. The item must be returned to the seller. It makes no sense for the buyer to go through the trouble of buying the item and then demanding that the seller take it back. We assume that the buyer accepted the higher price and has waived his rights of *ona'ah*.

Items with Set Prices

Price discrepancies of less than ⅙ are tolerated because of the imprecise nature of prices.[26] An item that has a set price that does not fluctuate at all will be subject to *ona'ah* on any amount overcharged.[27] An example would be a government-subsidized item that is always sold for the same exact price.

Inadvertent Violations

These laws apply even when the *ona'ah* was done inadvertently.[28] Once the buyer or seller realizes that the price was inappropriate, he should inform the other party and offer a refund.[29]

Passing on Higher Costs

If a merchant is overcharged by his supplier, he may not pass on the higher costs to his customers. Being the victim of *ona'ah* does not give one the license to commit a similar crime on one's customers.[30] The merchant may try to recover the overcharged amount from his supplier, or be forced to absorb the loss.

26. See footnote 16 for two interpretations of this concept.

27. *Aruch HaShulchan* 227:2. See also *Machaneh Ephraim, Ona'ah* 7.

28. *Rashi* (*Bava Metzia* 51a) points out that although a customer may be unaware that he is underpaying for the merchandise, the laws of *ona'ah* apply. See also footnote 32.

See *Maharit* 2:19 that implies that the prohibition is not violated when the *ona'ah* was done inadvertently. See also *Tur* in the beginning of 227 and *Bach* that maintain the prohibition is violated.

29. To rectify the violation of *ona'ah*. (See *Taz* [7] that even after *mechilah*, one should return the money overcharged. See also footnote 36.)

30. *Kitzur Shulchan Aruch* 62:3.

Determining Market Value

In practice, it is often difficult to determine the true market value of an item. Vendors who provide different levels of service are entitled to charge different prices to reflect these services. One cannot compare the price of a soda in a restaurant to the cost in a neighborhood grocery.

Price will also vary with location. Different cities have different market dynamics and their prices are not expected to be the same.[31]

These variations place an enormous responsibility on the seller. To avoid the prohibition of *ona'ah*, he must take steps to ensure that all his prices are appropriate. In practice it is very difficult to know exactly how high one may mark up each of his products to avoid violating *ona'ah*.[32] However, because of the many variables, it is difficult to recover money based on a claim of *ona'ah*.

Some items do not have a set market price. They are sold for a wide range of prices without any clearly defined value. There is a debate among the *poskim* whether *ona'ah* applies to such items.[33]

---

31. *Rabbeinu Yerucham, Sefer Meisharim, Nesiv* 9 *Chelek* 3.

32. *Rosh, Bava Metzia, Perek HaZahav Siman* 20 implies that the prohibition will not apply to inadvertent discrepancies of less than ⅙.

33. *Beis Yosef, Choshen Mishpat* 209:1 suggests that *ona'ah* would not apply to items that have no set price. (This opinion is not cited in *Shulchan Aruch*.)

Darkei Moshe 209 (1), *Shach* 209 (1), *Bach* 209(1) argue that *ona'ah* applies even when the price varies.

See also *Aruch HaShulchan* 227:7 that maintains that if an item is commonly sold at different price levels, any of the prices are acceptable and would not violate *ona'ah*.

Time Frame

Buyer

To claim a refund of *ona'ah*, the buyer must act immediately.[34] He is given adequate time to bring his purchase to an appraiser, to determine if the price was fair, and to confront the seller and ask for a refund. If he delays and does not act right away,[35] he loses his rights to claim *ona'ah*.[36]

If there is no one available to properly assess the true value of the purchase, the time frame is extended until such an expert becomes available.[37]

If the buyer immediately brought the item to an assessor, who erred and told him that the price was fair, the buyer may claim *ona'ah* whenever he discovers the error.[38]

This halachah applies only to a cash sale. If the item is bought on credit, the buyer may wait until he has to pay for the item to have its value assessed.[39]

---

34. *Choshen Mishpat* 227:7.

Chinuch 337 explains that this time limit was instituted to protect commerce.

35. There is no fixed length of time. It will vary depending on the availability of an expert.

36. There would be a *middas chassidus* for the seller to refund the money even after this time frame, according to *Chinuch* 337, *Rav Hai Gaon*, quoted by *Ramach* in *Shitah Mekubetzes, Bava Metzia* 52b, *Aruch HaShulchan* 227:18.

Meiri, Bava Metzia 51b seems to disagree.

If the buyer can prove that he did not show the purchase to an assessor simply because he did not imagine that he had been overcharged, *Aruch HaShulchan* 227:18 holds that the seller is obligated to provide a refund even after the time frame has elapsed.

37. *Choshen Mishpat* 227:15.

38. *Nesivos* 227:3; *Shach* 306 (12).

39. See *Mishneh LaMelech, Mechirah* 15:3 and *Shach* 227:4 for two explanations of this halachah.

Aruch HaShulchan 227:10 writes that if the buyer used the item for an extended period of time, all opinions agree he loses his right to claim *ona'ah*.

Seller

If the seller is underpaid, he may claim *ona'ah* whenever he discovers the price discrepancy.[40] Because he no longer has the item in his possession, he has no practical way of showing it to a professional to ascertain its true value. Therefore, his time frame is extended until he chances upon another one of the items and has the opportunity to have it assessed.

Standard commodities whose value can be determined without showing the actual item to an assessor do not enjoy this extended time frame.[41]

Today, virtually all items are mass-produced, and their prices are readily available. Most items can be priced with a model number, and the seller does not need to have physical possession of the item to determine its true price. Accordingly, the time frame for either a buyer or seller to claim *ona'ah* is very brief.

Using the Item

If the *ona'ah* is greater than ⅙, the buyer may not use the item once he discovers that he was overcharged.[42] *Ona'ah* greater than ⅙ nullifies the sale. If the buyer intends to exercise his right to claim *ona'ah*, the item belongs retroactively to the seller. Using it without permission and/or payment would be stealing from the seller. If the buyer nevertheless uses the item after noticing the discrepancy, he loses his right to void the sale.[43]

---

40. *Choshen Mishpat* 227:8.

41. Ibid.

42. *Ritva, Bava Metzia* 50b; *Nesivos* 232:1; *Machaneh Ephraim, Ona'ah* 5.

43. Presumably, the buyer would not steal from the seller by using the item without permission. We are forced to conclude that the buyer chose to waive his claim of *ona'ah* and to maintain the sale. (*Ritva* 50b; *Nesivos* 232:1; *Machaneh Ephraim, Ona'ah* 5).

(See *Pischei Teshuvah* 232 (1) for a discussion about a buyer who claims he was unaware of this halachah and did not intend to waive his rights.)

However, if the buyer first notifies the seller that he intends to return the item, and then proceeds to use it, he retains the right to claim *ona'ah.* Although using

These laws apply to *ona'ah* of greater than ⅙. If the *ona'ah* was exactly ⅙, the buyer may continue using the purchase and will not lose his right to demand a refund of the overcharge.[44]

Leases

The laws of *ona'ah* apply to leases and rentals.[45]

Real Estate and Debt

Ona'ah on a real estate transaction[46] or the sale of debt is not actionable in *beis din*.[47] While many *poskim* maintain that the *prohibition* still applies,[48] the sale remains in force and the wronged party has no legal recourse. A possible exception is if the sale[49] price was more[50] than double the fair market value. According to some *poskim*, when the price is so markedly unfair,

---

the item is inappropriate, it is clear there is no intention to waive any right to claim *ona'ah*.

44. *Nesivos* 232:1. If the *ona'ah* is exactly ⅙, the sale is valid. The wronged party's sole recourse is to demand a refund of the money that were overcharged. Because the sale will remain in force, the buyer may continue to use the item, and will not lose his right to claim *ona'ah*.

45. *Choshen Mishpat* 227:35. The rules regarding real estate apply to leases as well (although see also footnote 49).

46. Ibid. 227:32.
See, however, *Mordechai, Bava Metzia* 305 regarding rentals.

47. *Choshen Mishpat* 227:29.

48. *Chinuch* 337; *Ramban, Vayikra* 25:17; *Ohr HaChaim, Vayikra* 25 17; *Rabbeinu Yonah, Bava Basra* 77b; *Aruch HaShulchan* 227:35 and *Shaar Mishpat* 42 interpret the Gemara as excepting *karka* (land) from the monetary obligations of *ona'ah*. The prohibition remains in force.
Sma 227(51) quotes *Maharshal* that intentionally selling land for more than its true value is a violation of *ona'as devarim* and *geneivas daas*.

49. See *Nachalas Tzvi* who limits this to sales of real estate. Rentals would not be subject to this cap.

50. *Choshen Mishpat, Rama* 227:29.
Sma 50 writes that charging exactly double the true price will also void the sale.

the transaction may be voided.[51] This exception is subject to the same time limitation described above.[52]

Labor

Halachah differentiates between salaried workers and independent contractors.

Salaried Workers

Salaried workers, who are paid for their time (for example, an hourly, weekly or monthly rate) and work set hours (for example, a typical 9 to 5 employee), have a status similar to real estate.[53] An employer who underpays his worker is violating the prohibition of *ona'ah*, according to many *poskim*. However, the worker will not be able to recover the "lost" wages in *beis din*.

Independent Contractors

Shulchan Aruch rules that an independent contractor is subject to regular *hilchos ona'ah*.[54] Any discrepancy of ⅙ of the fair market price or greater must be returned.[55] An independent con-

51. As there is no clear ruling on this issue, we apply the rule of *hamotzi meichaveiro alav harayah*. See Appendix II (*Darkei Moshe* 4), *Maharashdam* 376.

Maharashdam 376 writes that if the property was sold at double its value, we may not force the seller to return the the money paid.

R' Akiva Eiger quotes *Maharit, Choshen Mishpat* 20 that when a property is sold for less than half its true value, the property must be returned to the seller (who has the status as a *muchzik* because of the concept of *merei kama*; see Appendix II).

See also *Shach* 66 (122) who concludes that *ona'ah* will not apply, regardless of the amount overcharged.

52. *Sma* (16).

53. *Choshen Mishpat* 227:33.

54. Ibid. 227:36. See Chapter 9 note 33 for a definition of an independent contractor.

See also *R' Akiva Eiger* who quotes *Rashba* and *Ramban* that independent contractors are exempt from *ona'ah*.

55. Discrepancies of greater than ⅙ allow the wronged party to void a sale. However, if

tractor is defined as a worker who is paid by the job (as opposed to a worker who is paid by the hour) and is not obligated to work at specific times.[56]

An exception to this rule is when a contractor was hired to improve land. Such cases are treated as real estate transactions and are not subject to recourse in *beis din* for the amount overcharged.[57]This applies only to work done directly improving land. A contractor who builds a house will not be subject to *ona'ah* on the portion of the job that involves the actual construction. Parts of the job that were done before the actual construction, such as preparing materials, etc, are subject to the laws of *ona'ah*.[58]

Cost Plus

Transactions based on a cost-plus basis are not subject to the laws of *ona'ah*.[59] For instance, if a distributor agreed to sell his entire inventory for a 15-percent markup, there is no *ona'ah* regardless of the inventory's true value.[60] *Ona'ah* by definition is cheating a person by not providing the appropriate value. The price in a cost-plus transaction is not designed to reflect the actual value of the goods. Rather, it is structured to give the seller a specific level of profit. As such, *ona'ah* has not been violated.

This exception only applies when the transaction is structured

---

the job has already been completed, the work cannot be "returned" to the contractor, and the price must be adjusted instead. The entire amount overcharged must be refunded.

56. See Chapter 9 note 33.

57. *Nesivos* 227:20; *Amudei Ohr* 107.

58. *Amudei Ohr* 107; *Dvar Avraham* 2:19:4.

If one price is given for the entire job, we prorate the amount based on the percentage of the work that would be subject to *ona'ah*.

Bach (42) maintains that we may prorate a bill only if the components have clearly defined prices.

59. *Choshen Mishpat* 227:27.

60. See *Shach* 227 (15) that this exception may not apply if the discrepancy is greater than ⅙.

in this manner because neither party knows the true value of the item. If, however, one party is aware that the agreed-upon price does not reflect the true value of the item, he will be subject to the prohibition of *ona'ah*.[61]

Ona'as Devarim — Hurtful Words

Ona'ah is not limited to overcharging in financial transactions. Causing a Jew pain through words is prohibited as well.[62] The Mishnah[63] provides an example of what is, unfortunately, a frequent occurrence. One may not walk into a store and inquire about the price of an item if he has no intention of purchasing it from that store. Raising the owner's expectations of making a sale and then disappointing him causes pain and is a violation of *ona'as devarim*.

If a person intends to buy the item, he is permitted to shop around to discover who will offer the best deal. However, if he intends to order the item online or directly from the manufacturer, he may not go into a Jewish-owned showroom to see the item, since he has already decided not to purchase from the retail establishment.

A buyer is trying to negotiate a better price on a piece of real estate. As a tactic to convince the seller to accept a lower offer, the buyer has several of his friends look at the property and put in very low bids. While this may be an effective negotiating tool, the friends who view the property without any intention of actually purchasing it have violated ona'as devarim.[64]

---

61. *Chochmas Shlomo* writes that the seller has violated *ona'ah*, but maintains that he has no obligation to return the money.

Nesivos 227:19 writes that the amount overcharged must be refunded.

62. ולא תונו איש את עמיתו ויראת מאלקיך (ויקרא כה:יז).

63. *Bava Metzia* 58b.

64. If they mislead the seller about the true value of the property, they are guilty of *geneivas daas* as well.

This prohibition applies to sellers as well.[65] A seller may not represent that he is willing to sell a property if he is not serious about selling it. Listing a property simply to find out its value is prohibited.

Case Study

A person hires a foreman to oversee a construction project. The foreman's responsibilities include buying the necessary supplies, retaining subcontractors, and overseeing the actual construction. As the project nears completion, the homeowner has someone audit the bills. He discovers that he has been overpaying for virtually every aspect of the job, from the cost of supplies to the foreman's salary. How do the laws of ona'ah *apply to this scenario, and what are the homeowner's rights?*

Level of Ona'ah

When dealing with *ona'ah*, the first question is the amount of the price discrepancy. Any price discrepancy of less than ⅙ is not actionable in *beis din*. Although it may be a violation of the prohibition of *ona'ah*, the wronged party will not recover any damages.

If the *ona'ah* was exactly ⅙, the price discrepancy must be returned.

Ona'ah of greater than ⅙ allows the wronged party[66] to void the sale. (However, see "Wages," below).

65. *Sefer Chassidim* 311.

66. See note 9.

Time Frame

The next question is the time frame. To claim *ona'ah*, the homeowner must immediately verify the true value of the item. If he procrastinates, he loses all rights to claim *ona'ah*. In our case study, the homeowner waited until the project was almost completed to verify the fairness of the bills. He has no recourse on any old bills regardless of the amount of overpayment.

This rule has a few important exceptions:

- It applies only to cash sales. If the homeowner had not yet paid for an item, he may claim *ona'ah* regardless of the amount of time that has passed since the purchase.[67]
- Wages that are subject to *ona'ah* (see below, "Wages") are not subject to this limit. If an independent contractor is overpaid/ underpaid, the wronged party may claim the *ona'ah* whenever it is discovered.[68]
- If the buyer tries to find a fair market value of the item, and the assessor misleads him, the buyer retains his right to claim *ona'ah*. If the customer relied on the expertise of the foreman to determine a fair price, this exception will apply.

Wages

The next area that must be explored is the type of transaction. Wages for a salaried worker (*poel*) are not subject to the laws of *ona'ah*. If the foreman worked set hours, he is classified as a *poel*, and would not have to return any excess wages.[69] However,

67. If, however, the buyer used the item for an extended period of time, the usual time frame for *ona'ah* applies regardless of whether or not the item was paid for (*Aruch HaShulchan* 227:10).

68. *Choshen Mishpat* 237:36.

69. If he was being paid twice the prevailing rate, see "Real Estate and Debt."

a *kablan*, or independent contractor, would be subject to *ona'ah*. If the foreman were not obligated to work set hours, and was paid a predetermined fee for the entire job, he is classified as a *kablan* and would have to return any excess wages.

However, as mentioned above in "Independent Contractors," even an independent contractor will not be subject to *ona'ah* if he was hired to improve land. The portion of the foreman's salary that was attributable to the actual construction, or for the hiring of other workers who are classified as *poalim*, would not be subject to the recourse of *ona'ah*. However, the percentage of his pay attributable to other work, such as purchasing materials and supplies, would be subject to *ona'ah*.

When dealing with workers, there is no difference between *ona'ah* of exactly ⅙ or greater than ⅙. Because the work was already done, the transaction cannot be reversed. The only recourse is to return the amount overcharged.

Agents

This case study has an additional variable that will completely change the halachah. The laws of *ona'ah* apply when the buyer personally buys an item and is overcharged. However, if an agent makes a purchase on his behalf, different guidelines will apply. The reson for this is simple. An agent is not authorized to pay inappropriate prices for any type of goods. Any agreement that entails any level of *ona'ah* is beyond the scope of his authority and is therefore void. Therefore, any amount of *ona'ah* is actionable.[70] Even when dealing with real estate or wages (that are not subject to the regular laws of *ona'ah*), the principal may demand a full refund of the amount overcharged. In our scenario, the foreman was acting as an agent, and the homeowner may demand a refund of any amounts overcharged regardless of the amount or type of purchase.

70. *Choshen Mishpat* 227:30. See also ibid. 182:4 for limitations of this concept.

This reasoning applies to suppliers, vendors, and subcontractors. However, the foreman negotiated his salary directly with the homeowner. As such, his salary is subject to the regular laws of *ona'ah*, as explained above.

2 Marketing, Disclosure, and Mekach Ta'us

Introduction

An individual who is selling an item or service often faces a dilemma when marketing it. What is his responsibility to his clients? Must he disclose every defect, or does it behoove the buyer to exercise due diligence and fend for himself?

There is a well-known concept called *caveat emptor,* buyer beware. Under this concept, as long as the seller does not conceal a defect or make any misrepresentation, it is the buyer's responsibility to exercise due diligence and to inspect the property. If the buyer fails to exercise due diligence, he has little recourse.

Halachah has a very different approach. All sales are presumed to have been made with the expectation that they are free of any defect. Therefore, selling an item without disclosing its defects is *geneivas daas* (deception) and is prohibited.[1] If a defective item is sold, the buyer has the right to void the sale and demand a

1. *Choshen Mishpat* 228:6.

Ritva, Chullin 94, *Smag Lav* 155, *Yere'im* 124 all hold that *geneivas daas* is included in the Biblical prohibition of stealing.

Nesivos 60:4 rules that according to the *Rambam,* cheating a buyer is a violation of the prohibition of *ona'ah*.

full refund.[2] The sale is considered a *mekach ta'us*, a transaction based on error, and is void. This applies both when the seller maliciously duped the buyer, and also if the seller himself was unaware of the defect.[3] The prohibition applies when dealing with either a Jew or a non-Jew.[4]

An investor buys, and immediately "flips," a property. Three days after moving in, the buyer discovers a serious structural defect in the building. The "flipper" must refund the buyer's money and then take action against the original seller.[5] *If the seller refuses to reimburse him, the flipper will suffer the loss, although he acted in good faith.*

Disclosure

The seller is obligated to clearly disclose any defect in the item. This disclosure must be specific.[6] The buyer must be told the exact deficiency of the purchase. A vague statement such as "the item is defective" is not a valid disclosure.[7]

A universal waiver that the buyer accepts any possible defect is not recognized by halachah. The buyer may void the sale by claiming that he either did not believe there were any defects, or that he would not have agreed to the waiver had he been aware of the extent of the damage.

2. *Choshen Mishpat* 232:3.

3. Ibid. 232:18.

4. Ibid. 228:6, *Shulchan Aruch HaRav, Hilchos Ona'ah* 11, *Chacham Tzvi* 68.

5. If the property was sold "as is," see the following section and "As Is" later in this chapter.

6. *Choshen Mishpat* 232:7.

7. See section "As Is" later in this chapter.

Leases

The laws of *mekach ta'us* apply to leases as well.[8] If a unit is defective, the tenant may void the lease.

Damaged Goods Sold at a Fair Price

The requirement to disclose all defects applies regardless of whether the defect impacts the value of the property. Even if the price was appropriate for the condition of the item and the buyer did not suffer a financial loss, selling a defective item without disclosing its defects is *geneivos daas*[9] and is grounds for a *mekach ta'us*.

A used-car dealer notices that the odometer in one of his cars has been turned back. He lowers the price to reflect the true value of the car, and sells it without notifying the customer that the mileage was inaccurate. This sale is a mekach ta'us and the customer is entitled to a full refund even though he paid the appropriate price for the car.

Type of Defect

To determine whether a defect creates a *mekach ta'us*, and is grounds to void the sale, "*minhag hamakom*," the prevailing norm, is examined.[10] All existing properties have some level of wear and tear. As such, minor defects are expected, and need not be disclosed. However, an unexpected defect that people consider unacceptable[11] creates a *mekach ta'us*.

8. *Pesachim* 4b.

9. *Perishah* 228 (5).
Overcharging a customer, *ona'ah*, is discussed in Chapter One.

10. *Choshen Mishpat* 232:6.

11. *Shulchan Aruch* 232:6 states that any defect that would cause most people to *return* the item creates a *mekach ta'us*. Although, if given a choice, everyone would

Repairable Defects

For a sale to be considered a *mekach ta'us*, the defect must be irreparable. If the item can be repaired[12] and the seller offers[13] to do so,[14] the buyer may not back out of the deal.

This applies only if the buyer will not suffer any loss if the seller fixes the item. If, however, the buyer needed the item immediately, and cannot wait until the repairs are done, he may void the sale.[15] Similarly, if a house is sold and the buyer is not informed that there is a tenant in the house who cannot immediately be evicted, the buyer may void the sale if he planned to move in right away.[16]

A person notices water seeping into the basement of his new home. Although this defect creates a mekach ta'us, if the seller agrees to waterproof the basement, the buyer may not claim mekach ta'us.

Obvious Defects

The concept of *mekach ta'us* is that all purchases are predicated on the assumption that the merchandise is in good condition.

---

prefer an item that is perfect, there are minor defects for which people would not bother returning an item. Such defects would not create a *mekach ta'us*.

See also *Bach* (4) ונ"צ.

12. *Choshen Mishpat* 232:5. This applies to a defect that can be satisfactorily repaired; if the item must be completely rebuilt *(panim chadoshos)*, the sale is void.

13. The sources cited by *Shulchan Aruch* and *Rama* give the seller the option of fixing the defect to avoid a claim of *mekach ta'us*. (See also *Ran, Pesachim* 4b.) The implication is that if the seller chooses, he may refuse to make the repair and instead allow the buyer to void the sale.

Ulam HaMishpat 232:5 **requires** the seller to fix the item.

14. *Shulchan Aruch* allows the seller to give the buyer a credit to compensate for the defect. The responsibility of making the actual repairs would fall upon the buyer. *Ulam HaMishpat* 232:3 requires the seller to actually make the repairs.

15. *Bach* (4).

16. *Knesses HaGedolah* 237:52.

Had the buyer been aware of the defect, he would not have purchased the item. Because the purchase was based on a false assumption, it may be voided. It follows that if the buyer was aware of the defect before the sale, it will not create a *mekach ta'us*.[17] In addition, an obvious defect will not create a *mekach ta'us*, since presumably the buyer noticed it before the sale.[18]

Recourse

If a defect creates a *mekach ta'us*, the buyer has the right to void the sale and demand a full refund. It is a "take it or leave it" proposition. He may not keep the item and force the seller to give him a discount to compensate for the defect.[19] If he really needs the item, he will be forced to waive his rights of *mekach ta'us*.

The seller, too, is required to accept the returned item and give the buyer a full refund. He may not force the buyer to accept a discount to compensate for the defect. (See "Repairable Defects" for an exception to this rule.) These halachos apply regardless of any store policy regarding returns.[20]

Time Frame

There is no time limit for a claim of *mekach ta'us*. Whenever the defect becomes apparent, the buyer has the right to void the sale.[21] However, once the buyer notices the defect, he should

17. *Choshen Mishpat* 232:3.

18. *Sma* 245:16.

19. *Choshen Mishpat* 232:4.

20. A buyer has the right to claim *mekach ta'us* unless he was specifically told about the defect. See later in this chapter regarding "As Is" sales.

If the *minhag hamakom,* prevailing norm, is to limit returns within a specific time frame, *Maharsham* 3:128 rules that the policy is enforceable *provided* that the buyer could have inspected the item and discovered the defect within this time frame. This applies only if such policies are the norm.

21. *Choshen Mishpat* 232:3. In contrast, *ona'ah* has a very limited time frame, as described in Chapter 1. See *Galya Masechta* 10 for an explanation of the difference.

notify the seller as soon as possible. If he delays, he will not be able to force the seller to refund his money.[22]

A proud father-in-law bought a beautiful leather-bound Shas for his new son-in-law. A few years later, the son-in-law noticed that a number of pages were missing from one of the volumes. He may claim mekach ta'us regardless of how many years passed before he noticed the defect.

Rent

When the buyer voids the sale because of a defect, the seller may charge him rent at the prevailing rate for the period of time during which he resided in the property before the defect was discovered.[23] Since the sale is nullified retroactively, the property always belonged to the seller, and he is entitled to charge the buyer for using his property.

Using the Defective Item

A buyer may not use the item after he discovers the defect.[24] If he continues to make use of it, he loses the right to claim *mekach ta'us*. The reason for this is that claiming *mekach ta'us* voids a sale retroactively. Accordingly, the item always belonged to the seller. Using it without permission and/or payment would be stealing from the seller. [25] If the buyer continues to use the

22. Not confronting the seller indicates that the buyer is willing to accept the defect. *Rif* (*Bava Metzia* 50b), *Ba'i Chayei, Choshen Mishpat* 82, *Maharitatz* 105, *Machaneh Ephraim, Ona'ah* 4 quoting *Rav Hai Goan.*

See *Mishneh LaMelech, Mechirah* 15, *Machaneh Ephraim, Ona'ah* 4, *Maharitatz* 225, who infer that *Rambam, Mechirah* 15:3 argues.

23. *Choshen Mishpat* 232:15.

See also *Nesivos* 232(5) with *Sma* 232:33.

24. *Choshen Mishpat* 232:3.

25. Until the defect was noticed, the buyer has the right to use the item, and is not responsible to pay the seller for the use (*Ritva, Bava Metzia* 50b). The issue arises

item, he must have decided[26] to waive his rights of *mekach ta'us* and to keep the item.[27]

A buyer notices that the engine of the used car that he has recently purchased is making strange noises and misfiring. Although the buyer knows that he is going to return the car, he continues driving it for another week before bringing it back to the dealer. By doing so, the buyer forfeits his right to claim mekach ta'us.

If the buyer informs the seller that he intends to return the item because of the defect, and subsequently uses the item, it is questionable whether he may still return the item.[28]

---

if the buyer continues using the item after he is aware of the defect and intends to void the sale.

Kiryas Melech Rav (15 *Mechirah* 3) points out that this halachah contradicts the previous halachah requiring the buyer to pay rent for the period during which he resided in the property before the defect was discovered.

Ohr Gadol (*Mishnayos Bava Metzia Perek* 4) differentiates between land, for which the buyer must pay rent, and movable objects (*mitaltelin*) for which the buyer is not obligated to reimburse the seller.

See however *Ohr Same'ach* 16 *Mechirah* 8 that even by movable objects (*mitaltelin*), the buyer must pay for his usage וצ"ע.

26. Even if a particular buyer is unfamiliar with these laws and does not realize that he is relinquishing his rights by using the item, the halachah remains the same. *Pischei Teshuvah* 232(1). See however *Aruch HaShulchan* 232:4.

27. If the buyer has no option but to temporarily use the item, he retains the right to void the sale. *Pischei Teshuvah* 232 (2).

28. *Machaneh Ephraim, Ona'ah* 5 states that one may return the item. He reasons that although it was improper for the buyer to use the item after he realized it was defective, notifying the seller of the defect makes it clear that he is not waiving any of his rights.

Nachalas Tzvi offers an alternative explanation. He suggests that by notifying the seller of the defect, the buyer has already nullified the sale. Once the sale is void, it is no longer possible to waive the rights of *mekach ta'us*. Therefore, subsequent usage, while improper, cannot enforce a sale that no longer is valid.

Galya Masechta 10 argues that the sale remains in force and the buyer may not return the item.

Pischei Teshuvah 232:1 writes that if the seller was already paid, he cannot be forced to return the money, as he can rely on the opinion of the *Galya Masechta*.

Damaging the Item Before the Defect Was Noticed

If the buyer damaged his purchase through normal use before realizing that it was defective, he may nevertheless return the item for a full refund. This applies only if he used the item in a normal manner. However, if he caused damage by using the item in an unusual manner, he must reimburse the seller for any damage.[29]

An exception to this rule is if the buyer had notified the seller that he intended to use the item in an unusual manner. In such cases, he would not be liable for the damage that results.

A developer purchases a small home on a large lot. The seller is aware of the buyer's intention to tear down the house and build a development in its place. After demolishing the house, the developer discovers that the land has environmental pollution. He is entitled to receive a refund[30] *of the entire purchase price and is not responsible for razing the house.*

Buyer's Responsibility to Safeguard the Item

The buyer is responsible to safeguard the item until he returns it to the seller.[31] He must act to protect the seller from any loss. If, for instance, the buyer waited to inform the seller of the defect, and because of the delay the seller was no longer able to return the item to his supplier, the buyer is responsible for the loss.[32]

29. *Choshen Mishpat* 232:13. See *Nesivos* (5) that limits this halachah.

30. See section "As Is" later in this chapter.

31. *Choshen Mishpat* 232:22.

32. Ibid. 232:18, according to the explanation of *Nesivos* (7).

A person discovers a defect in his brand-new computer. Although he immediately decided to return it, he nevertheless threw out all of the packaging after noticing the defect. Because the storeowner will not be able to return the computer to his supplier, the buyer would be responsible for the loss.

Improvements

The seller must reimburse the buyer for any improvements he made to the property.[33] The buyer has the status similar to a *yored bershus,* which is explained in Chapter Nine.

When the Buyer Fails to Inspect the Purchase

Some *poskim* maintain that if the buyer had an opportunity to inspect the purchase and neglected to do so, he loses his right to claim *mekach ta'us*.[34] By neglecting to check the item, he is demonstrating that he is not particular about its condition. There is considerable debate among the *poskim* about this ruling.

The *poskim* who accept this ruling make the following exceptions.

- It applies only when the buyer does not bother checking the item before purchase. If he inspects the purchase but inadvertently overlooked the defect, the buyer has not waived his rights to *mekach ta'us* and may void the sale.

33. *Choshen Mishpat* 232:14.

34. The general presumption is that the buyer expects the merchandise to be in perfect condition. However, a buyer who fails to verify the condition of the merchandise is demonstrating that he is indifferent. *Maggid Mishneh, Mechirah* 15:3, *Sma* 232 (10).

Radvaz 4:136, 139 writes that all opinions concur with this concept. See also *Pischei Teshuvah* 232 (1).

- It applies only if the buyer had the opportunity to inspect the item before the purchase.[35]
- If the seller represented that the item is not defective, this halachah will not apply.[36] The buyer is entitled to rely on the seller's word and need not inspect the item.
- If the custom is not to inspect the item purchased, this halachah will not apply.[37] For example, customers generally do not open a camera at the time of purchase in order to inspect all its features.
- It applies only to common defects that a customer would anticipate and inspect for.[38]
- It applies only if the buyer paid for the item.[39] If the item was bought on credit, the buyer may claim *mekach ta'us*.
- It applies only if the buyer can inspect the item easily[40] and without any expense.[41]
- It will not apply to a significant defect that makes the purchase worthless.[42]

According to some *poskim*, it applies only to instances where the buyer ***used*** the item without inspecting it.[43]

---

35. *Shevus Yaakov* 3:169, *Terumas HaKri, Maharam Shick Choshen Mishpat* 33.

36. *Divrei Chaim, Even HaEzer* 92, *Beis Shlomo* 62, *Maharashdam* 385, *Chochmas Shlomo; Pnei Moshe* 55, *Kiryas Melech Rav, Mechirah* 15:3.
See *Ranach* 41, *Radvaz* 4:136 that disagree.

37. *Kesef HaKadoshim; Radvaz* 4:136, *Pnei Moshe* 55.

38. *Chachmas Shlomo, Pnei Moshe* 55, *Divrei Mishpat* 232:3 (2).

39. *Mishneh LaMelech, Shaar Mishpat* 232:1. The buyer has little incentive to check the item before he pays, since he knows he may renege on the deal if a defect is found.

40. *Maharashdam* 385, *Kiryas Melech Rav, Mechirah* 15:3, *Mishpat Shalom* 232:3.

41. *Kesef HaKadoshim.*

42. *Beis Shlomo, Choshen Mishpat* 62, *Kiryas Melech Rav, Mechirah* 15:3.

43. *Nesivos* 232:7.

"As Is" Sales

Real estate is often sold "as is." The seller does not disclose defects, and the burden of discovering them is placed on the buyer. This compels the buyer to accept any possible defects without the knowledge of what the actual defects are. If the buyer had the opportunity to discover the defect through an inspection, the guidelines mentioned in the previous section would apply. Otherwise, it would seem that since universal waivers are not effective according to halachah (see section "Disclosure"), a buyer should not be bound to "as is" clauses. However, *Radvaz*[44] argues that if there is a *minhag hamakam*, if it is customary to honor such clauses, the waiver is accepted by halachah.

Case Study

Reuven buys a used car for $10,000. At the time of purchase, the odometer reading is 48,000 miles. Reuven drives the car for three years without any problems.

One day, Reuven receives a phone call from an investigator who informs him that the true mileage of the car at the time of purchase was actually 95,000 miles. Reuven is very upset. He feels he was taken advantage of, and had no intention to buy a car that had such high mileage. May Reuven demand a full or partial refund of the purchase price? What are his rights?

Geneivas Daas

This case touches on three separate issues: *geneivas daas*, *ona'ah*, and *mekach ta'us*.

Geneivas daas is the prohibition against misleading another

44. *Radvaz* 4:136.

Maharashdam 3:128 validates "as is" clauses, provided that the buyer had an opportunity to inspect the item. See also section "Inspections."

person. If the dealer was aware that the mileage was inaccurate, he violated *geneivas daas* by misleading the buyer. It is immaterial whether or not he was the one who actually turned back the odometer. However, *geneivas daas* is a prohibition. It is not actionable in *beis din*. The recourse available to Reuven will depend on the laws of *ona'ah* and *mekach ta'us*.

Ona'ah

Ona'ah, overcharging, depends on the amount that Reuven was overcharged. If the amount was greater than ⅙, Reuven has the right to void the sale and return the car for a full refund.

Ona'ah generally has a limited time frame. The buyer must check out the true value of the item immediately following the purchase. If he does not, we interpret his inaction as an indication that he is not particular about getting a fair price. However, this limitation will not apply to our scenario. Reuven was under the impression that the car had lower mileage. Based on that belief, the price seemed appropriate. His inaction does not prove any waiver of his rights.

However, if he continues to use the car after he finds out about its true mileage, he will lose his right to claim *ona'ah*.

Ona'ah is not dependent on the seller's knowledge. Even if the dealer sold the car in good faith and had no reason to suspect that the odometer had been tampered with, he is obligated to give the buyer a full refund.

If the amount of *ona'ah* was exactly ⅙, the sale remains valid. The buyer has the right to demand a refund of the amount overcharged. However, in this particular case (see footnote for an explanation), the seller may refuse to give a partial refund and demand that the buyer return the car.[45]

45. *Nesivos* 233:1, *Aruch HaShulchan*, explaining *Shulchan Aruch*. In a typical case of *ona'ah* of ⅙ the seller may not void the sale and must give a partial refund. However, if the *ona'ah* is a result of a **defect**, the seller may void the sale if the customer asks for a refund. *Nesivos* adds that this halachah is not universally accepted. However, the seller, who has already been paid, may rely on these opinions and refuse to give

There is another important factor. When the buyer returns the car and demands a full refund, the seller is entitled to payment for the use of the car.[46] We will have to determine the value of using the car for three years and subtract that from the sale price.

In addition, if the buyer damaged the car, he will be responsible for any loss. He will not have to pay for normal wear and tear. However, if he was in an accident, or if his children wrecked the interior, he will have to reimburse the dealer.

Mekach Ta'us

If the dealer sold the car at a deeply discounted price, it is possible that even based on the true mileage, there was no *ona'ah*. In such cases, the buyer may void the sale by claiming *mekach ta'us*. The buyer agreed to purchase a car with 48,000 miles. What he got was a car with 95,000 miles. This constitutes a defect that voids the sale. Regardless of the sale price, the buyer has the right to return the car and receive a full refund. He would, however, be responsible to pay for the use of the car and for damage that he caused, as described above.

If the buyer continues to use the car after he finds out about its true mileage, he will lose his right to claim *mekach ta'us*.

Mekach ta'us is also (like *ona'ah*) not dependent on the seller's knowledge. Even if the dealer sold the car in good faith and had no reason to suspect that the odometer had been tampered with, he is obligated to allow the buyer to return the car and give a refund.

---

a refund.

46. See however, footnote 25.
See also *Nesivos* 232:5.

3 Tortuous Interference / Ani Ha'mehapech B'chararah

Introduction

Ani ha'mehapech b'chararah[1] is the prohibition regarding interfering with another Jew's business deal. It is imperative that anyone involved in negotiations be aware of these halachos. Understanding the concept and recognizing its parameters will enable one to avoid potential disputes.

1. Literally, "A pauper who is pursuing a *chararah* cake." This phrase is derived from *Kiddushin* 59a: *Rav Gidal was pursuing a property. Rav Abba went and bought that property. Rav Gidal complained [about the incident] to Rav .... He asked Rav Abba, " If a pauper is pursuing a chararah, a cake, and another person comes and takes it, what is [the halachah]?" [Rav Abba] answered, "He [that takes it] is considered a rasha." [Rav Yitzchak then confronted Rav Abba.] "Why did you do the same [take the field that Rav Gidal was pursuing]?" Rav Abba responded, "I did not know [that Rav Gidal was pursuing the field]." Rav Yitzchak responded, "Then give the field to Rav Gidal (to redress the violation) ...."*

Maharit, Peirush L'HaRif; Rashi, Kiddushin 59a; and *Sheirus Yosef* 17 explain that *ani ha'mehapech* is based on the prohibition of being *yored l'chayav*, inappropriately interfering with another Jew's livelihood.

Mordechai, Kiddushin 524; *Ran, Kiddushin* 24a (*Dafei HaRif*) cite the verse of *V'asisa hayashar v'hatov* as the source of these laws.

Yerushalmi, Kiddushin 27a (according to the interpretation of *Pnei Moshe*) cites the verse, *La'mas mei'rei'eihu chased v'yiras Shakai ya'azov* (*Iyov* 6:14).

These halachos can be found in *Shulchan Aruch, Choshen Mishpat* 237.

Parameters

Once a buyer and seller reach an agreement, it is forbidden for another person to interfere by offering a competing bid. According to some *poskim*, these halachos apply only after the first bidder has reached a final agreement with the seller. If the parties are still negotiating,[2] anyone is free to make a competing offer.[3]

Other *poskim* maintain that the custom is to apply the concept of *ani ha'mehapech* even while the parties are still negotiating. If the negotiations are in their final stage and an agreement is imminent, one may not interfere with the negotiations.[4]

---

2. The Gemara does not define the point at which someone who is interested in a property becomes a "*mehapech*" and has first rights. *Rama* 237:1 quotes *Mordechai* (*Bava Basra* 551) that these halachos apply only after an agreement has been completely finalized and the parties are ready to make a formal *kinyan*. However, if the parties did not reach an agreement on all of the terms of the deal, these laws do not apply. *Mordechai* explains that if the prohibition against interfering with another's deal began the moment anyone began negotiating with the seller, the seller would be at a disadvantage. Other buyers would be prevented from offering competing bids and it would be difficult for the seller to receive a fair price for his property. In order to protect the seller, *Chazal* limited these laws to instances in which a deal had already been reached.

Nachalas Shivah 65 adds that it is difficult to verify whether a person had begun negotiations. Even someone who had only inquired about a property in passing could later make a claim of *ani ha'mehapech* against the buyer. To avoid problems, *Chazal* made a clear and verifiable requirement that an agreement must have been reached for these halachos to apply.

3. See *Yerushalmi, Kiddushin* 31a; *Mordechai, Kiddushin* 523; *Kesef HaKadoshim* 171:6 about bidding up the price of an item that another person is interested in buying.

4. *Perishah* 237, *Igros Moshe, Choshen Mishpat* 1:60. This applies only once it is clear that, in the absence of any outside influence, the parties will shortly come to an agreement on the minor issues that remain.

Pischei Teshuvah questions why the *Perishah* does not mention this custom in the *Sma*, his commentary on *Shulchan Aruch*. Contemporary *poskim* maintain that the *Perishah* is describing a custom that is not in use today (heard from *HaGaon R' Y. S. Elyashiv* and *HaGaon R' N. Karelitz*).

The *Aruch HaShulchan* adds that in a busy marketplace where there are many buyers and sellers, the halachos are more stringent. Once a person is negotiating with a seller, it is forbidden for another to interfere. (Presumably there is no loss to the seller by enacting these rules in a busy marketplace. If he is unhappy with the offer, he can break off the negotiations and easily sell the item to the next buyer.)

See also *Mateh Shimon* 237:9 and *R' Avraham of Jerusalem*, quoted by *Maharashdam, Choshen Mishpat* 224, that *ani ha'mehapech* applies even before a price was agreed upon.

These laws apply even before the buyer and seller sign a contract. Although, at that point, neither the buyer nor seller is legally[5] bound to consummate the deal, once an agreement has been reached, another party may not interfere.

These halachos apply regardless of whether or not the seller is Jewish.[6]

Reuven has been pursuing a particular property for years. He contacts the owner every few weeks,[7] but the owner is not especially motivated to sell and they never reach an agreement. One day Reuven notices a competitor speaking to the seller about the property. Reuven may not claim ani ha'mehapech since he never actually had an agreement with the seller.

Simultaneous Negotiations

According to some *poskim*, if two parties are simultaneously negotiating with the seller, once one party reaches an agreement with the seller, the other party is obligated to withdraw from the negotiations. He may not offer a higher bid in a last-ditch effort to get the deal. Although he may have started negotiating with the owner first, since they never reached an agreement, the second party was permitted to bid on the property. Once the second party's offer was accepted, trying to undermine it is a violation of *ani ha'mehapech.*[8]

A buyer is prepared to purchase a property, but feels that if he puts in a low bid and waits a few days, the seller will come down in price. A few days later, the buyer hears that another bidder has come

5. A verbal agreement creates an ethical, but not legally enforceable, imperative to consummate a deal. See Chapter Four for more about *mechusar amana*.

6. *Mordechai, Bava Basra* 551; *Rama* 237:1.

7. See Chapter Five for the laws of *Lo Sachmod* and *Lo Sisaveh*.

8. *Az Nidberu* 7:84, and heard from *HaGaon R' Y. S. Elyashiv* and *HaGaon R' N. Karelitz*.

See, however, *Ramban* to *Bava Basra* 54b.

in and agreed to pay the asking price. If the first party offers a higher bid to the seller, he will violate the laws of ani ha'mehapech.

If the Seller Solicits Bids

Chazal instituted safeguards to ensure that these halachos would not be used to harm the seller.[9] Therefore if the seller is dissatisfied with the current deal and solicits a bid from another party, anyone is free to enter the bidding.[10] Even if the first bidder invested a significant amount of money or effort to obtain the property, if the seller prefers to deal with another party, *ani ha'mehapech* would not apply.[11]

However, once the seller indicates that he will accept the current offer, it is forbidden for someone else to tell him that he can get a better price.[12] Although he merely intends to be helpful, he is doing so at the buyer's expense.[13]

Third Parties

These halachos apply to third parties as well.[14] Once the buyer and seller have reached an agreement, a third party may not

---

9. *Mordechai, Bava Basra* 551.

10. *Sh"ut Maharshal* 36, *Maharam Alshich* 67, *Sma* 386:10.

If the seller had already committed to sell the property to another buyer, he may be bound to honor his commitment, depending on the factors discussed in Chapter Four. It would be inappropriate for another party to aid and abet in this violation by bidding on the property.

11. Although see section *"Ani Ha'menakef."*

12. Once a seller accepts a bid, preventing people from making additional higher offers is not considered causing a loss (*Mordechai, Bava Basra* 551). Contrast to footnote 2.

13. This applies only if the parties are not being cheated. If there is *ona'ah*, one has an obligation to inform the other party. See Chapter 1 note 16.

14. *Chofetz Chaim* (*Hil. Rechilus, Klal* 9, *Be'er Mayim Chaim, Hakdamah*) points out that one is not allowed to interfere with another's deal even when one wants the property for himself. It is certainly forbidden to interfere when one does not expect

inform the seller that he can obtain a better price elsewhere. Although the third party does not intend to purchase the property for himself, interfering with an existing deal is a violation of *ani ha'mehapech.*[15]

A buyer approaches a real estate agent and indicates that he is interested in a property. If the agent knows that the seller has already agreed to sell the property to another buyer, he may not put in a bid.

Unique Opportunities

Many *poskim*[16] argue that *ani ha'mehapech* does not apply when the property being contested represents an extraordinary opportunity. The classic example is an ownerless item lying on the street. Even if someone is about to take possession of the item, another person may preempt him. *Ani ha'mehapech* is predicated on the argument that it is inappropriate to interfere with another's deal if one may find other opportunities elsewhere.[17] It follows that when an opportunity is unique and cannot be found elsewhere, one is permitted to preempt another to obtain the item.[18]

Some *poskim* limit this exception to instances where the item

---

to reap any personal gain.

Sh"ut Maharshal 36 asserts, "*Ein adam chotei v'lo lo.*" People typically sin because they expect to benefit from the sin. To sin merely as a favor for someone else is especially offensive.

15. If the seller is actively seeking a better offer, there would be no *ani ha'mehapech,* as per footnote 10. However, if the seller is satisfied with the tendered price, but the agent continues to seek a better offer, the agent and any new bidder would be in violation.

16. *Rabbeinu Tam* (*Tosafos, Kiddushin* 59a); *Rama* 237:1.

17. However, see footnote 1 for alternate explanations.

18. *Mordechai, Kiddushin* 524; *Ran, Kiddushin* 24a (*Dafei HaRif*) explain that the obligation of *ve'asisa hayashar v'hatov* does not require any individual (such as the new bidder) to suffer a loss.

See also *Kesef HaKadoshim*.

is available for free.[19] Others extend this exception to purchases that are available at an unusually inexpensive "bargain" price[20] or if the property is unique and special.[21]

However, all opinions agree that this exception applies only when the property being contested represents a true windfall[22] or is a truly unique item. A slightly reduced price or an item with a minor or subjective advantage would not qualify for this exception.

Reuven is searching for a new home. When he is at last prepared to make an offer on a house, the seller informs him that he has already committed to sell the house to Shimon. Reuven may not persaude the seller to renege on the deal, even if the house is the only one in the neighborhood with a two-story entranceway. The advantage offered by this particular house is not sufficient to effect its status as a windfall.

There are a number of *poskim* who reject this exception completely and rule that *ani ha'mehapech* will apply even to unique opportunities.[23] As a matter of halachah, the consensus of *poskim* is to allow this exception. However, a *baal nefesh* (one who is meticulous regarding his observance of mitzvos) should leave the deal for the first bidder.[24]

---

19. *Shach* 237 (3); *Ramban, Bava Basra* 54b; and *Aruch HaShulchan* 237:1 based on *Yerushalmi.*

20. *Rama* 237:1; *Mordechai, Bava Metzia* 238; *Maharik* 132; *Maharshal* 36; *Nesivos, Beurim* 183:6; *Avnei Nezer, Choshen Mishpat* 17; *Shulchan Aruch HaRav, Hefker* 10; *Ulam HaMishpat* 237.

21. Such as an adjacent property (*Rama* 237) or a local job opportunity (*Maharshal* 36 and *Masas Binyamin* 27).

22. *Mordechai, Bava Metzia* 238 rules that it must be an exceptionally cheap price that cannot be found elsewhere.

Kesef HaKadoshim requires that the price be at least 16.6 percent below its actual market value.

23. *Rashi, Kiddushin* 59a; *Mateh Shimon* 237; *Hagahos Beis Yosef* 2; *Knesses HaGedolah to Beis Yosef* 2; *Admas Kodesh* 1:70.

24. *Shulchan Aruch HaRav, Hefker V'Hasagas Gevul* 10; *Igros Moshe, Even HaEzer* 91. Note: This *chumrah* (restriction) will not apply if the *mehapech* is a wealthy person and could purchase the item elsewhere (*Rama* 237:1 according to the interpretation of *Sma*).

Employees

These guidelines apply when hiring an employee as well.[25] It is forbidden to approach someone who works for a competitor and offer him a better salary in order to lure him to your firm. However, if the worker is actively looking for a different job, one is permitted to make him an offer.[26] If the worker is unusually talented and there is no one else available that can do the job as well, the exception made for unique opportunities (see previous section) may apply.[27]

An investor is seeking a partner to manage a building that he intends to buy. The investor may not approach a friend who is presently managing buildings for a competitor, unless he is certain that this manager is unhappy with his job and is seeking other opportunities. Although this job represents a great opportunity for the worker to become a partner, one may not enlist him at his current employer's expense.

Career Opportunities

A worker may not try to convince an employer to hire him if the employer had already agreed to hire someone else. Causing the other prospective employee to lose a job opportunity is a violation of *ani ha'mehapech*.[28]

25. *Tosafos, Kiddushin* 59a; *Avnei Nezer, Choshen Mishpat* 17.

26. As per footnote 10.

27. *Tosafos, Kiddushin* 59a. Here too, the worker must be the only one available who is capable of doing this particular task.

Minchas Pitim 237:1 distinguishes between hiring a rebbi, where anyone may claim that this particular rebbi is best suited to teach his child, and hiring other workers, whose superiority must be clearly established.

28. *Tosafos, Kiddushin* 59a interprets *ani ha'mehapech* to be a dispute over an employment opportunity.

Customers

Ani ha'mehapech applies to clients as well.[29] If a client agreed to close a deal with a particular firm, a competitor may not step in and try to win the business.

Preempting Another's Mitzvah

According to some *poskim*, the restrictions of *ani ha'mehapech b'chararah* do not apply to mitzvos.[30] For example, if one sees a beautiful esrog, one may purchase it even though another person was about to buy it.

Recourse

One who violates these halachos is called a *rasha*[31] and is obligated to rectify the situation by allowing the first deal to go through. If, before the fact, *beis din* becomes aware that a party is trying to preempt a deal, *beis din* may take action to prevent the violation of *ani ha'mehapech*.[32]

If, however, a party has violated *ani ha'mehapech* and bought a property, after the fact, *beis din* is not authorized to compel them

29. *Maharam (Prague)*148; *Rama* 386:3.

30. *Aruch HaShulchan* 237:5; *Minchas Pitim* 237.

Chochmas Shlomo (*Maharshal*), *Kiddushin* 58b states that *ani ha'mehapech* does not apply to a *shidduch* because of the mitzvah of *p'ru u'r'vu* (see, however, *Igros Moshe, Even HaEzer* 91).

See *Sh"ut Maharshal* 36 (at the end of the first *Shem*) that contradicts *Chochmas Shlomo* and argues that mitzvos are not exempt from the laws of *ani ha'mehapech*.

See also *Shaarei Teshuvah, Orach Chaim* 482 that discusses a situation where two people are competing for one *kezayis* of matzah in order to fulfill the mitzvah. *Shaarei Teshuvah* quotes various sources that maintain *kol d'alim gvar*, each person should try his utmost to be the one to perform the mitzvah. In spiritual matters, the rule is *chayecha kodmin*, a person's own spiritual growth takes precedence and one need not politely allow an opportunity to do a mitzvah to slip away. (These sources do not refer to *ani ha'mehapech* directly; they seem to assume that it would not apply.)

31. *Kiddushin* 59a.

32. *Mishpat Shalom* 237; *Maharashdam Choshen Mishpat* 259.

to resell the property to the first party. However, *beis din* may publicize what was done in order to shame the offending party into complying with these halachos.[33]

The *Chofetz Chaim* holds that one may not tell the original bidder the name of the person who preempted him.[34]

Unintentional Violation

Ani ha'mehapech applies even if the second bidder was unaware of the existing agreement when he bid on the property. Although he acted in good faith and did not intend to hurt the first party, he must withdraw his bid once he learns about the prior agreement.[35]

Disputed Ani Ha'mehapech

If there is a dispute about *ani ha'mehapech*, a person is believed if he claims that he did not violate the laws.[36] For example, if a buyer claims that he is not subject to *ani ha'mehapech* because the seller solicited his bid, he is believed, and need not substantiate the claim.[37]

---

33. *Sma* 237:1 states that *beis din* should announce in shul that the person committed an act of *rishus* (wickedness).

34. *Rechilus* 9:15. After the deed was done, there is no recourse in *beis din*. There is no point in informing the prospective buyer of who preempted him, since that will only create animosity.

It would seem that if the issue arose before the closing, and the buyer was prepared to call the other party to a *din Torah*, it would be appropriate to disclose the information.

35. *Maharam (Levov)* 305; *Ranach* 125; and *Igros Moshe, Choshen Mishpat* 1:60 conclude that one has an obligation to resell the property to the first bidder.

Pischei Teshuvah quotes *Chemdas Shlomo* 4 that inadvertent violators are not **obligated** to resell the property to the first bidder. They should, however, do so as a *middas chassidus*.

36. *Sh"ut Maharshal* 36. *Ani ha'mehapech* is a prohibition and not a monetary claim. As such, if a party claims innocence, they are believed.

37. See *Mateh Shimon* 237:2 for a discussion of how to deal with a situation where the halachah of *ani ha'mehapech* is unclear.

Steady Clients

There is a related issue in halachah involving a *maruphia*,[38] a steady client. Some *poskim* maintain that one may not try to lure away someone else's steady client.[39] This differs from *ani ha'mehapech* in the sense that *ani ha'mehapech* is a prohibition against interfering with a specific deal that is about to be completed. *Maruphia* prohibits going after another's steady client even though at the moment there may not be any imminent deals.

Only loyal clients who do business exclusively with the competitor qualify for these laws. If the clients are not completely loyal and will occasionally use another firm, anyone is free to solicit their business.

The prohibition of *maruphia* is to **pursue** another's steady client. If the client initiates the deal, these laws do not apply.[40]

Advertising

One may advertise to the general public, and need not be concerned that a competitor's *maruphia* will be influenced by the advertisements. However, targeted mailings to a competitor's steady customers would be included in this prohibition.[41]

R*ama* cites different customs regarding the laws of *maruphia*, and does not render any final verdict.[42] Today, the custom is to permit pursuing the business of a *maruphia*[43] (although see foot-

38. *Chavos Yair* 42 explains that the term *maruphia* comes from *yaarof kamatar,* referring to something steady and reliable. *Sridei Eish* 3:66 explains that *maruphia* is an Arabic word for a close associate.

39. See *Mordechai, Bava Basra* 515; *Hagahos Maimoni, Shecheinim* 6:8; *Rama* 156:5 for a discussion of this issue.

40. *Sma* 386:10. The prohibition regards luring away another's reliable client. If the *maruphia* is "shopping around," he cannot be considered a reliable client.

41. *Cheshev HaEphod* 90.

42. *Choshen Mishpat* 156:5 based on *Mordechai, Bava Basra* 515, and *Hagahos Maimoni, Shecheinim* 6:8.

43. *Divrei Chaim, Choshen Mishpat* 1:20. *Minchas Yitzchak* 2:94 explains that we compete with both Jews and non-Jews. Enforcing the laws of *maruphia* will not

note). However, a *yarei Shamayim* (G-d-fearing individual) should refrain from doing so.[44]

Ani Ha'menakef

There is a related prohibition of *ani ha'menakef b'rosh hazayis*[45] wherein if a person invested significant effort to obtain an item, one may not preempt him. This concept is more severe than *ani ha'mehapech*, and is considered a form of theft.[46] It applies even to windfalls, as opposed to *ani ha'mehapech* (see "Unique Opportunities"). However, it applies only where the first person invested significant effort to obtain the item. There are differing opinions as to exactly what level of effort is required to qualify for these laws. *Maharshal*[47] maintains that the person must actually put his life in danger while pursuing the item to qualify for this halachah. *Masas Binyamin*[48] does not require that one endanger his life, but rather that he has overcome all obstacles and is assured that he will obtain the item (in the absence of any outside interference). Others[49] suggest that investing "significant money and effort" is enough, even though there are still obstacles and there was no physical danger.

---

necessarily protect a business' steady clients since a non-Jew, who is not bound to the laws of *maruphia*, may step in and woo the client away. Since the steady client cannot be completely protected, the *minhag* is to allow anyone to compete over a *maruphia*.

It would stand to reason that in an industry where it is unlikely for an *akum* to compete, such as Judaica, kosher food, etc., one should be *machmir* (stringent).

Chasam Sofer 69 suggests that if the steady client is a Jew, all *poskim* agree that one may not try to woo him away. (See also *Masas Binyamin* 27 who takes the opposite position and maintains that the prohibition of *maruphia* does not apply at all to a Jewish client.) See also *Cheshev HaEphod*.

44. *Shulchan Aruch HaRav, Hefker* 13. See also *Sh"ut Maharshal* 36.

45. *Gittin* 59b.

46. *Gezel Mipnei Darkei Shalom*.

47. *Sh"ut Maharshal* 36.

48. 27.

49. *Nachalas Tzvi* 237 (explaining the opinion of the *Maharik*).

"Ani ha'mehapech" is an illustration of the beauty of the laws of Choshen Mishpat. No formal contracts have been executed, no papers signed, and there are no legal obligations. Yet, halachah demands that we respect our competitors' space, and that we do not interfere with their dealings. We work because we must do our hishtadlus (effort). But the Ribbono Shel Olam does not want hishtadlus that comes at the expense of another person. Only a nation that lives with absolute bitachon and faith in Hashem could accept such laws. These ideals create a powerful Kiddush Hashem, and are an ongoing testimony to the uniqueness of Klal Yisrael.

Unfortunately, the reverse is also true. When people see Jews fighting with each other and trying to interfere with each other's deals, it creates a terrible Chilul Hashem and conveys a message of disunity.

Experience has also shown that when these halachos are violated, all too often, nobody gains. The first buyer loses the deal. The seller frequently becomes suspicious; he wonders why people are suddenly agitating to break the deal and to present better offers. If the first price he agreed to was too low, perhaps this offer is also a mistake. The seller often either chooses to hold on to what has suddenly become such a desirable piece of prime real estate, or looks elsewhere to see if he can get a still higher offer. In the end, the rasha gains nothing from his effort.

Case Study

A group is negotiating with a builder to purchase a cluster of houses in a new development. When they are about to sign the contracts, they learn that the builder has agreed to sell an adjacent house to a very undesirable neighbor. The group delivers an ultimatum to the builder: either promise us that you will not sell a house in the development to this person, or our entire group will not purchase houses. The builder has no choice and acquiesces to their demands. Assuming that their concerns about the neighbor are valid, did the group act appropriately, or have they violated the laws of ani ha'mehapech?

The first question is whether there was a final agreement between the undesirable neighbor and the builder. If they were still negotiating over the price and had not yet reached an agreement, there would be no *ani ha'mehapech*. As explained before, *ani ha'mehapech* applies only when the negotiations reach a stage where an agreement is imminent.[50]

Another issue that must be dealt with is *mechusar amana*. If the builder gave his word to this undesirable person that he would sell him a house, it may be inappropriate to encourage the builder to renege on his commitment. See Chapter Four for further discussion of *mechusar amana* and *trei tarie*.

Another issue that can be raised is that according to most *poskim*, if the property being contested represents a unique value or a windfall, the prohibition of *ani ha'mehapech* will not apply (see section "Unique Opportunities"). If the development is being sold for an unusually low price, or if it is the only area where there is such a large cluster of houses for the group to purchase together, perhaps it qualifies for this exception.

The exception of a windfall is limited. As per the *psak* of both the *Shulchan Aruch HaRav* and *Igros Moshe*, a *yarei Shamayim* should not rely on this exception. Secondly, there is a debate about whether this exception is limited to an ownerless item that may be obtained gratis, or if it extends to an item being purchased at an unusually low price. Our case study involves a purchase and may not qualify. Even if we will follow the *poskim* who extend the concept to sales, the sale must be a clear bargain that cannot be found elsewhere. If similar homes are available at comparable pricing, there will be *ani ha'mehapech*.

If a cluster of houses cannot be found elsewhere, and the group could not buy if the undesirable neighbor moves in, the group's action was permissible, but not appropriate for *baalei nefesh*. The appropriate response to such a situation would be to simply walk away from the negotiation without saying anything to the builder that would jeopardize the neighbor's deal.

50. See section called "Parameters" at the begining of the chapter.

This scenario differs from a classic *ani ha'mehapech* since the group had no intention to purchase that particular house for themselves. Their objective was to prevent an undesirable from moving into their neighborhood. Nevertheless, the rules of *ani ha'mehapech* would apply. The prohibition of *ani ha'mehapech* is to interfere with another person's deal. Whether the offending party will take the deal himself is irrelevant.[51]

51. See footnote 14.

4 Contracts, Commitments, and Kinyanim

Introduction

The Torah doesn't simply tell us not to tell lies. The Torah warns us, "midvar sheker tirchak," we must distance ourselves from falsehood.[1] *What is the necessity for this specific warning?*

"Shearis Yisrael … lo yedaberu chazav"[2] *may be interpreted in the following way: The remnant of the Jewish nation that will survive until the time of redemption will be those who do not speak falsehood.*

The middah necessary to survive galus and to be worthy of redemption is the virtue of truthfulness.

"Titein emes l'Yaakov." Yaakov Avinu, who represents the Jew in galus, is defined by the middah of emes.

What is the connection?

Torah and avodas Hashem are truth. The mission of the yetzer hara is to confuse us; to blind us and convince

1. *Shemos* 23:7.
2. *Tzephaniah* 3:13.

us that evil is actually good.[3] *Especially in the long and dark night of galus, it is easy to fall prey to the yetzer hara.*

If we are to have any hope of recognizing emes, we must be truthful people. We must be totally committed to truth, and refuse to accept even the slightest deviance from it.

Shearis Yisrael, those who are successful in living a life of truthfulness, will be the ones who will witness the ultimate geulah.[4]

The ability to enforce agreements is crucial for commerce. It would be impossible to conduct business if commitments were meaningless, and contracts could not be enforced. Yet, it is also clear that not every statement that a person utters is intended to create a binding contract. This chapter will explore the various stages of negotiations, and their halachic ramifications.

Every transaction can be divided into the following four stages:

- The owner decides to sell an item.
- The buyer and seller reach a verbal agreement concerning the sale.
- The buyer pays for the item.
- A formal act, or *kinyan,* is made to transfer ownership of the property.

3. *Chovos HaLevavos, Yichud HaMa'aseh* Chapter 5.

4. *Hakdamah* to *Niv Sefasayim.*

1. Decision to Sell — Dover Emes Bilvavo

The first halachic stage of an agreement is when one party makes a decision to accept an offer. Although this decision was never communicated to the other party, there is a concept of *doveir emes bilvavo*,[5] "speaking truth in one's heart." Once a person decides to accept an offer at a certain price, it is praiseworthy for him to carry through with this decision even if the buyer subsequently tenders a higher bid. This is not an obligation. Rather, it is a *middas chassidus*, an especially pious behavior.[6] Although the buyer was never aware that the seller was prepared to accept his original price, once the seller decided in his mind, this *middas chassidus* applies.

2. Verbal Agreements — Mechusar Amana

Once the parties agree to the terms of a deal and make a verbal commitment to buy/sell a property, they have an obligation to honor their commitment. This applies even though no formal contract or *kinyan* has been made. One who reneges on a verbal commitment is called *mechusar amana,* untrustworthy.[7]

The concept of *mechusar amana* applies to sales, rentals, services, and gifts. If one informs an acquaintance that he intends to give him a gift, hire him for a job, or rent a property from him, one may not change his mind and renege on the commitment.

The source of this obligation is *"Shearis Yisrael lo ya'asu avlah*

5. *Tehillim* 15:2.

6. *Kitzur Shulchan Aruch* 62:16; *Shulchan Aruch HaRav, Mechirah U'Matanah* 1, based on *Makkos* 24a.

7. *Choshen Mishpat* 204:7.

v'lo yedabru chazav"[8] or *"hin tzedek."*[9] A person is obligated to be honest and to honor his word. Although this obligation is not enforceable in *beis din*, a person who violates his word is called a *rasha*. Because no formal *kinyan* (as explained later in this chapter) was executed, *beis din* cannot force a party to fulfill his commitment. However, *beis din* is authorized to exert significant pressure to persuade one to honor his words.[10]

Size of Commitment

Mechusar amana applies only to a commitment that is taken seriously by the recipient. An offer to sell an item or to give a small present would qualify for these laws. However, an offer to give a large gift (*matanah merubah*) will generally not be taken seriously, and *mechusar amana* would not apply.[11]

Commitment to a Pauper

A pledge to give a large gift does not meet the criteria of *mechusar amana*. However, if the recipient is a pauper, the pledge is treated as a vow to give charity, and one is obligated to fulfill his commitment.[12]

8. *Tzephaniah* 3:13. *Sma* 204:12; *Baal HaMaor, Bava Metzia* 50; *Peirush Mishnayos L'HaRambam*; *Rav, Sheviis* 10:9; *Mordechai, Bava Metzia* 451; *Minchas Chinuch* 259.

9. *Vayikra* 19:36. *Nimukei Yosef, Bava Metzia* 29a (*Dafei HaRif*); *Mordechai, Bava Metzia* 312; *Ohr Zarua, Bava Metzia* 149.

See *Minchas Pitim* 204:11 that these opinions maintain that *mechusar amana* is a Biblical obligation. The opinions mentioned in the previous footnote that the source is *"Shearis Yisrael"* interpret *mechusar amana* as a Rabbinic concept.

10. *Agudah, Bava Metzia* 4:66; *Ranach* 118; *Maharam Mintz* 101; *Mishpat Shalom* 204 11; *B'tzel HaChochmah* 5:159.

11. *Choshen Mishpat* 204:8.

See *Pri Yitzchak* 51 that nevertheless, it is a *middas chassidus* to honor these commitments.

See footnote 21 for an application of this concept to an employment agreement.

12. *Choshen Mishpat* 243:2; *Yerushalmi, Bava Metzia* Chapter 4, halachah 2.

Meeting of the Minds

Mechusar amana applies only when there is a meeting of the minds regarding the commitment. To fall into the category of *mechusar amana*, both the granter and the recipient must be aware of the commitment. Therefore, if the seller does not make the commitment directly to the buyer, but rather to a third party, and then changes his mind before the buyer hears about the commitment, the seller would not be subject to *mechusar amana*.[13]

Trei Tarie — Change in Price

Because *mechusar amana* does not involve any binding legal contract, it has an important limitation. If the price of an item *unexpectedly*[14] changes[15] after the agreement, many *poskim* maintain that the buyer or seller may back out.[16] Their commitment was to buy or sell the item at the market price; now that the price has changed, their commitment is no longer binding.

This exception applies to any significant change in the buyer's

13. *B'tzel HaChochmah* 5:160; *Pri Yitzchak* 51.

See also *Machaneh Ephraim, Zechiah U'Matanah* 28; *Minchas Pitim* 204:8, 243:2; *Hafla'ah, Kesubos* 55; *Shulchan Aruch HaRav, Mechirah* 6 (*Hagoah*); *Chelkas Yoav, Even HaEzer* 30.

14. In a situation where the price regularly fluctuates, one may argue that the commitment to sell at the agreed-upon price was a commitment to forgo an expected price increase. For example, a long-term contract will almost always change in price over time due to inflation. It is difficult to justify backing out of a commitment because of a small increase that was expected to occur. This may apply as well to buying a house "on paper." It is understood that the value of the house is likely to increase when it is actually built and *mechusar amana* will apply. See *Beis Ephraim, Choshen Mishpat* 4 that advances a similar argument regarding the laws of *ona'ah*.

15. Some *poskim* maintain that this exception applies only when the market value actually changes. If the market price remains the same, but the buyer finds a seller willing to sell it below market price, *mechusar amana* will apply (*Shevet HaLevi* 7:236:4).

16. *Choshen Mishpat* 204; one opinion of the *Rama*; *Vilna Gaon* based on *Yerushalmi*; *Nesivos* 183; *Aruch HaShulchan*; *Chasam Sofer, Choshen Mishpat* 102; *Yoreh Deah* 246; *Chacham Tzvi* 70. *Pischei Choshen, Kinyanim* 1 n5 writes that most *Acharonim* rely on this opinion.

circumstances.[17] If one agrees to purchase an item and subsequently receives an identical item as a gift, one is not obligated to make the purchase.

If the buyer is aware that other stores may be selling the item at a lower price[18] and still chooses to make a verbal commitment to this particular seller, he may not back out later simply because he decided to look into other options and found something less expensive.

A customer signs a contract to buy a house and then applies for a mortgage at a local mortgage broker. Because the mortgage broker was an old friend, he felt compelled to use him regardless of how competitive his rates were. He fills out the necessary paperwork, and, after being approved, makes a verbal commitment to use the broker for his mortgage. If the seller reneges on his commitment to sell the house, the buyer has no obligations to the mortgage broker.

However, if the borrower decides to investigate online mortgage brokers and finds a slightly better rate, he still has an obligation to use the first broker. The rates have not changed; he had been aware all along that a better deal could be found elsewhere and is still bound to honor his commitment.

Other *poskim* argue that one must consider any oral agreement as final and binding.[19] Even if the price changes after the agreement, one should honor his word.

Aruch HaShulchan writes that although as a matter of halachah one is permitted to renege on a commitment if the price changes, it is a *middas chassidus* to honor one's commitment regardless of the circumstances.[20]

17. *Chasam Sofer* 102.

18. See Chapter One for a discussion of *ona'ah*, the laws of overcharging.

19. *Shulchan Aruch* 204:7; *Rambam, Mechirah* 7:8 (according to *Sma* 12); *Rama* 204:11.

Meiri, Bava Metzia 49a writes that the majority of the *Rishonim* apply *mechusar amana* even when the price changed.

20. *Aruch HaShulchan* 204:8.

See *Shevet HaLevi* 7:236:7 that if one receives an identical item as a gift and has

Attorney Review

Many real estate agreements are subject to an attorney-review period. During the review period, either party may cancel the contract if his attorney finds fault with the terms. If the contract is not reviewed by an attorney, it is legally binding.

If a legitimate issue is found with the contract, either party clearly has the right to cancel the contract and would not be considered *mechusar amana*. The agreement was reached subject to the approval of the attorneys, with the understanding that if the attorney disapproves, the deal will be canceled.

However, people occasionally use the attorney-review period to back out of a deal even though the contract is perfectly acceptable. They use the attorney-review period as a legal loophole that allows them to renege on their commitment. One could argue that this is a violation of *mechusar amana*. *Mechusar amana* applies to a verbal agreement even when there is no contract. The legal loophole permitting one to void a contract does not release a person from his obligation to honor his word.

This halachah will depend on the nature of the contract. If at the time the contract was signed it was understood that the parties would take advantage of the attorney-review period to finalize their decision, the agreement was only tentative and either party would be allowed to back out of the deal.

Furthermore, if the transaction had real issues that needed to be addressed, neither party would have *semichas daas*: they would not be confident that the deal had been finalized. As such, if the parties choose to back out for any reason, they would not be considered *mechusar amana*.[21]

---

absolutely no reason to buy a second, all opinions agree that there is no *mechusar amana*.

See also *Maharshag* 3:113, who, in situations where there is an extraordinary price increase, relies on the opinion that *mechusar amana* does not apply (based on *Taz, Even HaEzer* 114(2)).

21. See *Nachalas Tzvi* 237 quoting *Knesses Yechezkel, Orach Chaim* 8 that a rabbi may back out of an employment agreement. He explains that when a rabbi accepts a position, there are many unknowns. Because of the significant unknown variables, any

On the other hand, if the deal was finalized and there was a meeting of minds on all major issues, the legal right to void a contract would not release the parties from their responsibility to honor their commitments.

Inspection Periods

Backing out of a contract during an inspection period would be subject to the same parameters as the attorney-review period. Any real issues revealed by the inspection would justify canceling the deal. However, if the parties are aware of the general condition of the house, and the inspection is more of a formality, one may not take advantage of the inspection period to change his mind, unless there was an understanding to use the inspection period to reconsider.

A buyer signed a contract to purchase a house. During the inspection period, he had second thoughts and decided that he would rather live in a different neighborhood. He ordered an inspection for the property. The report contained no major defects, other than the expected wear and tear that exists in virtually all houses. If the buyer backs out, he will be subject to mechusar amana.

Non-Monetary Commitments

The concept of *mechusar amana* is discussed in the context of a business transaction. The cases discussed by the *poskim* usually involve commitments to buy, to sell, or to give a gift. In *Yoreh Deah Hilchos Milah*[22] there is a discussion whether a father who offers a *mohel* the opportunity to perform his son's *bris* may change his mind and offer the *milah* to a different *mohel*. The

---

commitment is considered a *matanah merubah* (see section "Size of Commitment") and is not binding.

22. *Yoreh Deah* 264.

mohel is not charging for his services, and there is no monetary dispute. The question is whether *mechusar amana* would apply to such agreements.

Most *poskim*[23] maintain that *mechusar amana* will apply, and the father should have the first *mohel* perform the *bris*.[24]

This debate has important ramifications for many different business transactions. Many modern-day business agreements are structured in ways that are not recognized in halachah as enforceable monetary commitments. (These issues will be explained at the end of this chapter. See "Contracts.") According to halachah, even in instances where an agreement does not create a binding financial obligation, the requirement to honor one's word will apply.

3. Payment

According to halachah, a formal act, or *kinyan,* is necessary to consummate a sale. Simply agreeing to sell an item does not transfer ownership to the buyer. [25](See Section "Formal Kinyan" for examples of appropriate *kinyanim.*) Paying for an item will have different halachic ramifications, depending on the nature of the sale. The primary factor is whether the transfer involves movable items, *mitaltelin,* or real property, *karka.*

---

23. *Rama* 264:1; *Taz* (5); *Shach* (7); *Chavos Daas, Yoreh Deah* 168 (38).

See *Yad Avraham* and *Maharshag* 3:113 who argue that the above-mentioned *poskim* based their verdict on an erroneous version of the *Teshuvas HaRosh* (102:10). However, according to the correct version, *mechusar amana* is restricted to commitments of monetary nature and will not apply to a *bris milah*. See also *Imrei Binah, Halvah* 51.

Minchas Pitim in *Shiyurei Minchah* 204 cites the correct version of the *Rosh* but nevertheless concludes that *mechusar amana* does apply to non-monetary cases.

24. This halachah has an interesting application. What happens if a seller commits to sell a property, and then makes a second conflicting commitment to sell the property to another party? At this point, regardless of whom the seller sells the property to, he will be a *mechusar amana* to the other bidder. Does the seller now have the right to choose whom to sell the property to, or does one of the buyers have precedence? This halachah implies that he must sell to the first party. However, see *Kesef HaKadoshim* 204 and *Shiyurei Minchah* 204:11.

25. *Choshen Mishpat* 204:1, 189:1.

Movable Objects — Mitaltelin

Payment for *mitaltelin* is not a valid *kinyan* and will not effect a change in ownership.[26] The Gemara[27] explains that according to Biblical law, payment should be an acceptable *kinyan* and should effect an immediate transfer of ownership. However, *Chazal* were concerned that if the buyer becomes the legal owner of the merchandise immediately after payment, the seller would have no incentive to safeguard the merchandise, which is still in his possession. If, for example, a fire broke out in the seller's warehouse, he would have no incentive to rescue the merchandise. He could allow it to be destroyed and the buyer would be compelled to suffer the loss. All buyers would therefore assume significant risk between payment and delivery.

To eliminate this risk, *Chazal* enabled either party to back out of the deal until the parties make another *kinyan*.[28] Even if the buyer paid in full for the merchandise, either party may change their minds and cancel the sale. This gives the seller an incentive to safeguard the merchandise until delivery.

On the other hand, *Chazal* did not want to allow buyers or sellers to indiscriminately renege on their commitments. To discourage people from taking advantage of this loophole, *Chazal* instituted the *me shepara*. *Beis din* curses the party who wishes to back out, saying, "*Me shepara*, Hashem, Who exacted payment from the generation of the *Mabul*, the *Dor Haflagah*, from the peoples of Sodom and Amorah and Who punished the Egyptians

26. *Choshen Mishpat* 204:1.

27. This reflects the opinion of R' Yochanan, quoted in *Bava Metzia* 47b.

28. Most *kinyanim* require the buyer to take physical possession of the goods. Once he takes possession of the goods, the buyer is no longer dependent on the seller to safeguard the merchandise.

Other *kinyanim* do not require the buyer to take physical possession of the goods. Nevertheless, until the buyer actually pays for the goods, the seller has a strong incentive to safeguard them. The risk that motivated *Chazal* to intervene arises only if the buyer has paid for the merchandise but had not taken physical possession of it. *Sma* 198(7).

at the Yam Suf,[29] will ultimately bring justice to those who do not stand by their word."[30]

Me shepera is a deterrent to prevent people from reneging on their commitments. Nevertheless, if the person is willing to accept the curse and insists on reneging on his commitment, *beis din* will allow him to do so.

This creates a unique situation. While either party has the legal right to renege on the agreement, because of the significant level of commitment created by paying for the item, halachah strongly discourages either party from taking advantage of this ability.

Parameters of Me Shepara

Me shepara is a very serious matter. It applies even if the price of the item changes after the agreement. The only instance where the buyer is permitted to back out of the deal is if the purchase is lost or destroyed.[31]

29. This is a listing of some of the more prominent examples in history when Hashem took vengeance on those who defied His Will. *Sma* (8).

30. *Shulchan Aruch* 204:4.

Rama 204:4 writes that *beis din* curses the person specifically, i.e., Hashem will punish **you**.

31. According to some *poskim*, the buyer need not wait until the item is actually destroyed. Even the threat of its destruction justifies reneging on the deal (*Shulchan Aruch* 204:2).

Aruch HaShulchan 204:7 (based on *Sma* 4) limits this exception to instances where the entire object may be destroyed. A threat of a partial loss does not justify reneging on the agreement. This applies only to a potential loss. If, however, the item is actually damaged, the buyer may back out of the deal even if the item is only partially damaged.

Shaar Mishpat 204:1 argues and extends this distinction between partial and complete loss to instances where the item was actually damaged. If it is only partially damaged, the parties must honor the terms of the deal. *Me shepara* is only waived if the entire purchase is destroyed.

Shaar Mishpat maintains that the distinction of partial damage applies only if the entire purchase is still intact, but somewhat damaged. For example, if a person pays for a barrel of wine, and it spoils and becomes vinegar, the item is still usable. Although it has less value than wine, because it is completely usable, one would be required to consummate the deal to avoid a *me shepara*. In contrast, if even part of a purchase is destroyed and completely unusable, the buyer may back out. For example, if a buyer places a deposit on a set of dishes, and one dish breaks before

Real Estate — Karka

Payment is a valid *kinyan* for real estate and can immediately transfer the ownership of real property.[32] The buyer need not pay for the entire purchase. Even a token payment can create a *kinyan*.[33] However, all *kinyanim* need *daas*; the parties must intend to transfer ownership. Nowadays, the parties typically do not want the transfer to take place until the deed and all of the appropriate documents are executed. As such, payment itself will not create a *kinyan*.[34] However, according to many *poskim*, *me shepara* will apply if a payment is made.[35]

Installments and Security Deposits

Me shepara will apply even if there was only a partial payment to the owner.[36] However, if the buyer does not actually pay the seller, but rather gives him an item as collateral (*mashkon*), to secure the deal, he would not be subject to *me shepara*.[37] The

the buyer takes possession, the buyer has no obligation to buy the set.

32. *Choshen Mishpat* 190:1.

33. Ibid.

34. Ibid. 190:7.

35. *Tosafos, Kesubos* 93a; *Pischei Teshuvah* 204:2; *Igros Moshe, Choshen Mishpat* 1:44; *Chazon Ish, Choshen Mishpat, Likkutim* 15:11.

See also *Beis Yosef* 204; *Shitah Mekubetzes* (*Ritva*), *Bava Metzia* 14a; and *Mishpat Shalom* 190:7 who quote sources that *me shepara* does not apply to real estate.

In a case where it is unclear in halachah whether a *me shepara* is appropriate, *Erech Shai* 204:2 (based on *Bach* 204 (9)) writes that if a party chooses to back out, a *me shepara* warning is not administered.

Mishpat Shalom 204:2 argues that since there is a doubt, the seller may refuse to refund the money until the buyer accepts a *me shepara*. However, because there is a doubt, *beis din* does not refer specifically to the buyer when making the *me shepara*. *Beis din* makes a general statement that Hashem will punish those who do not honor their commitments.

36. *Choshen Mishpat* 204:1

37. Ibid. 204:5.

See, however, *Ketzos* 204:1 who quotes *Ramban* and *Rashba* who disagree.

halachic status of a security deposit[38] or **money** given as collateral is questionable.[39]

4. Formal Kinyan

As explained earlier a formal act, or *kinyan,* is necessary to finalize a sale.[40] Until a *kinyan* is made, the item still belongs to the seller. If it is damaged or destroyed, the seller suffers the loss. After the *kinyan*, the item belongs to the buyer and the transaction is final. Neither party can reverse the transfer.

The most prevalent[41] *kinyan* for movable objects (*mitaltelin*) is taking physical control of the merchandise.[42] Neither payment[43] (see section "Payment") nor a contract[44] is a valid *kinyan* for *mitaltelin.* The classic *kinyanim* for *karka* (real property) are paying

38. *Chazon Ish, Likkutim* 15:11 writes that if the sales contract specifies a penalty for breach of contract, there may be no *me shepara*. The clause may be interpreted as an agreement to impose a financial penalty for breach of the agreement, and is an implicit waiver of any other remedies.

See also *Choshen Mishpat* 12:9, *Even HaEzer* 50:6.

39. *Bach* 204 (5); *Darkei Moshe, HaAruch* 204 (5); *Beur HaGra* 204:5 (10); *Mishpat Shalom* 204:5; *Nimukei Yosef, Bava Metzia* 29a (*Dafei HaRif*); based on *Yerushalmi, Sheviis* 10:4, write that although collateral does not create a *me shepera*, if **money** is given as a deposit, *me shepara* will apply. Accordingly, if a deposit is released to the seller, *me shepera* will apply.

However, a security deposit held in escrow by a third party is perhaps less binding than a *mashkon* and may not be subject to *me shepara* וצ"ע לדינא.

40. *Choshen Mishpat* 204:1.

41. Taking physical possession of the item is the most common form of *kinyan* for movable objects. Other *kinyanim* include *chalifin, suddar, agav,* or *odiysah.* See Appendix II for definitions of these concepts.

42. Lifting, pulling, holding the item, and bringing the item into one's property are the *kinyanim* of *hagba'ah, meshichah, yad,* and *chatzeir* respectively.

43. See *Mishpat Shalom* 201:2 as to whether payment is effective as a *situmta.*

44. See *Imrei Eish* 21, *Divrei Malkiel* 4:139 who write that a contract for the sale of *mitaltelin* would be an effective *kinyan* as a *situmta* (see "Accepted Business Norms").

for the property,[45] *chazakah*,[46] or *kinyan shtar* (contract).[47]

Accepted Business Norms — Situmta

Minhag hasochrim plays an important role in monetary transactions. If there is a prevaling custom to recognize a particular act as consummating a transaction, the act will be treated as a *kinyan* even though it does not conform to any of the classic forms of *kinyanim*.[48]

Contracts

There are a variety of halachic problems that may arise if a contract is structured incorrectly. *Kinyan devarim*,[49] *asmachta*,[50]

45. *Choshen Mishpat* 190:2, *Kinyan Kesef.* The buyer need not pay the entire sale price for the *kinyan*. A partial payment is sufficient. See *"Me Shepara — Karka."*

46. *Choshen Mishpat* 192. Improving the property in a manner that demonstrates ownership, such as enclosing it with a fence or plowing it in preparation for planting.

47. Ibid. 191. For a contract to be a valid *kinyan shtar,* there are a number of requirements regarding its form and structure. One should have the contract reviewed by a *rav* as well as a licensed attorney to ensure that it meets the necessary requirements.

48. Ibid. 201:2.

49. Halachah recognizes transactions that transfer ownership, create debts, liens, employment agreements, or any other monetary obligation. Contracts that call for other types of actions without monetary obligations are not enforceable and are known as *kinyan devarim*.

If one wishes to enter into an agreement that is a *kinyan devarim,* there is no direct way to make it enforceable in halachah. However, such agreements can be indirectly enforced by creating a monetary penalty that penalizes the party who does not abide by the agreement. The parties will be forced to comply with the agreement in order to avoid the penalty. To be effective, the penalty must be large enough to act as a deterrent.

50. Speculative agreements. A conditional liability that (1) the obligating party does not expect to occur, and (2) either (a) the event is not under his direct control, or (b) the liability he accepts is greater than the obligee's loss, is considered an *asmachta.* Such agreements are not binding in halachah even if a *kinyan* is made (*Choshen Mishpat* 207). A text to attach to a document to avoid issues of *asmachta* can be found in Appendix I.

and *lo ba l'olam*[51] are common in secular contracts, yet may be unenforceable according to halachah. Penalty clauses, non-compete agreements, and contracts for the future sale of goods are examples of common contracts that often have serious halachic repercussions. People often invest significant amounts of time and money negotiating a contract. They engage top-notch attorneys to ensure that their interests are well protected. Yet, *frum* Jews have an obligation to litigate their disputes in a *beis din*, which will not necessarily follow the secular guidelines with which the contract was drafted. Although in practice *beis din* will often insist that the parties honor a contract,[52] it is advisable to have a contract reviewed by a *beis din* or a *rav* before it is signed to ensure that it can be enforced by a *beis din* if the need to do so arises.

If it is not practical to have a contract reviewed by a *beis din*, a text may be added to the contract to enable it to be enforceable in *beis din*. This text will resolve many, but not all, of the common halachic problems that are found in contracts. See Appendix I.

It is recommended to make a *kinyan* when executing a contract.[53]

---

51. *Lo ba l'olam* occurs when one agrees to buy or sell an item that has not been manufactured, or that he does not yet own (*eino b'reshuso*). These transactions have become increasingly common as just-in-time delivery systems have become more popular. Selling new construction "on paper" before it is built and custom-made furniture are common examples. A *kinyan* is not effective on such transactions. These halachos are discussed in *Choshen Mishpat* 209.

52. Although none of these categories is binding according to strict halachah, many *poskim* honor certain agreements when they are consistent with *minhag* and *dina d'malchusa* (government law). See *Aruch HaShulchan, Choshen Mishpat* 201:3; *Chasam Sofer, Choshen Mishpat* 66; *Kovetz Teshuvos* 2:166.

(See, however, *Chazon Ish, Choshen Mishpat, Likkutim* 15:11 that *dina d'malchusa dina* will not eliminate the invalidation of *asmachta*.)

53. As explained before, an agreement, even in writing, is not enforceable in strict halachah without a *kinyan*. Although *minhag* and *situmta* may apply, it is advisable to avoid these issues by making a *kinyan*. This can be accomplished by executing a *kinyan suddar*. Each party should give an item of relatively negligible value such as a pen or handkerchief to the other party. By acquiring the *suddar* (uneven exchange), the parties obligate themselves to the terms of the contract.

Arbitration Clause

It is very difficult to force an uncooperative party to come to *beis din*. While *beis din* can exert strong communal pressure on a non-compliant party, there is no guarantee that the pressure will prove effective. The most effective way to avoid such issues is to include a dispute-resolution clause in all contracts. The clause should specify that any issues will be resolved through binding arbitration by a *beis din*. If executed properly, such a clause is legally binding and will force the parties to submit any dispute to a *beis din*.

Specifying a Beis Din

When a dispute arises, there is often strong disagreement over which *beis din* should adjudicate the issue. The parties involved will often try to ascertain which *beis din* will be most sympathetic to their claims. Choosing a *beis din* can become a difficult and time-consuming battle. Worse, an unscrupulous party may attempt to have the case tried by an ad-hoc corrupt *beis din*. Such incidents are not unheard of and can cause tremendous difficulties.

To avoid these problems, the parties may include a specific *beis din* in the dispute-resolution clause. When a contract is first signed, the parties generally have sufficient goodwill and trust to agree upon which *beis din* to use if necessary. Later, if an issue arises, the parties will be bound to use the *beis din* that they originally agreed upon. A sample specific dispute resolution clause can be found in Appendix I.

Two business partners from Tanzania expand their business to the United States. Before initiating the venture, they hire a top Tanzanian law firm to draft the necessary documents and partnership agreements.

Years go by. The new division is wildly successful and develops into a hugely profitable business. However, the partners begin to argue. The situation deteriorates and they decide to dissolve the partnership. The buy-out negotiations quickly fail and the partners begin what proves to be a messy and protracted litigation.

During the discovery phase of the trial, the partners present various documents to support their claims. They are confident that the Tanzanian attorneys had done their job well, and that their interests are well protected.

This proves to be a mistake. The Tanzanian documents had been drafted in Swahili, and were based on legal traditions that were radically different than those of the United States. In form and in substance, the documents are deemed unacceptable and unenforceable in the U.S. legal system.

When the partners receive the verdict, they are shocked. Unable to comprehend that they had blundered by using a Tanzanian lawyer, the partners blame the judge. They conclude that the judge is incompetent, corrupt, and probably incapable of reading plain Swahili.

All too often, people come to a din Torah with documents and agreements that are simply incompatible with Choshen Mishpat. When beis din issues its ruling, the losing party cannot accept the fact that his documents were not drafted according to halachah. He concludes that the dayanim are incompetent, corrupt, and incapable of reading plain English.

In addition, many clauses that are common in legal documents can lead to violations of various mitzvos or to prohibitions. To avoid these pitfalls, and to guarantee that a contract will be honored and enforceable by a beis din if necessary, one should have all contracts reviewed by a competent rav or dayan.

5 You Shall Not Covet / Lo Sachmod and Lo Sisaveh

Introduction

Middos are not counted among the 613 mitzvos of the Torah. Rav Chaim Vital[1] explains that proper middos are the prerequisite and foundation upon which the Torah is given. Without the necessary middos, it would be impossible for a person to serve Hashem properly. He would struggle to perform mitzvos, and would ultimately not succeed. Because an unrefined middah will cause a person to violate multiple commandments, it is too broad to be counted as one specific sin.

In a sense, a person needs to be more particular about his middos than about a specific mitzvah, since achieving one proper middah will empower him to perform many future mitzvos.

The root of any violation of Lo Sachmod is jealousy. Yet as Rav Chaim Vital explains, Lo Sachmod is just

1. *Shaar HaKedushah, Shaar Sheni.*

one of the many prohibitions that a person whose personality is controlled by envy will violate. If he is unable to obtain the item he covets legitimately, he will eventually come to cheat, steal, or even murder in his uncontrolled quest to fulfill his desires.[2]

Lo Sachmod is unique in that the prohibition is based on an emotion. One is not allowed to covet an item that belongs to someone else. Jealousy is a very human emotion; how can we be expected to overcome human nature?

The Ibn Ezra explains that we are only jealous of something that that we believe could be ours. When we see a friend or classmate being successful, we feel jealous. But when we see a king of royal lineage bask in the splendor of his riches, we don't feel a bit envious.

The difference is clear. We recognize that we are not kings. We were not born into royal families, and we don't yearn for something that we know cannot possibly be ours. But we might be envious of our neighbor, who we believe is no more capable than ourselves.

Lo Sachmod teaches us that our friend's possessions are out of reach. Hashem has given each person what is appropriate for him and anything belonging to another is no more in reach than is royalty.

If we would live with this emunah, we would never be tempted by another's possessions.

There are two related prohibitions regarding coveting — "Lo Sisaveh" and "Lo Sachmod."

2. *Rambam, Gezeilah* 1:11.
Even Shlomo Chapter 3 states that all sins arise from uncontrolled jealousy.

Definition — Lo Sisaveh

Lo Sisaveh[3] is the prohibition against desiring another person's belongings, and *making plans to obtain it.*[4] Even if these plans are never executed, *Lo Sisaveh* is violated by desiring the item and making plans to obtain it.[5] However, one who desires an item does not necessarily transgress the prohibition. Only if he makes plans to obtain it does he violate this prohibition.

Definition — *Lo Sachmod*

Lo Sachmod is a related prohibition. When a person takes action and pressures the owner to sell or give him the item that he desires, he violates *Lo Sachmod.* [6] Although the seller ultimately agrees to sell the item, if he was coerced or pressured into making the sale, *Lo Sachmod* has been violated. The prohibition applies both when the buyer pressures the owner directly, or has other people apply pressure on his behalf.[7] Every time a person

3. *Devarim* 5:18.

4. *Choshen Mishpat* 359:10 based on *Rambam, Gezeilah* 1:11.

However, see *Chinuch* 416 and *Rambam, Sefer HaMitzvos* 266 who imply that one violates *Lo Sisaveh* simply by desiring an item without making plans to obtain it.

5. *Choshen Mishpat* 359; *Chinuch, Mitzvah* 416.

6. *Rambam, Gezeilah* 1:10; *Choshen Mishpat* 359:10; *Chinuch, Mitzvah* 38.

Tosafos, Sanhedrin 25b maintains that the prohibition applies only when one takes the item **without** paying for it. If one pressures the owner to sell the item, according to *Tosafos, Lo Sachmod* has not been transgressed.

Shulchan Aruch follows the ruling of the *Rambam* that *Lo Sachmod* applies even if one pays for the item (*Sma* 359:9 (14)).

See, however, *Ba'er Haitev* 359:9 (6) who maintains that even *Rambam* and *Shulchan Aruch* concede that the Biblical prohibition applies only if the item is taken without payment. Coercing the owner to sell would be a Rabbinic violation.

7. *Hichbid Alav Brayim V'Hiphtzir. Rambam, Gezeilah* 1:9.

This would appear to conflict with the rule of *ein shaliach l'dvar aveirah*, one is not liable for a sin done on his behalf by an agent. However, there is an important distinction. *Lo Sachmod* is coveting an item and then causing the owner to relinquish it against his will. Sending an agent to pressure the owner to sell a particular item is itself the violation. The person applying the pressure is not violating the prohibition on behalf of the buyer; he is simply the means whereby the buyer is pressuring the owner to sell.

violates *Lo Sachmod*, he will violate *Lo Sisaveh* as well.

To violate the prohibition, the person must be successful in obtaining the object. If the owner refuses to sell, the bidder has not violated *Lo Sachmod*. However, he has violated *Lo Sisaveh*.

Most items today are mass-produced and are readily available. If a person desires such items, he can simply purchase them in any store, and has no reason to pressure any particular owner to sell it to him. It is therefore uncommon to find violations of *Lo Sachmod* involving standard mass-produced items.[8] Antiques, custom one-of-a-kind works of art, and real estate are examples where the prohibition is more relevent.

Guidelines

If one desires an item, it is permitted to approach the owner and inquire if the item is for sale. If the owner indicates that he is willing to sell the item, one may negotiate without any fear of *Lo Sachmod*. The prohibition is to pester and pressure the owner to sell against his wishes.[9]

As a general rule, asking the owner once or twice if he is willing to sell is permitted.[10] Asking three times is considered pressure and is a violation of *Lo Sachmod*.

There are exceptions to this rule. If the owner is approached in a manner that makes it difficult for him to refuse the offer, it is possible to violate *Lo Sachmod* on the first approach. For example, a distinguished member of a community, whom the owner cannot refuse, may violate *Lo Sachmod* by approaching the owner even once.[11]

According to some *poskim*, making an exorbitant offer on a property is a violation of *Lo Sachmod* if the owner did not intend to sell the property. Although the owner may now be thrilled to

8. Although see *Derech Pekudecha*. ורצ״ע

9. *Hichbid Alav Brayim V'Hiphtzir. Rambam, Gezeilah* 1:9.

10. *B'tzel HaChochmah* 3:43:9.

11. *Shaarei Teshuvah, Shaar* 3:43.

sell at such a high price, since the item was not for sale and he only consented because of the irresistible offer, *Lo Sachmod* has been violated.[12]

The *Aruch HaShulchan*[13] suggests that one avoid purchasing from anyone who is not selling the item for his *parnassah* (livelihood), in order to avoid these issues. However, if the owner approaches a buyer to offer him the item, one need not hesitate.

A developer requires a particular parcel of land to complete a development. If the owner indicates that he is not interested in selling, and the developer pressures him to sell, the developer has violated the prohibition of Lo Sachmod.

Brokers

Lo Sachmod applies when a person covets an item and takes action to obtain that item. A broker who pressures someone to sell his property has not violated *Lo Sachmod*,[14] since the broker does not want to purchase the item. He is merely convincing the owner to list the property so that he can sell it on his behalf.

However, if a buyer asks a broker to pressure the owner to sell a property, the buyer has violated *Lo Sachmod*. The broker may violate *lifnei eveir* by assisting the buyer in violating *Lo Sachmod*.[15]

---

12. *Chareidim* Chapter 21 (2-5); *Birchas Peretz, Yisro*.
This would apply to an item that the owner had no intention of selling until "coerced" by the offer. For example, making a high offer on a person's home. However, one could argue that an investment property would always be considered for sale, subject to an appropriate offer.

13. *Choshen Mishpat* 359:13.

14. *Divrei Yatziv* 6:65.
See, however, *Sefer Rav Berachos, "Lo Sachmod,"* who discusses this halachah but does not render a final verdict.

15. See Ch. 6 footnote 7 for more about *lifnei eveir*.

Non-Jewish Sellers

The prohibition applies only when the item belongs to a Jew. If an item belongs to a non-Jew one does not violate the prohibition by convincing him to sell.[16]

Lo Sachmod is one of the Ten Commandments.[17] *Yet, many people cannot properly define the prohibition or identify situations where it applies. With even a basic understanding of this commandment, it becomes clear that it is very relevant in today's business environment. There are many common situations in which applying standard business practices will lead to a violation of the prohibition. It is especially important for those involved in real estate to become familiar with the parameters of these halachos.*

16. *Minchas Chinuch* 38; *Sefer HaMakneh, Kuntreis Acharon* 28; *Shulchan Aruch HaRav, Orach Chaim* 440; *Kuntreis Acharon* 11. However, see *Pri Megadim* 604.

A non-Jew is obligated to honor the prohibition of *Lo Sisaveh* (*Chinuch* 41). [Although a non-Jew is obligated to honor only the seven mitzvos of Noach, *Lo Sisaveh* is a precursor to, and is included in, the prohibition against stealing.]

17. *Lo Sachmod* is the last of the Ten Commandments. Its severity is equal to all of the others combined. *Even Shlomo* Chapter 3; *Pele Yoetz, Chemdah.*

Financing

6 Ribbis – Heter Iska and Mortgages

Introduction

Imagine in your mind's eye the world's largest kosher restaurant. The restaurant is always bustling, serving thousands of customers each day. It is a full-service restaurant that serves both milchig and fleishig. Incredibly, the restaurant manages to do this out of only one kitchen and with only one set of dishes.

Now imagine that this restaurant has no hechsher, no Rabbinical supervision to ensure its kashrus. The owners are fine ehrliche (upright) Yidden who wouldn't dream of serving tarfus (not kosher) to the public, and people rely on them completely.

Now imagine that the owners of this establishment are completely ignorant of the laws of kashrus. They have never studied the laws of kashrus, and their knowledge is limited to several tidbits that they have heard from a few well-intentioned customers over the years.

Would anyone patronize such an establishment?

Sadly, our parable is reality when it comes to Hilchos Ribbis. Our financial dealings are highly sophisticated, and the slightest misunderstanding could easily lead to ribbis. Yet, the financial-service companies that we deal with have no supervision, no hechsher ribbis, and no one involved who can examine our transactions to determine whether they are kosher, i.e., meet the basic standards.

The Sma[1] *writes that each family should have a talmid chacham familiar with the laws of ribbis with whom they consult before every transaction. He continues that if a heter iska is written without proper guidance, a beis din should not accept it, even if it happened to be executed properly.*

We are fortunate to live in a time where Rabbanim, batei din, and poskim are only a phone call away. It is inexcusable for people to spend weeks carefully drafting a loan agreement and negotiating over each and every word, and then nonchalantly pulling out a heter iska form at the closing and signing without even reading it.

Ribbis, the prohibition of charging or paying another Jew interest, is one of the most difficult areas of halachah to master. Seemingly minor changes in an investment relationship can have major implications in *Hilchos Ribbis*. It is important that every businessman be aware of at least the basic guidelines of *ribbis*, so that he is able to recognize an issue when it arises. In fact, the *Nesivos HaMishpat* instructed his descendants[2] to master the laws of *ribbis* ***before*** entering the workforce.

The following chapters outline some of the *ribbis* concerns that a businessman may face. It must be stressed that these chapters are only an outline and are intended to create a general aware-

1. End of *Kuntreis HaRibbis*.

2. *Tzava'ah* paragraph 20.

ness of the issues and to offer several practical suggestions on how to deal with them. One should consult with a Rav who has experience with *Hilchos Ribbis* whenever a question arises, as each case has its own nuances that impact the halachah.

What Is Ribbis?

A Jew may not charge or pay another Jew interest on a loan. There are six separate prohibitions of *ribbis*.[3] The lender, borrower,[4] guarantor, witnesses, and even the lawyer who drafts the loan document[5] all violate *ribbis* prohibitions.[6] In addition, anyone assisting the parties may violate *lifnei eveir*.[7]

---

3. *Rambam, Malveh V'Loveh* 4:2.

4. This is unique to *ribbis*. A thief violates *gezel*, not the victim. *Ona'ah* is violated by the one who overcharges and not by the one who is cheated. Only in *Hilchos Ribbis* do we find that the victim (borrower) violates a prohibition. *Tur, Yoreh Deah* 160 explains that since *ribbis* is such a common and tempting sin, the Torah places a prohibition on the borrower to discourage him from creating an opportunity for the lender to charge interest.

5. *Rambam, Malveh V'Loveh* 4:2 and *Shach* 160:1. The Mishnah discusses a scribe who wrote the loan document. A modern-day equivalent would be a lawyer or secretary.

6. *Yoreh Deah* 160:1.

7. There are three levels of prohibitions against facilitating a *ribbis* transaction.

Lifnei eveir is a Biblical prohibition against enabling another person to violate a prohibition. It is limited to instances where the parties were incapable of violating the prohibition without your help. (If the parties were incapable of violating the prohibition without help, but other Jews were willing to provide assistance, see *Mishneh LaMelech* 4:2, quoted in *Pischei Teshuvah* 151:2, 160:1. See also *Chazon Ish, Avodas Kochavim* 62:13.)

The second level is *mesayei'a*. This is a Rabbinic prohibition and applies to anyone that helps a person violate a prohibition. Although the sinner was capable of violating the prohibition without any outside help, assisting him is prohibited.

There are certain leniencies that may apply to cases that involve only *mesayei'a* and not *lifnei eveir*. For example, *Pri Megadim Aishel Avraham, Orach Chaim* 163:2 maintains that this halachah does not apply to Rabbinical prohibitions (see however *Pischei Teshuvah, Yoreh Deah* 160:1 who disagrees). In addition, *Shach, Yoreh Deah* 151:6 and *Dagul Mervavah* limit this halachah to instances where the sinner is unwittingly violating a prohibition. If, however, a person deliberately violates a prohibition, one is not forbidden to assist him.

Ribbis is a third category. Drafting or guaranteeing a *ribbis* transaction is itself a violation of *ribbis*. It is irrelevant whether the parties could have completed the transaction without help. The problem is not causing the transgression; the prohibition of *ribbis* applies to all those that are involved in the loan. Therefore, the

Akum

The prohibition applies only when a Jew charges another Jew interest. A Jew may charge[8] or pay an *akum* (non-Jew) interest.

Business Loans

The prohibition against charging interest applies to both personal loans and to money advanced for business purposes.[9] It makes no difference whether the borrower needs the money to put food on his table or if he intends to invest the money in a lucrative business deal. *Ribbis* is prohibited even if the borrower expects to earn more on his investment than the interest that he is paying.

Corporations

Some *poskim* write that a Jewish-owned corporation may pay interest to another Jew.[10] This ruling applies only to loans that

---

argument that the parties could have done it without outside assistance or that the parties were willfully violating the prohibition will not relieve the involved parties of their responsibilities.

A broker who negotiates a loan is not considered a party to the *ribbis*. Therefore, the guidelines of *lifnei eveir* and *mesayei'a* would apply.

8. There is nothing inherently wrong with charging interest on a loan (see introduction to Chapter 8). The prohibition of *ribbis* arises from the requirement to treat a fellow Jew as a brother and to help him with a free loan. As such, these laws do not apply to an *akum*.

See *Bava Metzia* 70b that there was a Rabbinical injunction against charging an *akum* interest. See *Tosafos* for various reasons why this injunction does not apply today.

9. Interest on a loan is *ribbis*. However, if the money is advanced as an investment, where the investor is liable for losses, and will earn a return based on the profits that his money engendered, there may not be a *ribbis* violation. See below for an explanation of *heter iska*.

10. *Igros Moshe, Yoreh Deah* 2:63; *Maharshag* quoted by *Minchas Yitzchak* 4:16. The Torah prohibits charging interest on a loan. A loan by definition implies that there is a borrower who is responsible to ensure that the debt is repaid. When a corporation borrows money, there is no personal liability. No one is personally responsible to repay the debt. *Igros Moshe* ruled that such transactions are not classified as loans

have no personal liability.[11] If the owner of the company guarantees the loan, this leniency would not apply.[12] If the owner pledges collateral for the loan, this leniency will still apply, provided that there is no personal liability. However, when relying on this leniency, careful attention must be paid to any clauses that may create personal liability in the event of a default.

This ruling applies only when the corporation borrows money. A corporation may not charge interest to an individual.

Many *poskim* disagree with this ruling. A person should follow the ruling of his Rav.[13]

Heter Iska

From the times of the Rishonim, there were various suggestions on how to structure a transaction that would have many of the characteristics of an interest-bearing loan, yet be halachically permitted. What evolved is a partnership structure known as a *heter iska*.

To understand a *heter iska*, one must understand the difference between a loan and an investment. A loan must be paid back under any circumstances. Even if the borrower loses the money that he borrowed, he is obligated to return the funds to the lender. While borrowers do occasionally default on loans, that simply means that they are not honoring their obligations to repay the loans.

In contrast, an investment is a risk. It is repaid only if the business retains its value. If the business suffers a partial loss, so

---

and are not subject to the laws of *ribbis*.

11. *Igros Moshe* extends this concept to a personal loan in which the borrower accepts no personal responsibility to repay the loan, but rather pledges assets as collateral for the debt.

12. *Igros Moshe* 2:63.

13. Many contemporary *poskim* disagree with this leniency. See *Minchas Yitzchak* 3:1, 4:16, 4:17; *Bris Yehudah* 7 n66; *Minchas Shlomo* 1:28.

It should be noted that some of the *poskim* who disagreed with this ruling concede that the violation in such cases would be Rabbinic. Accordingly, certain leniencies that apply to Rabbinic cases of *ribbis* will apply (*Maharshag Yoreh Deah* 3,5; *Minchas Yitzchak* 4:16:7).

will the investor. If the business does not generate any profits, the investor will not earn any returns. If the business loses all its value, the recipient has no obligation to make any payments to the lender. This is not a default of his obligations; there is simply no liability for a legitimate business loss.

A *heter iska* is an investment that is structured in a way that virtually guarantees that the investor will receive both the principal and "interest" payments. It accomplishes this by creating a partnership with the following terms.

All profits and losses from the investment are shared equally[14] between the "lender" and the "borrower."[15] To ensure that the "lender" receives his principal and "interest," the agreement requires the "borrower" to clearly demonstrate how well the business venture has performed before the profits are divided. The "borrower" must either provide two halachically acceptable witnesses,[16] or take a solemn oath[17] to account for the investment.

Neither of these options is especially appealing to the borrower. Finding two halachically acceptable witnesses who have direct knowledge of his business affairs is difficult. Solemn oaths are discouraged under any circumstances.[18]

The "borrower" is given another option. He may return the principal together with a previously agreed-upon profit payment

---

14. This applies to the classic *heter iska* known as a *chatzi milveh v'chatzi pekadon*. Half the money advanced is treated as a loan, for which the "borrower" has full responsibility. The remaining funds are treated as an investment for which the "lender" is liable. The profits are also divided equally. The investor is entitled to the profits generated by his half of the money, and the "borrower" is entitled to the profits generated by the funds that he borrowed. An alternate form known as a *kulo pekadon* is described in footnote 36.

15. A *heter iska* creates a partnership, and the terms "lender" or "borrower" are inaccurate. Nevertheless, I have used these terms in quotation marks to make this section easier to understand.

16. To verify any claim of loss. The investor is entitled to demand witnesses to account for the lost money.

17. To verify a claim regarding the amount of profits generated. One may not require witnesses for the amount of profits (*Levush*, *Taz* 167).

18. See *Chasam Sofer, Choshen Mishpat* 90.

("interest") in exchange for the lender/investor waiving his rights to demand proof of the investment's return. The "borrower" generally chooses to make this payment.

What results is a relationship which is a partnership in halachah, yet acts like a loan in practically every situation.

Risk

It is important to realize that every *heter iska* carries with it a minimal level of risk. The "borrower" has the right to make an oath that no profits were generated, or to bring witnesses that the investment lost money. If he does, the "borrower" is not obligated to repay the investment.[19] While this risk is certainly minimal, it is an absolute necessity for the validity of the *heter*. If steps are taken to completely eliminate any risk, the *heter iska* is invalid.

Permissible Use of Heter Iska Funds

An *iska* partnership is predicated on the rights of the investing partner to receive the profits generated by his funds. If the recipient intends to use the money for personal non-business use, there will be no profits generated and therefore no justification for the investing partner to receive any payment in lieu of profits. If the recipient owns a business or has investments worth the amount that he is receiving as an *iska*, he may use a special *heter iska* form described in the next chapter. If the recipient has no investments, he may not use a *heter iska*.[20]

19. When a standard *heter iska* (*chatzi milveh v'chatzi pekadon*) is executed, the "lender" is always entitled to repayment of at least half his funds, even if the "borrower's" business suffers a complete loss.

20. See *Bris Yehudah* 38 n18 that permits the use of a *heter iska* if the recipient is buying a house. Although it will not generate steady rental income, it may appreciate in value over time.

Although a "borrower" is prohibited from taking money for an *iska* if he has no intention of investing it, the "lender" may presume the money was invested as per the *iska* agreement and may demand verification of the business results, or the

Management Fee — Schar Tirchah

A *heter iska* requires the investing partner to pay[21] a management fee to compensate the recipient for managing the *iska* partnership. This payment is required by halachah.[22] If it is not paid, the fact that the recipient manages the *iska* partnership on behalf of the investing partner is itself considered *ribbis*. Nevertheless, the investing partner is not obligated to pay the full market value of the managing partner's services. A token payment will suffice, provided it is agreed to at the start of the *iska* partnership.[23]

Guarantors

The custom is to permit guarantors on a *heter iska*.[24]

Executing a Heter Iska

When a *heter iska* is executed, there are a number of important rules to bear in mind.

---

payment in lieu of such verification. Unless the "lender" has direct knowledge that the "borrower" diverted the funds for personal use, he may collect the agreed-upon profit payments (*Toras Ribbis* 16 n86 citing *Maharshag Yoreh Deah* 4 and *R' S. Z. Auerbach*).

See also *Shoel U'Meishiv* 1:3:160 who permits the recipient to accept *heter iska* funds for personal use if it will indirectly enable the recipient to engage in a profitable business. (For example, using *iska* funds to marry off a child may ultimately save the father the cost of supporting the child. Using *iska* funds for living expenses allows the recipient to work and earn a salary.)

21. An alternate form of compensation is to give the recipient a greater share of the profits generated.

22. *Yoreh Deah* 177:2.

23. Ibid. 177:2-4.

24. *Imrei Yosher* 189; *Maharsham* 1:20.

If the funds went directly to the "borrower," the guarantor never had the opportunity to invest the funds, and consequently could not have generated any profits. How can a guarantor make payments in lieu of profits that could not have been generated?

Maharsham 1:20 writes that the lender often does not have firsthand knowledge of what happened to the funds he advanced. Since the funds *may* have gone to the guarantor, the "lender" may demand either verification or the payments in lieu of verification.

- It is important that both parties understand the *heter iska.*[25] It should be studied carefully. Each party should be aware that the transaction is a partnership and not a loan.

- Many *iska* contracts call for a $1 payment. This is known as *schar tirchah* and is a management fee due to the "borrower" for managing the *iska* on behalf of the investing partner.[26] The "borrower" must actually receive this payment.[27]

- The *heter iska* should be written[28] and signed by both

Imrei Yosher 189 suggests that the guarantor is obligated to invest money on behalf of the "lender." Although the guarantor did not receive any funds, the *iska* partnership is created when the guarantor takes personal money and invests it on behalf of the "lender." If the guarantor swears that this investment did not generate any profits, he will not be liable for profit payments. If the guarantor is unable to swear, he would be obligated to pay even if the "borrower" swears that no profits were generated by his investment.

See *Minchas Elazar* 2:33 that implies that a *heter iska* cannot be executed between a guarantor and a "borrower."

25. A *heter iska* is a legal document that defines the parties' relationship. They are no longer "lender/borrower"; rather they are partners. The parties must have a clear understanding of what they are doing. See *Chochmas Adam* 143:3; *Igros Moshe, Yoreh Deah* 2:62; *Minchas Yitzchak* 4:16:5.

Igros Moshe, Choshen Mishpat 1:22 implies that if the parties did not understand the *iska*, it is, *bedi'eved*, still valid. See, however, *Igros Moshe, Yoreh Deah* 2:63 וצ"ע.

Tzemach Tzedek. See *Yoreh Deah* 88, *Shev Yaakov* 35, that if the two parties did not understand the *iska*, it would not be valid.

26. Although managing an investment is clearly worth more than $1, a token payment will suffice.

Some *iskas* avoid this payment by either including the dollar in the agreed upon profit payment, or by increasing the percentage of profits that the managing partner is entitled to, in the event that he chooses to take an oath to verify the actual amount of profits earned.

27. *Ginas Veradim, Yoreh Deah* 6:6 writes that the recipient may not waive the *schar tirchah* using the mechanism of *mechilah* (וע' שם שיכול לאמר הריני כאילו התקבלתי).

28. *Kitzur Shulchan Aruch* 66:7; *Tzemach Tzedek, Yoreh Deah* 88.

If the parties execute a promissory or mortgage note that characterizes the transaction as a loan, the "lender" would be able to use the promissory note to collect the principal even if the *iska* investment suffers a loss. Therefore, the recipient must have either a written *heter iska* or other evidence acceptable to *beis din* that the transaction was in fact an *iska* and not a loan (*Yoreh Deah* 176:24).

See footnote 31 for a discussion of whether the *heter iska* must be enforceable in secular court.

parties.[29]

- The *heter iska* should supersede any other conflicting documents.[30] If the "lender" is not observant of Torah law, the *iska* must be legally enforceable.[31]

- The recipient must retain the option of defaulting on the payments if he is able to produce acceptable proof that the venture did not produce profits, or suffered

---

If the money was advanced without any written documentation that describes a loan, and the parties understand the meaning of a *heter iska*, an oral *heter iska* will, *bedi'aved*, suffice. Nevertheless, it is preferable to have a written *iska*.

29. A *heter iska* form defines the rights and obligations of both the "borrower" and "lender." The "lender's" signature proves that he agrees to the terms. If the parties execute a legal promissory note, and only the "borrower" signs the *heter iska*, he will be unable to prove that the "lender" agreed to the terms. *Cheshev HaEphod* 1:96. See footnote 28.

30. *Igros Moshe, Yoreh Deah* 2:62. Executing a *heter iska* contradicts the terms of the loan document. If the parties sign both, it may not be clear which document is primary. Including a clause in the *heter iska* stating that it overrides any other document will make it clear that the transaction is in fact an *iska* partnership and not a loan. Alternatively, one may insert a clause in the loan document that specifies that it is subject to the terms of the *heter iska*.

Some attorneys object to including such clauses in a mortgage or promissory note because of the fear that these documents will be unenforceable in civil court. A secular court will not necessarily understand the nature of a *heter iska*, nor will it interpret the *iska* in a halachically appropriate manner. To allay such fears, one may write that the *heter iska* clause is intended to be interpreted by a *beis din*, and not by a civil court. However, this may only be written if the "lender" can be trusted to submit to a *beis din* in the event that a question concerning the *heter iska* arises. See footnote 31.

It should be noted that many loan documents have a clause that overrides any other document. This clause must be modified so that it does not override the *heter iska*.

31. *Minchas Yitzchak* 4:16:8. We typically give all Jews a *chezkas kashrus* and assume that they will act in accordance with halachah. Consequently, we are not concerned that a lender will use the secular loan documents to collect the "loan" if the recipient is able either to swear or to produce witnesses that the *iska* was not profitable.

However, this applies only when there is no clear evidence that the "lender" will ignore halachah. A "lender" who is not observant or has been known to charge interest without a *heter iska* does not have a *chezkas kashrus* and cannot be trusted to honor the *heter iska* in the unlikely event that the recipient manages to produce appropriate witnesses regarding losses. One may borrow from such a person with a *heter iska* only if it is clear that the *iska* can be enforced in court if the need arises.

Note: If loan documents are executed, a written *heter iska* is necessary regardless of who the "lender" is, as per footnote 28. *Minchas Yitzchak* is discussing a written *heter iska* that is not enforceable in secular court.

a loss.[32] Some erroneous *heter iska* forms **require** payments in lieu of providing testimony or an oath.[33] If one does not trust the recipient, and suspects he may be willing to make a false oath, one should not enter into an *iska* agreement with him.[34]

---

32. If a standard *chatzi milveh* form was executed, the "borrower" would be obligated to repay half the funds, even if there was a complete loss.

33. A commonly used, albeit misleading, *heter iska* form states, "However, the said______ has agreed that in lieu of such sharing of profits and losses, which would require substantiation of all losses by two trustworthy witnesses, and verification of all profits by oath, ______ shall accept my payment of _______ and waive all other profits ...."

This language seems to imply that the parties have agreed to make the predetermined-profit payment, and have waived their right to take an oath or to produce witnesses regarding the return of the investment. If this interpretation is correct, the *iska* would be invalid.

However, a careful reading of the text shows that while the "lender" has agreed to accept the set-profit payment, the recipient has never obligated himself to make such a payment and still retains the right to take an oath or bring witnesses. While this analysis is technically correct and the *iska* is valid, it does not seem appropriate to use an *iska* that is misleading, and could easily be misinterpreted by many users. The form can easily be corrected by changing the text to read, "We have agreed, that if I choose, I may make a payment of _______ percent for his share of profits."

This particular form has one signature blank for the recipient to sign. This reinforces the impression that the *iska* is a one-sided agreement that does not impact the "lender's" rights. It is recommended that both parties sign a *heter iska* to reflect the fact that it is restructuring the transaction in a manner that impacts, and is binding on, both parties.

See *Ginas Veradim* 6:6 regarding an erroneous *heter iska* form.

34. *Sma, Kuntreis HaRibbis, Kitzur* 3.

There are a number of clauses that may be inserted into an *iska* to give the "lender" additional security. One option is to require the recipient to make all his financial records available to the "lender" to verify the business results. This will "encourage" the recipient to make the profit payment.

Another option is to require the recipient to notify the investor within thirty days of any loss or shortfall of expected profits, and to require the immediate repayment of the remainder of the funds. Lack of such notice is construed as an admission that the expected profits have been generated. This clause precludes the "lender" from losing more than thirty days of "interest," and makes it even more difficult for the recipient to prove a loss (*Chochmas Adam* 143; *Imrei Yosher* 189; *Maharshag, Yoreh Deah* 4).

The Rate of Return Allowed in a Heter Iska

The agreed-upon profit payments of a *heter iska* must be based on the profits that the investment is expected to generate. If a standard *heter iska* form (known as *chatzi milveh v'chatzi pekadon*)[35] is executed, the rate of return may not exceed one-half of the project's projected rate of return. If a *kulo pekadon*[36] form is executed, the return may be as high as the investment's projected rate of return. These projections may be optimistic, but they must be realistic.[37]

If the investment will not generate enough profits to justify the agreed-upon rate of return, the parties may create an *iska* with other assets belonging to the "borrower." As long as the "borrower" owns any investment that will produce enough profits to justify the payments, he may create an *iska* on that asset. A *heter iska* form for such transactions may be found in Appendix I, but the *heter iska* for personal use form should be executed.

"Hard Money"

It is not uncommon for people who need short-term loans to turn to "hard money" lenders who may charge exorbitant rates. If the rate is above what the recipient can reasonably expect to earn during that short period, a *heter iska* does not make the

35. A standard *iska* form is *chatzi milveh v'chatzi pekadon.* This means that half the funds are advanced as a loan (*milveh*), for which the "borrower" accepts full responsibility, and the investor does not participate in any profits. The other half of the funds are advanced as a *pekadon*, for which the investor bears all the risks or profits. Accordingly, because the profit payment reflects the profits earned by only one-half of the funds, the agreed-upon payment cannot be greater then half the projected rate of return (*Igros Moshe, Yoreh Deah* 3:40).

36. A *kulo pekadon* form designates the entire advance as a *pekadon,* for which the investor receives all profits or losses. Accordingly, the rate of return may equal the investment's rate of return.

37. See *Mishpat HaRibbis* which states that R' Yissaschar Dov M'Belz instructed his *chassidim* not to charge more than 16 percent on an *iska.*

transaction permissible.

These lenders may justify the rates they charge as appropriate considering the level of risk involved in these transactions. This argument does not mitigate the prohibition of *ribbis*.

Occasionally, a borrower will offer the lender a fixed rate of return plus an equity stake in the investment. Care must be taken to ensure that the combined return does not exceed the expected rate of return of the project.

Points and Closing Costs

The "interest" paid on a *heter iska* is a payment in lieu of expected profits. As such, these payments may not be due before the investment could have produced profits. Points, which are paid at the time of the loan, can not be justified with a standard *heter iska*. One must subtract the points from the principal and create an *iska* partnership on the amount of money actually released to the recipient.[38] The rate of return may be adjusted to compensate for the resulting shortfall.

This applies to other fees as well. Origination fees, commitment fees, or any other fees relating to borrowing the money must be subtracted from the principal of the *iska*. However, fees related to the closing or preparing the loan and *iska* documents may be paid by the "borrower" and need not be reflected in the *iska*.

A Jewish bank "lent" a client $100,000 at the rate of 8 percent. The bank charged two points for the loan, an additional $1,000 for document preparation, and $700 for loan commitment and origination fees.

When drafting a heter iska, the principal amount should be $97,300 (the face value of the loan minus the points and loan fees). The profit payments should be 8 percent[39] *plus a one-time fee of*

---

38. *Kovetz Teshuvos* 1:79, 3:125.

39. Technically, because the face amount is $97,300 as opposed to $100,000, the rate should be slightly higher than 8 percent. One can either calculate the exact rate, or

$2,700 (the points and loan fees). The fee for preparing the loan documents need not be subtracted from the principal of the iska.

Default Terms

Many loan documents contain provisions that if violated, increase the amount of interest due. For example, the rate may increase if the borrower does not repay the loan by a certain date, or if he defaults on any of his obligations as defined by the agreement. Such increases must be reflected in the *heter iska* document drafted by the parties.[40]

Heter Iska Hashkafah

The entire concept of a *heter iska* needs explanation. The Torah clearly prohibits charging interest on a loan. The Torah also encourages Jews to extend free loans whenever another Jew needs help. Why did *Chazal* structure a formal way for people to circumvent the laws of *ribbis*? Is it proper to encourage people to take advantage of this arrangement?

Commentators explain that the prohibition against *ribbis* is related to the commandment of *v'chai achicha imach* (which requires that we ensure the financial stability of our brethren) and the obligation to help fellow Jews.

In a commercial (as opposed to agricultural society) society, people often require access to capital that generally cannot be made available interest-free. In order to enable lenders to fulfill these obligations, the Sages devised the *heter iska,* a vehicle which enables the financiers to advance funds while profiting in a way that the gains do not constitute *ribbis.*

---

simply write in the actual dollar amount that will be due per month.

40. The parties may either draft a detailed *heter iska,* specifying all of the terms, or they may incorporate into the *iska* a clause stating that additional terms and conditions are described in other documents. See Appendix I for an *iska* with attached document.

Accordingly, if a Jew is having difficulty earning a living, and one is able to give him an interest-free loan, it is appropriate to avoid using a *heter iska*. Extending an interest-free loan is a positive mitzvah of *im kesef talveh*.[41]

In a business environment, when someone is looking for a loan to expand his business and it is worthwhile for him to pay a return on the money, a *heter iska* may be appropriate.

Heter Iska — L'chatchilah or Bedi'eved?

People may be reluctant to rely on a *heter iska* because they feel that it is a *haramah*, a subterfuge to disguise what is actually *ribbis*. While there is certainly justification for such reluctance, it should be noted that the concept of a *heter iska* has been widely accepted throughout *Klal Yisrael*. Hundreds of responsa have been written regarding *heter iskas*, and numerous *sefarim* introduce new ideas and ways to structure an *iska*. With few exceptions, the *poskim* accept the concept and their discussion is about specific clauses or modifications to an *iska*.[42] A concept that has been validated for centuries by the greatest authorities may certainly be relied upon.

Mortgage Bankers

Mortgage bankers originate loans. They either lend their own capital or funds that they borrowed from other institutions. If the mortgage bank is owned by Jews, a *heter iska* is necessary. It is uncommon for a bank to be owned exclusively by either Jews or non-Jews. Most firms have mixed ownership, and there is considerable halachic debate on how to characterize these firms. There are three basic halachic categories for these "hybrid" firms:

---

41. *Shemos* 22:24.

42. It should be noted that there have been various clauses added to *heter iska*s to make them more secure. There is certainly basis to be *machmir* (stringent) and to refrain from relying on some of these new concepts.

- If Jews own most of the shares, the bank is considered Jewish owned and loans will be subject to the laws of *ribbis*. A valid *heter iska* would be required.[43]

- If Jews own an insignificant percentage of the bank and do not have any level of control, one may rely on the opinions that the bank is considered owned by non-Jews and is not subject to *Hilchos Ribbis*. [44]

43. It is unclear whether a bank may legally write a *heter iska*. An *iska* technically creates a partnership between the bank and the borrower. Banks are heavily regulated and are very limited in their ability to form partnerships with their clients. Additionally, banks may not take risks with depositors' money. An *iska* grants the recipient the right to default on the loan provided that he is able to produce acceptable evidence of a business loss. Accepting this additional risk may be a violation of banking regulation and could in theory open the bank to potential liabilities. Additionally, all public companies are obligated to disclose on their prospectus any risks involved with their business. One could argue that a bank would be liable for securities fraud if it fails to disclose the fact that it uses a *heter iska*.

In practice, it seems that bank regulators are willing to overlook *heter iskas*. Because the incremental default risk of a *heter iska* over a standard loan has historically been negligible, regulators seem to treat *iska*s as standard loans.

However, if a borrower defaults on a loan based on the terms of the *iska*, it is unclear whether the courts will enforce an *iska*. In fact, there have been a number of court cases regarding the enforceability of a *heter iska*, and the results have been inconclusive. See *Journal of Halachah*, Volume 25 for an article analyzing various court rulings regarding *heter iska*s. Consequently, if the bank in question is controlled by observant Jews, one may assume that they will honor the *iska* regardless of the court's stance. However, if a bank is controlled by Jews who are not observant and cannot be trusted to voluntarily honor a *heter iska*, one should not use the bank unless he is confident that the particular *iska* can be enforced if necessary. See also footnote 31.

See "Banks" regarding a *heter iska klali*.

See also *Maharit* 1:116 quoted by *R' Akiva Eiger, Yoreh Deah* 168/9:21; *Minchas Pitim* 168; *Cheshev HaEphod* 62 that if a non-Jew has complete control over the funds, there are no *ribbis* concerns regardless of who the funds belong to (although *Erech Shai, Yoreh Deah* 168 and *Maharshag, Yoreh Deah* 3 disagree).

44. *Igros Moshe, Even HaEzer* 7; *Kovetz Teshuvos* 3:123.

Similar arguments are suggested by *HaElef L'cha Shlomo, Orach Chaim* 238; *Mahariya HaLevi, Orach Chaim* 124; *R' Simchah Zelig Reger*, printed in *Kol HaTorah*, Vol. 40, p 103; *Teshuvos V'Hanhagos* 2:421.

Virtually every public bank has some Jewish shareholders. If the prohibitions of *ribbis* apply to a partnership with even a minority of Jewish ownership, it should be problematic to borrow from any public banking institution. Clearly, the *minhag* is to use public banks. What is the justification for this practice?

The above-mentioned *poskim* suggest that shareholders who own an insignificant number of shares in a public company are not considered real owners. They have no

- If Jews own a significant but minority stake in the bank, there is basis to be lenient.[45] However, one should preferably avoid using such a bank unless there is a valid *heter iska*.

Many *poskim*[46] maintain that a standard *heter iska* will not work if the lender intends to sell the *iska* to a non-Jew as a standard mortgage note.

Mortgage Brokers

Mortgage brokers arrange loans between a client and a third-party provider. The brokerage firm does not lend money; it

---

access to the company, have no rights to any of its assets, and their power is limited to voting for directors. Such ownership is not meaningful in halachah, and we view their shares as simply the right to share future profits or dividends of the company.

Accordingly, as long as there are no major Jewish shareholders, there would be no *ribbis* concerns.

R' Moshe *zt"l* does not define an exact percentage of ownership that would be considered meaningful in halachah. It likely will vary based on the size of the bank and the size of other blocks of stockholders. As a point of interest, the SEC considers a 5- or 10-percent stake significant regarding various legal issues.

This position leads to some interesting questions. R' Moshe was referring to situations in which the owners of the bank kept the majority of the shares. As such, these owners had absolute control of the company and were considered the "true owners." In today's market, many of the larger public banks do not have any single owner who owns more then a fraction of a percent. Presuming that these companies do in fact have owners, one could question whether and how the reasoning of R' Moshe would apply (see also *Teshuvos V'Hanhagos*).

This concept has other important ramifications as well. Owning a small number of shares in a company that does business on Shabbos or owns *chametz* on Pesach would be permitted according to *Igros Moshe*.

45. See *Bris Yehudah* 30:16, note 43 for an extensive discussion of the issue of minority ownership. *Bris Yehudah* concludes that most *poskim* permit using a bank that has a minority of Jewish ownership. However, many of the sources quoted consider this *heter* to be *bedi'eved*, to justify an existing practice. Also note that some of the arguments advanced to defend the use of banks would not apply in today's business environment.

46. If the transaction is structured as an *iska*, the "borrower" must retain the right to either swear or produce witnesses to verify the profits produced by the venture. If the mortgage is later sold to a non-Jew as a standard mortgage note, the new owner will not respect the conditions of the *iska*.

See *Kovetz Teshuvos* 3:124; *Yeshurin* Volumes 13 and 14; *Kovetz Meishiv B'Halachah* Volume 21 for a discussion of the issues and various solutions to the problem.

is the agent between the applicant and the lender. If the bank that is actually lending the money is owned by an *akum*, the mortgage itself is permissible. Even though the broker is paid a commission, the fee is for arranging the loan and is not considered interest. However, mortgage brokers often have some level of liability for the loans. If the borrower defaults within a certain time frame, the broker may be forced to buy the loan. Such arrangements may lead to *ribbis*, and a Rav should be consulted.[47]

General Iska — Heter Iska Klali

Under normal circumstances, a separate *heter iska* is required for each and every transaction. This requirement can be very challenging for businessmen, and it is all too easy for one to inadvertently neglect to execute an *iska* contract. To help avoid such scenarios, some people execute a general *heter iska*, or *heter iska klali.*

A *heter iska klali* is a document that states that all transactions done by this person/firm shall be in accordance with the terms of a *heter iska*. The *iska* is signed by authorized agents of the company and is publicized.[48]

The principle behind a *heter iska klali* is that by publicizing that all transactions are *iska* partnerships, anyone that does business with such an establishment is implicitly accepting the terms of this proclamation. Even if the parties do not execute a specific *heter iska* for their transaction, the general *iska* will govern.

For this argument to be valid, the *iska* must be properly publicized. A document on the wall of a backroom office will not suffice.

There is considerable debate about the effectiveness of a *heter iska klali*. The *poskim* who accept the concept of a *heter iska*

47. These issues will vary based on the type of transaction, and one should consult with a Rav on a case-by-case basis.

48. *Maharsham* 1:20 writes that the *heter iska* should be executed in front of a *beis din* and publicized in all of the shuls in the city.

klali do so with the assumption that both parties are aware of the restrictions of *ribbis*, understand the concept of a *heter iska* partnership, and are aware that the parties have executed the *heter iska klali*.[49] Because these conditions are often not met, one should not rely on a *heter iska klali* alone. Nevertheless, anyone who conducts business that may involve *ribbis* issues should execute a *heter iska klali* as a backup in case a regular *heter iska* is forgotten.

Heter Iska Klali for Banks

Banks are unique in that they are heavily regulated and have numerous bylaws that govern all of their transactions. Therefore, anyone dealing with a bank understands that he is subjecting himself to the bank's bylaws. If the bylaws include a *heter iska*, the customer will be bound to its terms, even if he was unaware of its existence. Therefore, the prevalent custom is to rely on *heter iska klali* when dealing with banks.[50]

However, the *heter iska klali* must be included in the bank's bylaws. Simply having a local branch manager hang a copy on the wall of the bank will not create a binding agreement. The *iska* should be executed by the bank's owners or directors.

A copy of a *heter iska klali* may be found in Appendix I.

Guarantor

It should be noted that there could be *ribbis* issues even when dealing with a non-Jewish bank. Banks often require a guarantor on a loan. It is forbidden to guarantee a loan on which a Jew will pay interest, even if the lender is a non-Jew.[51]

---

49. See *Bris Yehudah* 40, notes 19 and 20. See also *Cheshev HaEphod* 1:96.

50. *Bris Yehudah* 40 n11. This argument applies only to banks and is not valid for a typical firm.

51. *Yoreh Deah* 170. This prohibition applies to an *areiv kablan* and not to an *areiv stam*.

This creates a very common problem. First-time homeowners may not qualify for a mortgage. Very often, they ask a relative to co-sign the mortgage for them. Although they are borrowing from a non-Jewish bank, this arrangement is prohibited unless a *heter iska* is executed.[52]

This restriction does not apply if the borrower pledges collateral for the loan and the practice is for the bank to foreclose on the collateral before trying to collect from the guarantor.[53]

In instances in which one may guarantee a loan,[54] many *poskim* allow the guarantor to charge the borrower for providing the guarantee.[55]

If Ribbis Was Paid

If someone inadvertently enters into a *ribbis* agreement, he may not make the interest payments called for in the loan agreement. If the lender is not observant and threatens to foreclose if full payment is not made, a Rav should be consulted.

If the entire loan and interest were already paid, the lender is obligated to return the interest to the borrower.[56] However, the

---

An *areiv stam* is a guarantor who is liable to repay the loan only if the borrower defaults on his obligations. The lender must first take appropriate steps to collect from the borrower. Only after he is unable to collect from the borrower does he have the right to collect from the guarantor.

In contrast, the lender may collect from an *areiv kablan* immediately and he has no obligation to first approach the borrower to ask for payment.

Today, virtually every guarantor is an *areiv kablan*.

See *Maharshag* 107 that the custom is to be lenient and allow guarantors even in the case of an *areiv kablan*. (See also *Maharam Shick* 160; *Avnei Nezer* 3:197.)

52. See footnote 24.

53. *Mishnas Ribbis* 15:8.

54. For example, on an interest-free loan.

55. *Taz* 170:3, *Nekudas HaKesef*, *Shulchan Aruch HaRav* 63, and *Chochmas Adam* 132:7 permit even an *areiv kablan* to charge. See however, *Chavos Daas* 170:1 who prohibits.

56. *Yoreh Deah* 161:5. This applies only to Biblical *ribbis* (*ribbis ketzuzah*). To be considered *ribbis ketzuzah*, there must be a loan with an agreed-upon interest payment. *Ribbis* that arises from sales (i.e., prepayment discounts) or *ribbis* that was not agreed upon (as when the borrower voluntarily sends a present to the lender) are Rabbinical prohibitions and *beis din* will not force the lender to reimburse the

borrower may choose to be *mochel*, or forgive, the interest that is due him.[57]

If the loan was not completely paid, the borrower may not continue to make interest payments. Even if the borrower wants to make interest payments, it is still forbidden. He may not be *mochel*, or forgive, interest that he has not yet paid.[58]

Determining whether a loan has been paid can be difficult. Banks will credit all payments toward the interest that is owed. Only when there is no outstanding interest balance will the bank credit a payment toward the principal. In halachah, it is unclear how to account for interest payments. Because it is forbidden to charge interest, according to some *poskim* any payments will reduce the principal owed,[59] even if the parties explicitly agreed

borrower. There is, however, a *latzeis yedei Shamayim* obligation to refund the interest. (For exceptions to this rule, see *Yoreh Deah* 161:2.)

57. Ibid. 160:5.

58. Ibid.

59. *Igros Moshe, Yoreh Deah* 3, *Hilchos Ribbis* 23; *Avnei Nezer, Yoreh Deah* 186, 142; *Tiferes Tzvi, Yoreh Deah* 49.

See also *Pischei Teshuvah* 161 (6) and *Bris Yehudah* 8 (n51).

If all payments are credited toward the principal until the loan is completely paid, there is a tremendous *kulah* (leniency) regarding the prohibition of *ribbis* and a *chumrah* (stringency) regarding the money owed. As far as the prohibition is concerned, if the payments are credited toward the principal, no *ribbis* payments were made and the prohibitions were not violated (aside from the original agreement; see Ch. 7 footnote 3). As far as the money owed, it is a *chumrah* (stringency). Because the payments reduce the principal, the borrower must subtract all payments from the balance and may not pay the lender more than the outstanding halachic balance. He may not be *mochel,* or forgive, the interest that he has not yet paid.

If the borrower pays the entire balance without subtracting all interest payments, he will violate *Hilchos Ribbis.* The lender may make a *heter iska* for future payments, but may not recoup past-interest payments.

Accordingly, to determine the correct halachic balance one must add up all the payments that were made, including both the principal and interest. Subtracting this number from the original loan amount will yield the current halachic balance.

For example, Reuven borrowed $100,000 at 7 percent, and the agreement called for interest-only payments for the first three years, after which the entire principal was due. After two years, and $14,000 in interest payments, the parties realized that they had violated the prohibition of *ribbis.* Although according to the contract Reuven still owes the entire principal of $100,000, in halachah the current balance would be $86,000. If Reuven repays more than that amount, he will violate the prohibition of *ribbis.*

If interest payments are not credited against the principal balance and are considered interest, there is a *chumra* regarding the *issur* and a *kula* regarding the money. The interest payments were a violation of *ribbis.* However, because the

that all payments would be applied toward the interest balance first. Consequently, a person may have completely paid up a loan for halachic purposes, while his account statement may still show a large balance.

Converting a Loan into an Iska Partnership

If the money was originally advanced as a loan that called for interest payments, one may not retroactively change the loan into an *iska*. The interest that accrued may not be collected. However, the parties may convert the loan into an *iska* and begin to charge "interest" or profits from the time of the conversion and on.

In order to convert a loan into an *iska* partnership, a *kinyan* must be made. By making a *kinyan*, the borrower is paying back the loan by giving a share of his assets to the lender as an *iska* partnership. Merely telling the lender or borrower to consider the money an *iska* is not sufficient.[60]

A borrower may not give the lender a present after the loan in order to compensate him for "lost" interest.[61]

---

payments were already made, the borrower may choose to be *mochel,* or forgive, those payments. (Note: Forgiving the *ribbis* while the remainder of the debt is still outstanding may itself be a form of *avak rabbis* (see Chapter Seven). A Rav should be consulted in these situations.) He may execute a *heter iska* for future payments and the lender will not suffer a financial loss.

60. *Choshen Mishpat* 176:1; *Rama; Shach, Yoreh Deah* 177:15, 41.

See *Nesivos, Choshen Mishpat* 176 that a verbal agreement to convert a loan into an *iska* will take effect once the recipient actually invests the funds. See, however, *Erech Shai, Choshen Mishpat* 176:1 who quotes *Maharshal* who disagrees.

61. Giving the lender a present after the loan has been repaid is *ribbis me'ucheres* and prohibited in most cases (*Yoreh Deah* 160:6). If *both* of the following conditions are met, the borrower may give the lender a present after the loan has been repaid.

- The borrower does not tell the lender that the gift is in gratitude for the loan, and
- it is not obvious from the size or timing of the gift that it is because of the loan.

In practice, it is uncommon today for people to give presents without a clear reason. It will usually be very obvious that the gift is payback for the loan and would be prohibited. However, if the loan were between relatives, close friends, or neighbors who have given each other gifts in the past, it would be permitted.

If one waits a significant amount of time after the loan was repaid, even a large gift may be given (*Shach* 160 [9]).

These halachos apply to gifts after the loan was repaid. Gifts or favors while the loan is outstanding will be discussed at the end of the following chapter.

7 Ribbis in Partnerships

Introduction

The Mishnah[1] tells us that the world is supported by three pillars: Torah, Avodah, and Gemilas Chasadim.

R' Chaim Volozhin[2] explains that Torah is not merely one of the three pillars of the world. Torah also defines the other two pillars. What is Avodah? Before Matan Torah, man was free to offer to Hashem any sacrifices that he pleased. Man chose the offering, the venue, and the method of the service. This all changed at Har Sinai. Klal Yisrael was taught exactly how to serve Hashem. Offerings that had been considered Avodah before Matan Torah subsequently became a sin.

Gemilas Chesed, continues R' Chaim, is also dependent on the Torah. Before Matan Torah, lending a needy person money at a reasonable interest rate was a tremendous chesed, one of the pillars that support the entire world. After Matan Torah, not only is it not a

1. *Avos* 1:2.
2. *Ruach Chaim.*

chesed, charging interest is a terrible prohibition that Chazal tell us can preclude a person from Techiyas Hameisim, the Resurrection of the Dead at the time of the Final Redemption.

This, perhaps, explains why it is so difficult to understand the concept of ribbis. Lending money at a reasonable rate is inherently an act of chesed, helping the borrower stay afloat and enabling his business to survive.

Yet the Torah demands v'chai achicha imcha; a fellow Jew is our brother. Brothers do not take advantage of another brother's misfortune, and we are obligated to help without charging interest. The Avnei Nezer named his sefer on ribbis, Bris Achim. Extending interest-free loans truly is a sign of brotherhood, a potent symbol of how we extend a helping hand to every Jew and do chesed without expecting anything in return.

Partners often have agreements that create *ribbis* issues. Because of the nature of partnerships, these issues often need creative restructuring to be permitted. This chapter will focus on some of the more common problems.

Partnership Agreements

Partnership agreements typically include a clause governing future investments. Often, they stipulate that in the event additional capital is needed, the partners must each contribute a prorated amount. If a partner does not make his contribution, he is responsible for that payment plus an agreed-upon interest rate. This arrangement involves *ribbis* and a *heter iska* is necessary. It should be noted that executing a document that calls for future *ribbis* payments is problematic, even if one does not expect any *ribbis* to actually be paid.[3]

3. Aside from the prohibition against collecting *ribbis*, the very act of extending a

Borrowing on Behalf of a Partnership

Partnerships often need to raise capital to operate their business. In order to maximize the amount that they can borrow, a partner may take out a personal loan and deposit the money into the business. The business then makes the actual payments to the bank on behalf of the borrowing partner.

In halachah this situation is treated as two separate loans.[4] The first loan is between the bank and the borrowing partner. The bank has no relationship with the partnership; it recognizes only the person who signed on the loan. The second loan is between the two partners. When the borrower invests the money in the business, he is in effect extending a loan to his other partners. In exchange for the loan, the business makes payments to the bank *on his behalf*, and is effectively paying *him* interest. Even though the partner who "lent" the business money is not making any profit, and the business is just covering his personal interest expense, this arrangement is subject to the following guidelines:

---

loan with interest is prohibited – *"Lo sasimun alav neshech."* This applies at the time of the loan.

The Gemara in *Bava Metzia* 62a discusses a case in which money was lent with an agreement to pay interest. The parties realized their error before the loan was due and the *ribbis* was never paid. There is a debate whether the prohibition of *lo sasimun* applies to any agreement to pay interest, or only if the agreement is ultimately honored.

Taz 160:11 and *Shaar Deah* 159 rule that the prohibition is only violated if the *ribbis* is ultimately paid.

Gaon 168: 41, *Toras Emes* (*Mahara Sasoon*) 162, *Gedulei Terumah* 46:2:1, *Chasam Sofer* 6:26 conclude that one violates the prohibition with the agreement to pay interest.

The above-mentioned *poskim* discuss situations where a loan was extended with an agreement to pay interest. A typical operating agreement is less problematic. There is no loan that takes place at the time of the agreement. In fact, there may never be a loan since the partnership may not require additional capital. Even if capital is required, there is a possibility all of the partners will contribute their share. Perhaps an agreement that if there will be a loan, the parties will be obligated to pay interest is not a violation of *lo sasemun*. See *Minchas Shlomo* 2:68:15 (this responsa is printed in the first edition only).

Regardless of whether there is a technical violation in signing such an operating agreement, one should not put himself in a position in which he may be compelled to pay *ribbis*.

4. *Taz, Yoreh Deah* 170(3).

If the partner who signed on the loan is not actively involved in running the business (a silent partner), a *heter iska* is necessary under all circumstances.[5]

If the signatory on the loan is an *active* partner, and the other partners accept personal responsibility to reimburse him for any interest that he may pay, a *heter iska* is also necessary.[6]

If the partners do not indemnify the partner who signed for the loan, according to some *poskim* the business may make the interest payments using profits generated by the business.[7] Other *poskim* allow the business to make interest payments with its capital, even if no profits were generated.[8]

Other *poskim* reject this entire leniency.[9]

To avoid this dispute, and to protect the partner signing on the loan, a *heter iska* should be executed.

When executing a *heter iska*, one must include the various points or fees in the *iska,* as explained in the previous chapter ("Points and Fees").

Co-signing Loans

As mentioned in Chapter Six, one may not co-sign or guarantee a loan that calls for interest payments even if the lender is not Jewish. When a partnership borrows money, if the loan is to the company and the only liability is on the assets of the partnership, the arrangement is permissible. Each partner is using money attributable to his share of the partnership to repay the interest, and no partner is borrowing from, or paying interest to, another partner. If, however, some or all of the partners personally

5. Ibid.

6. *Chavos Daas* 170:1, *Divrei Chaim, Choshen Mishpat* 29, *Shulchan Aruch HaRav, Ribbis* 64, *Chochmas Adam* 132:8.

7. *Shulchan Aruch HaRav* 64 and the *poskim* mentioned in the next footnote.

8. *Divrei Chaim, Choshen Mishpat* 29, *Maharal Tzintz* 170 (4), *Maharsham* 7:63, *Chochmas Adam* 132:8.

9. *Chavos Daas* 170:1

guarantee the loan, a *heter iska* should be executed between the partners.[10]

Heter Iska Between Partners

When a partnership is being formed, it is common for one partner to lend another some of the needed start-up capital. In order to charge interest on the loan, a *heter iska* is required. However, there is a fundamental problem with using a *heter iska* in a partnership. To understand this problem, a brief review of the fundamentals of *heter iska* is necessary.

A *heter iska* is not a loan. It is an investment. All profits and losses from this investment are shared equally between the "lender" and the "borrower." To ensure that the "lender" receives his principal and "interest," the agreement requires the "borrower" to clearly demonstrate how well the business venture has performed before the profits are divided. The "borrower" must either provide two halachically acceptable witnesses, or take a solemn oath.

Neither of these options is especially appealing to the borrower. Finding two halachically acceptable witnesses who have direct knowledge of the business is difficult. Solemn oaths are discouraged under any circumstances.

The "borrower" is given another option. He may return the principal together with a previously agreed-upon projected-profit payment ("interest") in exchange for the "lender"/investor waiving his rights to such proof. The "borrower" generally chooses to make this alternative payment.

This approach is predicated on the fact that the "lender" can legitimately demand that the "borrower" verify the outcome of the business venture. If, however, the "lender" is an active partner in the business, he knows firsthand how well the business performed. If the business was not profitable, he has

10. In the absence of a *heter iska*, the partner will not be able to recover any interest payments that he makes as a guarantor.

no justification to demand proof from the "borrower," and cannot collect any payments in lieu of such proof.[11]

Heter Iska on Other Assets

In such situations, a *heter iska* can be executed to create a business venture on/with *other* assets belonging to the manager "borrower." (A copy of such an *iska* can be found in Appendix I.) In exchange for the money that the "lender" is investing in the partnership on his behalf, the "borrower" assigns a share of his other business/investments to the partner. In this way, although the money is advanced directly into the partnership, the actual *iska* is on other assets belonging to the recipient. Since the "lender" is not a partner in these other assets, he has no first-hand information on how well these investments have performed. He is justified in demanding that the "borrower" verify the profits or losses of the investment. The "borrower" then has the choice of either providing such proof, or paying the agreed-upon rate of return.

A *kinyan* should be executed when entering into this type of *iska* agreement.[12]

If the manager/"borrower" does not have any other businesses or investments in which to invest the *iska*, a *heter iska* should not be used.[13]

---

11. *Igros Moshe, Yoreh Deah* 2:63.

12. A *heter iska* requires that the funds be invested in a profit-making venture. In a standard *iska*, the receiver takes the funds and invests them in whatever business he is "borrowing" the money for. The partnership is created as soon as the money is spent for the venture.

Under the terms of this special *heter iska*, the "borrower" is not using these funds for a business transaction on behalf of the partnership. He must transfer to the "lender" a stake in other investments that he owns. Transferring assets requires a *kinyan*.

13. The parties may create an *iska* with the business in which they are partners. However, in the event the business does not generate profits, the "lender" will not be able to collect any "interest" payments. Furthermore, if the business loses money, the "lender" must share in that loss.

Profit-Sharing

Iska

An *iska* is a partnership where one partner provides all of the capital, and another partner manages the business. In the absence of any agreement to the contrary, the two partners share the profits and losses equally. Such arrangements require that the working partner be reimbursed for his labor.[14]

The partners may choose to divide the profits in any other manner *provided* that the investor's share in the profits is not greater than his share in the losses.[15]

Partnership

When both partners invest capital, the arrangement is considered a partnership.[16] As such, they may share the profits in any manner that they choose, even if only one partner is actually running the business (see footnote).[17]

---

14. If the parties discuss this in advance, a token payment is sufficient. If, however, the original agreement did not require any compensation, a Rav should be consulted.

15. The percentage of losses for which the managing partner is responsible is treated as a loan. Therefore, if he shares profits attributable to that share of the business, he is paying "interest." However, because the profits are only paid from income generated by the investment, the *ribbis* is Rabbinic in nature (*Ritva, Bava Metzia* 70b).

16. *Rama, Yoreh Deah* 177:3 based on *Rif, She'arim* 8, *Shach.*

In contrast, *Rambam* requires that both partners *work* to avoid the classification of *iska.*

17. *Chavos Daas* qualifies this ruling that the investor's share of profits may not be greater than his share of losses. However, the working partner need not be reimbursed for his labor, since this is a partnership as opposed to an *iska.*

Chesed L'Avraham 48 (the grandson of the *Chavos Daas*), *Eretz Tzvi* 35, and *Nachalas Avos* 37 limit the ruling of *Chavos Daas* to instances where the managing partner accepts personal responsibility for his share of the losses However, if only the investment is at risk, the parties may divide the profits and losses in any manner that they choose.

Preferred Returns

Partnerships are sometimes structured so that the investor receives his original investment plus an agreed-upon rate of return before any other profits are distributed to the other partners. There are different opinions among the *poskim* whether such an arrangement is permitted.[18]

Preferred Shares

Preferred shares are equity positions that have many characteristics similar to bonds. For example, the dividends of cumulative preferred shares accrue regardless of whether or not the company actually earned any income. Ultimately, the company pays the dividends using equity belonging to the regular shareholders.

In addition, if the company becomes insolvent, the regular shareholder's equity is used to pay off the preferred shareholders. The preferred shareholder's investment, is in a sense, guaranteed

18. In a preferred-return arrangement, the partners are generally not personally liable for the money. Accordingly, the *poskim* mentioned in Chapter Six, "Corporations," would permit this arrangement.

In addition, some *poskim* treat these returns as a legitimate way to divide profits, and not as a *ribbis* transaction, provided that the parties are not personally liable for losses (*Chesed L'Avraham* 48 and *Eretz Tzvi* 35 quoted in previous footnote).

This applies only when the deal is structured so that the investor receives his preferred return from the profits that are generated. If the investing partner receives his preferred return even if the business fails to generate profits, the arrangement would be prohibited (*Maharsham* 7:140, *Shevet HaLevi* 5:97).

In addition, these guidelines apply to partnerships in which both parties invested capital. If there is only one investor, the arrangement is treated as an *iska* and the investing partner may not receive more profits than his share in potential losses.

(Note: These *poskim* all discuss situations in which the investor participates to some degree in any loss. If the business loses money, the investor will not receive the full amount of the principal, even though the business still has enough capital to cover the advance. In contrast, modern preferred-return arrangements often require the business to return the investor's capital before that of any other shareholders.)

See also *Rashdam Yoreh Deah* 61 and *Radvaz* 1:247 that prohibit preferred returns.

See also *Maharal Tzintz* 177:9.

with the assets of the other shareholders. The company is effectively borrowing funds from the preferred shareholders, and repays the "loan" and "interest" with shareholder equity.

The authorities mentioned in Chapter Six, "Corporations," who permit loans to corporations would allow such transactions since there is no personal liability. Those that do not rely on this opinion would prohibit preferred shares of Jewish-owned companies.

Avak Ribbis

While a loan is outstanding, there are various halachos regarding the relationship between the borrower and lender. Partners, who often work closely with each other, need to be aware of these restrictions and act accordingly during the term of a loan. Any favor that the borrower does for the lender while the loan is outstanding may appear to be a payment for the loan and may be considered *avak ribbis*. The borrower may only do a favor for the lender only under the following circumstances:[19]

- If the borrower **would have done** the favor for the lender even had he not borrowed money, it is permitted as long as the favor is done in an inconspicuous manner.[20]
- If the borrower **actually had done** this particular favor for the lender in the past, it is permitted even if it is done in a conspicuous manner.[21]

Reuven owes money to his partner Shimon. Shimon decides to go to the country for the weekend, and asks to use Reuven's country house. This would be prohibited since the favor is quite conspicuous.

19. Another uncommon example of *avak ribbis* is if the lender takes the liberty of taking or using something that belongs to the borrower without asking permission.

20. *Yoreh Deah* 160:7.

21. *Yam Shel Shlomo, Bava Kamma* 9:11.

If Shimon was an old friend of Reuven's and had used his house in the past, Shimon would be allowed to use the house for the weekend.

Avak Ribbis with a Heter Iska

There are different opinions among the *poskim* whether the restrictions of *avak ribbis* apply to the parties of an *iska* partnership.[22] Accordingly, if one expects to encounter situations of *avak ribbis*, he should execute a *heter iska kulo pekadon* form.[23] A *heter iska kulo pekadon* is structured differently than a standard *iska*, and avoids the problem of *avak ribbis*. A form can be found in Appendix I.

22. *Shulchan Aruch HaRav* 39 prohibits *avak ribbis* with a *heter iska*. His reasoning is that since every standard *heter iska* is considered part loan and part investment, if any favors are done for the investing partner, we attribute them as payment for the portion of the *iska* that was advanced as a loan. *Chavos Daas* 166 argues and permits certain *avak ribbis* with a *heter iska*.

23. In a *kulo pekadon* form, the funds advanced are entirely owned by the investor. The borrower's liability for the funds is as a guardian (provided he is able to properly account for the investment). Consequently, no loan takes place and there are no *avak ribbis* concerns.

8 Miscellaneous Ribbis Concerns

Introduction

Ribbis is one of the weakest points in our chinuch. From the moment that a baby is born, we begin to teach him the fundamentals of Yiddishkeit. A child quickly learns that Shabbos is a special day. Kashrus, Yom Tov, and davening are mitzvos that our children are constantly exposed to. Over time, they develop an appreciation for these mitzvos, which become a natural part of their daily routine.

That very same child grows up with the concept of charging interest. From literally the day a baby is born, he begins to accrue interest on the savings bonds he received as a gift. As he grows older, he is exposed to bank accounts, credit cards, and mortgages. Interest is a very natural part of life.

It comes as no surprise that when someone discovers the issur of ribbis, he is totally shocked. He has no sensitivity toward the issur and finds it counter-intuitive.

This makes it all the more important to become

familiar with Hilchos Ribbis. It is strongly recommended that anyone who deals with ribbis issues on a regular basis should take the time to study the laws of ribbis.

Real Estate-Related Issues

Security Deposits

Virtually all lease agreements require the tenant to provide a security deposit. The deposit is held by the landlord to enable him to collect payment if the tenant damages the unit. If there is no damage, the deposit is returned when the tenant vacates the unit. Lease contracts often call for the deposit plus accrued interest to be returned to the tenant when he vacates the property. If the money was put into an escrow account, this arrangement is permissible. Because the landlord had no access or liability for the money, there was never a loan, and *ribbis* will not apply. However, if the contract allows the landlord to deposit the money into his personal account, he may not pay the tenant any accrued interest when he returns the deposit.

Tax Liens

Many municipalities sell tax liens at public auctions. The buyer of a tax lien pays the taxes that are owed for a particular property. In exchange, the investor buys the right to recover future tax payments, plus interest. If the property owner does not pay his taxes within a certain period of time (redemption period), the investor may foreclose on the property.

Is it permitted to buy a tax lien on a property that is owned by a Jew? May one collect interest that accrued while a Jew was holding the tax lien?

The interest that accrued on the unpaid taxes before the lien was purchased is certainly permitted, since the debt was owed to a non-Jewish government.[1]

The interest that accrues after the purchase is more questionable. It would seem that the interest is accruing on a debt that is between two Jews and should be prohibited. However, see footnote.[2]

---

1. *Rama, Yoreh Deah* 168/9:10.

Nekudas HaKesef does not allow the Jewish buyer to collect the interest directly from the Jewish property owner. However, if the borrower pays the non-Jewish lender, who in turn gives the money to the buyer, it is permissible. Tax liens are collected by the government, which then forwards the proceeds to the tax lien holder. The buyer never collects the money directly from the debtor, and therefore this arrangement is permitted.

Taz (12) permits even if the interest is paid directly to the Jewish buyer.

2. If the tax lien is attached to a property and the owner is not personally liable, the *poskim* mentioned in Chapter Six, "Corporations," would permit collecting the interest. However, it should be noted that while in practice governments typically sell the tax liens and do not try to collect from the owner, in some states the property owner is personally liable for the debt. As such, this leniency would not apply.

Another question is whether the government is actually selling the debt, or if it is selling the right to foreclose on the property subject to the right of redemption. If the latter interpretation is correct, there would be no borrower/lender relationship between the property owner and the lien holder. While the lien holder will profit from any interest paid to the government, he is not the lender and the arrangement would be permitted.

If the first interpretation is correct, and the actual debt is sold, the buyer may not collect interest that accrues after the sale (*Yoreh Deah* 168/9:10 based on *Rashba* 764, *Taz* 12).

Each state has different laws and regulations regarding tax liens. One should carefully research the legal status of his particular state before relying on either leniency.

Nekudas HaKesef discusses a case in which a non-Jew lent money to a Jew, and then sold the debt to another Jew. The sale was done in a manner recognized by secular law, but not by halachah. *Nekudas HaKesef* rules that the Jewish buyer may receive the interest, since according to halachah the debt is still owed to the non-Jew. There is no lender/borrower relationship between the Jewish buyer and Jewish borrower.

This concept cannot be applied to tax-lien sales since the procedure for the sale of tax liens is clearly spelled out in the property-tax code of many states. By definition, the sale will be recognized by halachah because of the concept of *dina d'malchusa dina*. The *Nekudas HaKesef* was presumably referring to a private sale which would not necessarily be governed by *dina d'malchusa dina* (although see *Choshen Mishpat* 66:25 ונצ"ע).

Late-Payment Fees

Many leases contain a late-payment fee. If the tenant pays his rent past a certain date, he is charged a penalty.[3] In effect, the tenant is being charged for "borrowing" the landlord's money. This may be *ribbis* and must be structured in accordance with the following guidelines.

One may impose a late-payment fee on a lease if it is only a one-time fee.[4] For example, a landlord may impose a $25 late-payment fee for payments that are more than two weeks late. However, the fee can be charged only once. One may not charge an additional $25 for every additional two weeks that the balance is outstanding.

One may charge this fee again if another month's rent is late. For example, if a tenant pays January's rent late, the landlord may impose a fee one time. Regardless how long the tenant delays payment on January's rent, the fee may not be imposed a second time. However, if the tenant pays February's rent late, an additional fee may be imposed for February's rent.

As a practical matter, this arrangement leaves little incentive for someone to pay his rent once he has already incurred the penalty fee. Once the penalty date has passed, there is no additional cost to the tenant for delaying payment. To avoid this situation, the landlord may choose to impose a large penalty after a longer grace period. For example, instead of a $25 fee after two weeks, the lease may call for a $100 penalty if the rent is more than four weeks late. This gives the tenant a very strong incentive not to delay payment past the four-week mark.

In addition, one may stipulate in the lease contract that any payment will automatically be credited toward the rent that is past due. Therefore, every month that the tenant is not current, he will be forced to pay another penalty.

3. Late-payment fees and other penalty fees may be unenforceable in halachah if they are an *asmachta*. See Ch. 4 footnote 50.

4. *Radvaz* 1:497.

A one-time penalty clause is acceptable because the debt originated from a lease.[5] In a loan agreement, any sort of penalty or fee would be prohibited.[6]

Buying a House Under Someone Else's Name

Someone with a poor credit rating who is unable to obtain a mortgage may elect to purchase a home under the name of a close friend or relative. The friend, who has a better credit rating, buys the house under his own name and takes out a mortgage. The real owner then makes the mortgage payments to the bank. While this seems to be an innocent arrangement and is usually done as a favor without any profit motive, this situation presents serious halachic challenges.

In halachah, there are two independent loans taking place simultaneously. The first loan is the actual mortgage between the bank and the titleholder. Because the titleholder is the one who signs all the paperwork, he is the actual borrower from the bank. The bank does not recognize the real owner, and has no claim against him. Although the collateral (the house) belongs to the true owner, he is not the borrower as far as the bank is concerned.

The second loan is between the titleholder and the real owner of the house. When the titleholder closes on the house on behalf of the real owner, the real owner takes responsibility for the mortgage payments. This creates a debt between the real owner and titleholder.

The real owner then proceeds to pay both the principal and interest to the bank. Ultimately, he pays the bank more than the principal that he originally borrowed from the titleholder.

5. Penalties on sales are permitted as well. In contrast, charging a customer a higher price for buying on credit is prohibited, as explained in section "Paying for Credit." See footnote 18 for an explanation.

6. *Yoreh Deah* 177:14.

According to most *poskim*, this is prohibited.[7]

There are two ways to avoid *ribbis* in this situation. The first is to use a *heter iska*.[8] The second option is to structure a rent-to-own agreement, which is described below.

Rent-to-Own[9]

A rent-to-own agreement is an alternative to a *heter iska* when a property is being sold. There are two parties to a rent-to-own agreement, the titleholder/landlord and the buyer/tenant. The titleholder purchases the property and obtains a mortgage. The titleholder does not act as an agent for the tenant; the house truly belongs to him, and he bears full responsibility for the mortgage. To protect him, and to transfer the property to the other party, the buyer/tenant enters into a long-term lease and purchase agreement with the titleholder.

Under the terms of the sale agreement, the titleholder agrees to sell the property slowly, over the life of the mortgage, to the buyer. The sale price equals the amount of the principal of the titleholder's mortgage. Each month, the titleholder sells a small portion of the property to the buyer. He charges the buyer the exact amount that he is paying to the bank for the principal on his

---

7. *Bris Yehudah, Ikrei Dinim* 21 n10; *Shevet HaLevi* 7:141.
See *Keren HaTorah, Hakdamah* 14 for a dissenting opinion.

8. To execute a *heter iska*, the recipient must either be investing the money that he receives, or have other investments of equal value with which he creates the *iska*. If the person buying the home does not have investments worth the value of the loan, the *iska* must be made on the house itself. This can be problematic. The titleholders often will have firsthand knowledge if the house is vacant or decreases in value. If this occurs, he may not demand from the recipient verification of the investment results, and will not be able to collect the loan (*Igros Moshe, Yoreh Deah* 2:62,63).

Another important point is that mortgages often have points and fees taken off the loan amount. The points and fees related to the loan must be subtracted from the principal of the *iska*, since the "borrower" does not receive that money and obviously cannot invest it. The rate of return can be raised in order to make up for the shortfall. See Chapter Six, "Points and Fees."

The *heter iska* must also reflect the various late-payment penalties that may be associated with the mortgage. See Appendix I for a *heter iska* for this scenario.

9. This concept was introduced in *Igros Moshe, Yoreh Deah* 2:62.

mortgage. By the time the mortgage is paid, he will have sold the entire property to the buyer.

Until the mortgage is completely paid, the titleholder owns a portion of the property. He agrees to lease his share of the property to the buyer. The rental payments are set at the amount that the titleholder pays the bank each month as interest on the mortgage. The lease requires the tenant to pay all property taxes, utilities, maintenance, and insurance[10] on the property as additional rent.

Each month there are two payments: an equity purchase and rent. Together, these two payments will exactly equal the amount of the mortgage that the titleholder is paying. Each month the composition of the two payments changes. The amounts track a standard amortization schedule. The buyer pays rent only on the portion of the property that belongs to the titleholder. Each month the buyer is purchasing a little more of the property, and therefore each month, the amount of rent he pays the titleholder decreases. The monthly payments are kept the same, but more of each payment is used to increase the buyer's equity. This arrangement continues until the house is completely paid for.

The advantage of this concept from a halachic viewpoint is that the buyer never borrows any money from the seller. Their relationship is as that of a landlord/tenant and seller/buyer and not of a lender/borrower. All payments made to the titleholder are either for the rent or the purchase.

A copy of this agreement may be found in Appendix I.

10. *Minchas Yitzchak* 4:19 writes that the tenant/ buyer may not accept liability for the property. To circumvent this issue, the seller may insure the property. The lease may require the tenant to pay for insurance. If a loss occurs that is not covered by insurance, the titleholder/seller must absorb the loss.

Refinancing

If one refinances a home that was financed with either a *heter iska* or a rent-to-own agreement, a Rav should be consulted.[11]

Ribbis in Sales

The following sections will discuss *ribbis* issues that arise from sales. Three types of *ribbis* will be discussed:

1. Paying for credit
2. Receiving a discount for prepayment
3. Locking in a price in exchange for prepayment

Paying for Credit

If a seller charges a higher price for a credit sale, he is in effect charging interest for the delayed payment. This may be *avak ribbis* and is subject to the following guidelines.[12]

If the item has a clear and well-known value, one may not charge a premium for a credit sale. Because the true value of the item is well known, it would be obvious that the higher price is because of the credit and it will be *avak ribbis*.

---

11. If a rent-to-own agreement was used, the titleholder is completely responsible for the mortgage. The other party is simply a tenant and there is no reason for his monthly rent or purchase payments to change simply because his landlord chose to refinance his property.

If the parties executed a *heter iska*, the titleholder has complete responsibility for the mortgage. The other party's responsibility to make payments arises from the *heter iska*, under which he accepted money for an investment and agreed to make certain payments if he could not properly verify the profits and losses of the investment. The refinance should not change his responsibility toward the titleholder.

While under either scenario there is nothing wrong with the parties "renegotiating" the terms of their agreement, there is certainly no obligation to do so. Furthermore, the expectation that the deal will change if there is a refinance undermines the integrity of the *heter* and indicates that it was simply a *har'amah*.

12. *Yoreh Deah* 173:1.

If the item does not have a clear and well-known value, a seller may charge a small premium for a credit sale. Because the price is not well known, it will not be obvious that the buyer is paying an additional fee for credit. However, this applies only to a small premium. If the item is sold for an exaggerated amount, it will be obvious that there is another factor (credit) influencing the price.

The seller may not explicitly tell the buyer that he is charging a higher price because he is extending credit. If he does, it will be *avak ribbis* and it is prohibited.

If the seller offers two prices, a lower price for cash sales and a higher price for credit, one may not choose the credit option and pay the higher price. Doing so makes it clear that there is a charge for credit, which is prohibited. If the seller anticipates that the buyer will need credit, he should offer the item for the higher price only, and include credit in the deal. As long as the item does not have a well-known price and the seller never offered a lower price for cash, the sale would be permissible.[13]

After discussing a sale price of $500,000 for a property, the buyer offered to pay $550,000 if the seller would provide an interest-free loan for two years. This is avak ribbis and is prohibited.

Prepayment Discounts

Prepayment discounts are another form of *avak ribbis*. The buyer advances money to the seller and, in exchange, the seller reduces the price. The "interest" for the prepayment is given to the buyer in the form of a cheaper price. This is prohibited under

13. *Chavos Daas* 173 (2) suggests that if the seller offers the property at the lower price, and then realizes that the buyer needs credit, he may withdraw his original offer. After the offer is withdrawn, he may raise the price and say that regardless of whether the buyer pays immediately, he will only sell for the higher price. Since the item does not have a clear value, and at this point there is only one price being offered, the arrangement is permitted.

most circumstances.[14] A notable exception is if the seller has the item in stock at the time of payment. Although the seller does not intend to deliver the goods until a later date, if he has the item in stock he may sell it at a discounted price.[15]

These restrictions apply only to sales. One is permitted to give a prepayment discount for leases or rentals.[16]

2/10 Net 30

Many vendors offer their clients incentives to pay promptly. A common business practice is "two/ten net thirty." If the bill is paid within ten days, the client is entitled to a 2-percent discount. Otherwise, payment in full is required within thirty days. According to many *poskim*, waiting thirty days and paying the full price is *avak ribbis*.[17] Although the higher payment is not called a fee, but rather the lower price is called a discount, the additional 2-percent payment is *ribbis*. This is because the true price of the item is determined by the amount due when payment is made at the appropriate time. According to halachah, sales require immediate payment. Therefore, the price that includes the 2-percent discount is, in reality, the price of the item. The higher price due after ten days includes a fee for the credit. Regardless

14. *Yoreh Deah* 173:7.

15. Ibid., 173:7 *Rama*. A person may sell his merchandise at a discount. Because the item is in stock, we consider the transaction as an immediate sale, and not as a loan. Even though no formal *kinyan* was made and the seller is not prepared to deliver the goods, there would be no *ribbis* concerns.

16. *Yoreh Deah* 176: 6.

As long as a binding *kinyan* takes place at the time of payment, the money advanced is not a loan. The payment is for the immediate purchase of the rental rights. Accordingly, this is comparable to selling an in-stock item for a reduced price. This applies even if the tenant does not immediately move into the rental unit (*Nekudas HaKesef*).

However, the unit must be completed and inhabitable. If the unit needs significant work, one may not receive a discount for prepayment.

17. *Bris Yehudah* 22 n8.

See *Hagaos* to *Imrei Yosher* 150 that permits this arrangement if the practice of extending credit is so widespread throughout the industry that a seller has no right to demand payment before the ten days.

of how it is described on the bill, such a fee is considered *ribbis*.[18]

Paying on time and taking the 2-percent discount is permissible, since there are no interest fees or payments being made. The issue arises when one pays late and incurs the additional 2-percent "fee."[19]

A *heter iska* can be executed to correct this problem.

Forward Contract / Locking in a Price

It is prohibited to accept prepayment for an item in exchange for locking in its price.[20] If the price of the item rises before delivery, the difference between the market value and the price being paid is viewed as "payment" for the advanced funds. This applies even to situations where the price of the item can either rise or fall. Although it is an even risk, if in fact the price rises, there will be *avak ribbis*.

Reuven ordered fifty tables from his Jewish supplier. The supplier warned him that the prices were subject to change. However, he agreed to lock in the current price if Reuven prepaid for the goods. This arrangement is prohibited. If the price does indeed rise before delivery, Reuven must pay the current value of the goods to avoid avak ribbis.

18. In contrast, a one-time penalty fee is permitted for late payment on a sale (discussed in "Late Payment Fees"). The difference is that a penalty does not permit the customer to retain the funds for a longer period in exchange for an "interest" payment. Rather, it is a "punishment" for breaching the agreement to pay on time. In contrast, when a customer is offered a higher price for credit, he is agreeing to pay a fee in exchange for the right to delay payment. By paying the fee, he buys the rights to retain the money for a longer period which, in effect, is *ribbis*.

19. If the merchandise is being ordered on behalf of a corporation and there is no personal liability for the payment, the *heter* discussed in Chapter Six would apply.

20. *Yoreh Deah* 175:1.

Exceptions

This prohibition will not apply if ***any one*** of these conditions is true:

- The seller has the item in stock.[21]
- The item is readily available at the agreed-upon price.[22]
- The item will not have a clear price at the time of delivery.[23]

Real Estate Sales

It is common in real estate transactions for a buyer to sign a contract, give a deposit, and then wait a few weeks or months before actually closing on the property. In effect, the seller agrees to freeze the price at the current level in exchange for the deposit. This would seem to be problematic. However, in most real estate transactions, the seller owns the property that he is selling and the first exception, *yesh lo,* having the item in stock, will apply.

Selling "On Paper"

However, developers often sell new construction "on paper," before the houses are built. Although the developer already owns the land, the house itself was not yet built and does not qualify for the first exception of "in stock."

Avak ribbis applies only if the deposit is released to the seller. If the deposit is kept in escrow, the builder/seller has no access to

21. Ibid 175:4. This is the concept of *yesh lo*. The item must be virtually completed for this exception to apply. If the item is being manufactured and requires three additional steps to complete, this exemption will not apply.

22. Ibid 175:1. The price must be stable. If it is constantly changing, this exception will not apply.

23. Ibid 173:7, *Rama. Avnei Nezer, Yoreh Deah* 210, *Binas Adam* 8 (139:14), *Beis Meir.* See, however, *Taz* (12) who disagrees. See also footnote 25.

or responsibility for the money and is not treated as a borrower. As such, any discount would be permissible.

Even when the deposit is released to the developer, these transactions are generally permissible because the third exception applies. Property often does not have a clearly defined value.[24] Consequently, at the time of the closing it will not be clear that the closing price is below the current value of the property. Such an arrangement would be permitted according to some opinions.[25]

This will apply to most real estate sales. However, in a large town house development where many of the units are the same, there may be a clear and well-known value for a standard unit. Because there are so many identical units, it is easy to determine the market value of the house. If at the time of closing equivalent houses are being sold for a higher price, the discount will be obvious and is prohibited.[26]

Deposits

Although one may not offer a discount or lock in a price in exchange for prepayment, one may require a security deposit in order to ensure that a buyer will close on the property.[27] If the deposit is only to secure the deal, the discount or lock in is not payment for a loan and would be permitted. This applies only when it is clear that the deposit is needed for security and that the discount offered is not because of the funds advanced. If the

24. *Baal HaTerumos* 46:4:29, *Teshuvas HaRif* (*Shitah Mikubetzes, Bava Metzia* 65a), *Ein Ona'ah Lekarkaos.*

25. This form of *ribbis* is prohibited because it appears to be *ribbis*. In the absence of a clearly defined market price, the transaction does not appear to be *ribbis* and is therefore permitted.

See *Taz* mentioned in footnote 23 who argues on this halachah. See also *Be'er HaGolah, Shaar Deah* who defend *Rama,* but their reasoning would not apply to this scenario.

26. *Minchas Yitzchak* 4:20:8. Although there is a concept of *Ein Ona'ah Lekarkaos*, real estate is not subject to the regular laws of *ona'ah*, it is still possible for real estate to have a price. In the example mentioned above, there can be a clear and well-known price for real estate, and the problem of locking in a price may apply.

27. *Mishpat Shalom* 209:25.

purpose of the deposit is unclear, this arrangement would be prohibited.[28]

Today, the norm is for the deposit money to be kept in escrow. If the builder asks for the deposit money to be released, it is usually because he needs the funds and this *heter* will not apply.[29] A *heter iska* may be used in such a scenario. See Appendix I for such a *heter iska*.

28. This halachah applies only to new construction or when the seller is "flipping" a property that he does not yet own.

If the sale is for an existing house that the seller owns, he may require a deposit based on the concept of *yesh lo,* in stock.

29. If the deposit were simply to secure the deal and ensure that the buyer would not back out, it would be most reasonable to put the money in an escrow account. If the builder insists that the money be released to him, it would indicate that his intention is to use the deposit. The deposit would then be considered a loan and the agreement to freeze the price would be considered interest.

Management

9 Employers and Employees / Hilchos Poalim

Introduction

The Rambam[1] writes:

"Just as an employer may not withhold the wages of his workers, so too the worker may not steal time from his work ...

And he is obligated to work with all of his strength, as Yaakov HaTzaddik declared, "For I have worked for your father [Lavan] with all of my strength."

The Rambam deduces the responsibilities of an employee from the relationship between Yaakov and Lavan. Let us explore the history and nature of this relationship.

Yaakov worked seven years for Rachel, Lavan's daughter. At the end of the seven years, Lavan tricked Yaakov and forced him to work an additional seven years.

After this period, Lavan hired Yaakov to tend his flock. The Torah describes how Lavan constantly changed

1. *Sechirus* 13:7.

Yaakov's pay, and tried again and again to defraud him of what he had rightfully earned.

Not only was Lavan a thief, he was a murderer as well. "Arami oveid avi"[2] — Lavan tried to destroy the entire nation of Israel.

One would think that when dealing with such an evil person, a thief, a cheat, and one willing to commit murder, a person would be entitled to "fight fire with fire" and resort to trickery to protect himself. Yet, Yaakov described his years of labor for Lavan as follows:

"A tereifah (an animal with a life-threatening defect) I never brought to you — I would bear the loss, from my hand you would extract it, stolen by day or stolen by night ...

"By day, heat consumed me, and snow by night; my sleep drifted before my eyes ...."[3]

Yaakov refused to lower his standards, and refused to compromise his personal integrity, even under such trying circumstances.

This truly should be our model on which our sense of honesty and obligation to our employers should be based.

Terms of Employment

Whenever a worker is hired, any terms that are not specifically discussed are assumed to be in accordance with local norms.[4] For example, the hours that an employee is obligated to work, the amount of vacation he is entitled to, and whether he is paid for overtime are all governed by the local norms. An employer who hired a worker without discussing specific terms may not

2. *Devarim* 26:5.

3. *Bereishis* 31:39.

4. *Choshen Mishpat* 331:1.

pressure an employee into working extra hours. He certainly has no right to threaten to terminate a worker for his refusal to work additional hours.

This rule applies even when the employee is being paid an unusually high salary. If the employer expects his employees to accept additional responsibilities in exchange for their higher pay, he must stipulate the terms in advance before hiring them.[5]

If there is a dispute between the employee and employer regarding what the terms of the employment agreement were, the burden of proof lies with the party who wishes to deviate from the accepted norm. An employer's claim that the worker agreed to work more than the norm would not be believed. Similarly, a worker who claims that the employer granted him unusual privileges would be required to substantiate the claim.[6]

Employment Contracts

An employment agreement need not be written to be binding. If the parties reach an oral agreement regarding the terms of employment, and the employee begins the job, both parties are bound to honor the agreement (see below, "Hiring Workers"). Nevertheless, it is prudent to have a written employment agreement. A written contract provides the parties with the opportunity to clarify their expectations and to define the exact responsibilities of each party.

It should be noted that certain terms often included in an employment contract may be halachically problematic. See Chapter Four, "Contracts," for a discussion of problematic contracts.

5. Ibid. 331:1. *Sma* (1) explains that the worker may claim that he is being paid a higher salary to produce better work. We have no proof that the extra wages were in exchange for longer hours.

6. *Choshen Mishpat* 330:5.

Employee's Responsibilities

An employee is responsible to ensure that he will be as productive as possible for his employer.[7] He may not do anything that will diminish his productivity. Staying up late at night, fasting,[8] overeating, and undertaking a second job are specific examples of inappropriate behavior cited by *Shulchan Aruch.*

Halachah does not give precise guidelines for these activities. It is self-evident that employees will, on occasion, show up at the office tired. However, the employee may not go beyond the norm. If he consistently stays up late and comes to work unusually lethargic, he is violating his employment agreement.

It is clear that halachah charges the worker with looking out for his employer's interests. A worker's responsibility is not simply to punch in at the appropriate time. He must act throughout the day, even after hours, in a manner that will enable him to be most productive for his employer.

Hiring Workers

Once a person makes a verbal commitment to hire a worker, he is bound to honor his commitment. If the employer rescinds the offer, the worker may have *tarumos*, complaints, against him. However, these complaints are not actionable in *beis din*.

If the prospective worker gave up other employment opportunities because of the job offer, the employer will be responsible for the loss.[9]

---

7. Ibid. 337:19.

8. *Dinei Mamanos* 3:7:1 writes that a worker may not even fast on a *yahrzeit* of a parent.

These issues are subject to *minhag*, the accepted norms.

9. He does not have to pay his full salary since the worker is not actually doing any work. He pays *k'poel batul*, which is explained in footnote 11.

Because the obligation is to pay for the damage caused by giving up other employment opportunities, the payments will be based on the salary that the

These halachos apply before the worker actually begins the job.

Firing a Worker — Without Cause

Once the worker begins a job, the employer is obligated to keep him until he completes the agreed-upon employment period.[10] If the employer fires the worker without cause during the employment period, the employer will be liable to pay his salary. However, the salary will be adjusted to reflect the fact that the employee will not actually be working.[11]

This applies only if the worker suffered a loss as a result of

---

employee would have earned elsewhere, and will not reflect the amount that was promised to him.

For example, a worker was offered a job paying $300 per day, and because of that offer, turned down a job paying $250 per day. If the employer rescinds the $300 offer, he is only liable for the loss of $250 that he caused. Contrast this to note 11, where the employer's obligation is to honor his commitment, and is not related to any damage that he caused.

10. *Igros Moshe, Choshen Mishpat* 1:75,76 writes that if the worker is hired without any specific time frame, the employment agreement continues indefinitely until the employer no longer needs the work.

Chazon Ish, Bava Kamma 23:2, and *Divrei Malkiel* 3:151 write that an employment agreement that does not specify a time period is binding for one pay period. If the worker is paid a monthly salary, his employment period is one month. If he is paid a yearly salary, his employment period is a year. Once he begins an employment period, he cannot be fired until the end of that period. This approach can also be found in *Shulchan Aruch HaRav, Orach Chaim* 243:12,

Chazon Ish suggests that if there is a *minhag* regarding how much notice must be given to an employer/employee, the *minhag* must be followed. Often secular laws will create a de facto *minhag*.

Chazon Ish continues that if there is a typical time period that a worker needs to find another job, or that an employee needs to replace a worker, that time frame is implicitly accepted as the employment period.

11. *K'poel batul.* Most workers would agree to reduce their salary if they were offered time off and not required to work. For example, an accountant who is paid $300 for a job would probably agree to accept $150 and take the day off. (*Taz* 333:1 gives a number of 50 percent as a base.) The dollar amount is based on what the employee was promised, and not on alternative offers.

Ketzos 316:1 writes that if the employer terminated the employee for no reason, he is liable for the full salary and does not reduce it to *k'poel batul. Nesivos* 316(2) disagrees.

being fired. If the worker finds an equivalent job for the same pay, the original employer will not be liable for any financial damages.[12]

Reuven, a prospective employee, goes to an interview at a large accounting firm. That evening, the manager calls him and offers him a job. He agrees to start the following Monday. Subsequently, the manager meets a distant relative of his who mentions that he is looking for an accounting position. The manager promptly notifies Reuven that the job offer is being withdrawn.

If this exchange takes place before Reuven begins the job, although the manager has acted inappropriately, he is not liable for any financial penalties unless Reuven passed on other employment opportunities because of this offer. However, if Reuven has already begun working, the manager does not have the right to fire him. If he fires him anyway, he will be responsible to pay k'poel batul (see note 11) until Reuven finds another job.

Unavoidable Termination

If an unavoidable event[13] occurs that makes it impossible for the work to be done, the employer may terminate the worker and bears no responsibility for the employee's pay.[14] This applies either to an event that neither the employer nor the employee could have anticipated, or an event that both of them could have anticipated. For example, if a factory burns down, the owner may fire the workers. He is not liable since he could not have anticipated the fire, and can no longer provide the employees with work.

However, if the employer was aware that the job may be

12. *Tarumos* and *mechusar amana* may apply, as explained above.

13. These halachos govern typical events that may occur. *Makas medinah*, widespread disruptions, have different halachos and are discussed in *Choshen Mishpat* 321.

14. *Choshen Mishpat* 334:1.

eliminated and did not bother to notify the worker, the employer will be liable for his pay.[15]

Reuven is hired by a large accounting firm to service a specific[16] *account. The firm is aware that the client is reevaluating their relationship, but they are hopeful that they will keep the account. If the account is ultimately terminated, the accounting firm may not fire Reuven. Because they were aware of the potential problem, they should have notified Reuven before they hired him.*

However, if the account were suddenly terminated without any prior warning, the firm would not be liable to Reuven.

Firing a Worker — for Cause

A negligent worker may be fired only after he has been negligent three times. At that point, he has a *chazakah*, and is considered an unreliable worker. However, the worker must be warned each time that he will be fired if his behavior continues.[17]

Irreparable Harm

If a worker's negligence caused his employer a loss that cannot be recouped, the employer may fire him even though he was never warned.[18] It is understood that such behavior will not be tolerated, and the employer has no obligation to specifically warn the employee. However, this applies only after he was negligent three times. One or two mistakes are not grounds for dismissal.

15. Ibid.

16. If he was not hired for a specific account, the employee may not fire him regardless since the worker is available to work and could be assigned to a different client (*Sma* 334:2 [10]).

17. *Choshen Mishpat* 306:8, *Beur HaGra* 23, *Nimukei Yosef, Bava Metzia* 66 (*Dafei HaRif*).

18. *Choshen Mishpat* 306:8.

Shulchan Aruch implies that this halachah applies only to one who works for the public. *Rama* extends it to all workers.

If the worker was specifically warned about such negligence, he may be fired after even one incident.[19]

Definition of Irreparable Harm

Often when a worker is negligent, he is obligated to reimburse his employer for the damage that he caused. Such scenarios are not classified as irreparable harm, since the employer will recover the damages from the employee.

If the damage can not be properly assessed, or if it was caused in an indirect manner for which the employee is not liable, the harm is considered irreparable. Furthermore, even if the incident causes non-monetary losses, it may still be considered an irreparable loss.[20] A missed opportunity to profit also qualifies under these halachos.[21]

The intent of this halachah is to protect an employer from future losses. It is not a punishment for the past. As such, if it is clear that the negligence will not continue, the worker may not be fired.[22]

A landlord hires a contractor to fix up a rental unit. The landlord warns the contractor that he needs it done immediately in order to be able to show the unit to potential tenants. If the contractor delays the project, he may be fired, since the delay will cause the landlord to lose rental income. Since the landlord has warned the contractor in advance, he may be fired after causing a delay even

19. *Rama* 306:8, *Nimukei Yosef, Bava Metzia* 66 (*Dafei HaRif*).

20. An example would be a teacher who neglects to teach his students. The knowledge his students "lost" can never be recovered. Although loss of knowledge cannot be measured monetarily, it is grounds for terminating the teacher's employment.

21. An example cited is a gardener who does not tend the field properly. Because we can not predict what would have happened had he done his job faithfully, the gardener cannot reimburse his employer for the losses that were caused by his neglect. The employer is justified in firing him.

22. *Igros Moshe, Choshen Mishpat* 1:47.

once.[23] *Without prior warning, he may only be fired after causing three delays.*

Collecting Damages from an Employee

In certain cases, *Chazal* exempted workers for damages that they inadvertently caused. A porter who drops an item is not responsible to pay for the damage.[24] Although the porter is a paid worker and should be liable for such losses, *Chazal* recognized that people would not accept such difficult and low-paying jobs if they had liability.[25]

Even in cases that do not qualify for this exemption, it is appropriate for an employer to forgive any damage that his workers cause, even if it was caused by the workers' negligence.[26]

Severance Pay

There is no obligation to pay severance to a worker unless there is a universal *minhag* to make such payments.[27] Nevertheless, it is commendable to give severance pay even in the absence of any binding obligation.[28]

---

23. The definition of an unacceptable delay and determining whether the contractor was at fault are issues that a *beis din* must determine.

24. *Choshen Mishpat* 304:1. They must, however, establish that there was no negligence involved. See also *Nesivos* 1 that limits this halachah to instances where the worker was carrying a heavy load.

25. *Shevus Yaakov* 3:176 adds that *Chazal* exempted porters since the majority of them are paupers.

26. *Bava Metzia* 83a, *Kitzur Shulchan Aruch* 185:5, *Sma* 304:1 (unless the worker was purposefully negligent).

If the workers are poor, one should pay them their wages as well.

27. *Minchas Yitzchak* 6:167.

28. *Chinuch* 482, *Minchas Yitzchak* 6:167.

Quitting a Job

A salaried worker has the right to quit his job at any time.[29] Although he was hired for a specific amount of time, he may resign before the end of the term (subject to the limitations described below). The *pasuk* tells us *Ki Li Bnei Yisrael Avadim, Avadai Heim*[30] – a Jew is bound only to serve Hashem. A Jew cannot become a "servant of a servant," and is free to leave his job, without suffering any penalty.[31] The worker is entitled to be paid the agreed-upon rate for the period that he worked.[32]

This applies to a salaried worker. A *kablan*, an independent contractor,[33] who is paid by the job and sets his own schedule, has greater restrictions on resigning and may suffer a financial penalty for doing so.[34]

There are a number of instances where a worker's right to resign in middle of a job will be limited:

- If the job is time sensitive, and quitting would cause the employer a loss.[35] This applies to either a financial

29. *Choshen Mishpat* 333:3.

30. *Vayikra* 25:55.

31. However, a worker who accepts a job and then reneges on the agreement will be subject to *tarumos*.

32. 333:4.

33. There are two criteria to determine whether a worker is classified as a *poel* or *kablan*; how the worker is paid (per job or per hour), and what his responsibilities are (to work set hours, or to complete the job).

A salaried worker who works set hours is clearly a *poel*.

An independent contractor who is paid by the job and sets his own hours is clearly a *kablan*.

The status of a worker who is paid by the job but must work at a set time (i.e., a car service may be paid a set price for a trip, yet must provide his services at a specific time) is debatable (*Nesivos* 264 7 (8); see also *Rashba* in *Beis Yosef* 334, *Terumas HaDeshen* 329).

A part-time worker who is paid by the hour but is free to work whichever hours he chooses will have the status of a contractor (*Chochmas Shlomo* 333(3)).

34. *Choshen Mishpat* 333:4, *Yado Al Hatachtonah*.

35. Ibid. 333:5. *Pilpulei Charifta, Bava Metzia Perek* 6 (90) explains that the concept of *Ki Li Bnei Yisrael Avadim* is Rabbinical, and does not apply when the employer will suffer a loss.

If the employer can find a suitable replacement for the worker, he will not suffer loss (e.g., an accountant resigning on April 14), or if the employer will not be able to accomplish the job that the worker was hired to do (e.g., a band walking off the job in the middle of a wedding. The couple will not suffer any financial losses, but they will not be able to find a replacement).

- According to many *poskim*, a worker may not quit a job in order to accept a better-paying job elsewhere.[36]
- If a craftsman has taken possession of an item that he will repair, it is questionable whether either party may back out.[37]
- If the worker makes a *kinyan*.[38]
- If the employer makes a *kinyan* on the worker's tools.[39]

---

any loss and this rule would not apply.

Alternatively, if there were never any other workers available for the job, the worker has not caused the employer a loss by accepting and subsequently declining the job. Had he not accepted it in the first place, the employer would have suffered the same loss (*Choshen Mishpat* 333:5, *Pischei Teshuvah* (11); although see *Shach* (28).

36. *Rama* 333(4), *Tur, Bach, Sma* 333(16), *Aruch HaShulchan* 333 (17), and others quoted in *Pischei Teshuvah* 333:4. Some *poskim* maintain that the worker may not resign. Others allow him to resign but impose a financial penalty (*Yado Al Hatachtonah*). See *Pischei Teshuvah* for dissenting opinions.

37. *Nesivos* 333:1 quoting *Ritva, Bava Metzia* 48a does not allow either party to back out.

Mordechai, Bava Metzia 359, *Sefer HaYashar L'Rabbeinu Tam* 608, *Nemukei Yosef Bava Metzia* 99 do not consider this a binding kinyan.

38. *Sh"ut Ritva* 117, *Pischei Teshuvah* 333, *Aruch HaShulchan* 333:8 apply this concept to all workers.

Shach 333(4),(14), *Ketzos* 333 3(5), *Nesivos* 181(4) apply this only to a *kablan*.

Appropriate *kinyanim* include contracts (*Noda B'Yehudah, Choshen Mishpat* 30:8); *kinyan suddar* (*Shach* [4] rules that a *kinyan suddar* is effective only for a *kablan* but not a *poel*; *Sh"ut Ritva* 117 applies this ruling to a *poel* as well); and payment (*Shut Ritva* 117; see, however, *Choshen Mishpat* 333:3 that disagrees).

39. *Choshen Mishpat* 333:1, *Rama*. An independent contractor (*kablan*) must complete the job. A salaried worker may resign, but the employer has a lien on his tools.

Shach (5) argues with this halachah and requires the employer to return the tools.

See also *Nesivos* (2) and *Chazon Ish, Bava Kamma* 23:3.

Yored — Unauthorized Work

The laws of *yored shelo bershus*[40] govern the amount of compensation that a worker is entitled to receive for unauthorized work. There are two typical scenarios that involve the laws of *yored*.

1. If a worker improves a property without being hired. This can occur if the worker confuses two properties and improves the wrong one.

2. The worker was hired to improve the property, but there was a significant misunderstanding of the nature of the job. Since the work done was not what was negotiated, the worker in effect improved the property without any employment agreement. The worker will be compensated as a *yored* (see footnote).[41] This may also apply if a worker does not complete the job in a timely fashion.[42]

In order to establish the amount of compensation that the *yored* is entitled to, we must determine whether the improvements made were appropriate for the property.

40. *Choshen Mishpat* 375.

41. Ibid. 306:3, *Shach* 5.

If the worker was at fault for the mistake, according to *Rama* 306:3, *Sma* (9), and *Nesivos* 6 (based on *Yerushalmi*), the worker is penalized. (See *Sma* and *Nesivos* for details on how he would be compensated. See also *Choshen Mishpat*; *Shach* 306(5); *Chazon Ish, Bava Kamma* 22:23 who disagree.)

If the worker was not at fault for the misunderstanding, the guidelines described above would apply.

42. *Kesef HaKadoshim* 375. Delays are normal and do not nullify an employment agreement. However, if the employer clearly stipulated that the job must be completed by a certain date, and the worker missed the deadline but completed the job anyway, he has in effect improved the property without being hired.

For example, if a homeowner hired a painter, and specified that the job needed to be completed before an upcoming *simchah*, if the painter procrastinated and the job was not completed on time, the original agreement is void.

Appropriate Improvements — Sadeh Ha'asuyah Lita

When the improvements are appropriate for the property, *sadeh ha'asuyah lita*,[43] the worker is entitled to be paid the full value of his services.[44]

Atypical Improvements — Sadeh She'ein Asuyah Lita

If the improvements that were done were atypical for the property, and the owner would not have made them, the property has the status of a *sadeh she'ein asuyah lita.*[45] The worker is entitled to the lower end of the expenses he incurred (including his labor)[46] or[47] the appreciation in value caused by the improvement.

A person arrives home one day and is shocked to see a crew putting finishing touches on a huge new deck in his backyard. It becomes clear that the crew was supposed to build the deck for a neighbor, but had confused addresses. Assuming that such a deck is not the norm for the neighborhood, the homeowner is only responsible to pay the lesser of the costs of the materials and labor, or the amount that his home appreciated in value because of this new addition.[48]

43. Literally, "a field that is typically planted." The Gemara discusses a situation where a *yored* planted trees in a field.

44. *Choshen Mishpat* 375:1. See also *Beis Yosef* and *Aruch HaShulchan* 375:5 for a discussion about how the rate is calculated.

45. *Choshen Mishpat* 375:1. Literally, "A field that is not typically planted."

46. *Shach, Choshen Mishpat* 306 (5). He is paid as a basic laborer.

47. The homeowner is receiving benefit from the work, and it is only right that he pay for it. Yet, the worker had no right to improve the homeowner's property, and should not profit from it. Therefore, the homeowner pays for his benefit, but not more than the *yored's* expenses.

48. If the homeowner refuses to pay even this amount, see the next paragraph.

If the Owner Is Not Interested in the Improvements

If the owner does not want or like the improvements that were done, or if he cannot afford to pay for them, he may demand that the improvements be removed.[49] Once the improvements are removed, he will not be liable to pay the worker.[50] According to many *poskim*, this applies even to improvements that are appropriate for the property *(sadeh ha'asuyah lita)*.[51]

Changes that Are Not Improvements

If a person makes changes that do not increase the value of the property, he is not entitled to compensation. For example, if a *yored* repainted a room that did not need to be painted, he will not be able to charge the owner for the expense. Although the *yored* may believe his color is nicer, there is no appreciation in the value of the house. Because he did not provide the owner with any value, he cannot charge him. If, however, the room needed to be repainted, the *yored* will be entitled to compensation even though the homeowner may have preferred a different color.[52]

49. This right is limited if the worker was hired but made the wrong improvement. See *Choshen Mishpat* 306:3.

50. Ibid. 375:2.

51. Ibid.; *Sma* (4); *Rosh, Bava Metzia* 8:22; *Rama* quoted by *Tur*, *Nesivos* 158 (8). See *Gaon* for other opinions. *Shevus Yaakov* 1:112 writes that in the absence of a clear ruling, the owner of the property may refuse to pay.

Chazon Ish, Bava Basra 2:3 suggests that it depends on the circumstances. If the owner has a legitimate reason to demand the removal, he is entitled to do so. However, if the norm is to make such improvements and the owner does not present any legitimate reason why he does not want them, we will presume that he is trying to take advantage of the *yored* and he will be liable to pay for the improvements.

52. Subject to the following section concerning the owner's right to demand the improvement be removed.

Improvements that Cannot Be Removed

There are instances where it is not practical for the *yored* to remove the improvements. For example, it is not practical for a painter to undo his work without suffering a complete loss. According to some *poskim*, the owner must pay for the work and does not have the right to demand that the worker remove it.[53]

If the Owner Shows that He Values the Improvements

If the owner refuses to pay for the improvements and demands that the worker remove them, but then demonstrates that the improvements have value to him, he must pay the worker the full value of these improvements.[54]

A gardener mistakenly plants extra flowers and shrubs in a customer's yard. The customer not only refuses to pay for the extra work, claiming that he doesn't like the shrubbery and they do not make the lawn look any nicer, but also demands that the gardener uproot the shrubs and repair the property. If the customer is later seen watering and trimming the plants, he will have to reimburse the gardener for his work.

53. *Nesivos* 375:2, 306:7; *Chukos Chaim, Choshen Mishpat* 84.
Ketzos 306:6 disagrees. See also *Chazon Ish Bava Kamma* 22:6, *Bava Basra* 2:6.

54. *Choshen Mishpat* 375:3. *Rosh* limits this halachah to a situation in which, although the improvements were appropriate (*sadeh ha'asuyah lita*), the owner refuses to pay and demands that the improvements be removed. If the owner proceeds to use the improvements, he must pay for them.
Rama applies this concept even when the improvements were not appropriate (*sadeh she'ein asuyah lita*). If the owner shows that he values the work, he must reimburse the worker for the full value of his services (see also *Aruch HaShulchan* 375:6).

If the Work Was Necessary

By definition, any work that was necessary to maintain the property is *asuyah lita*, and the owner is obligated to pay the full value of the services provided.[55]

A plumber notices water pouring out of a window of a vacant building. The plumber enters the building and makes the necessary repairs on the burst pipes. He is entitled to the full market value of his services since the owner clearly needs to make these repairs.

A builder hires an electrician to do rough electrical work in a new-construction house. The electrician mistakenly includes a number of electrical upgrades. If the property is an apartment building in a slum neighborhood, the work has minimal value to the owner and he may tell the electrician to remove the upgrades. If the house is a mansion in an upper-class neighborhood where all of the houses are significantly upgraded, the electrician may demand full payment for his work.

Partners

Partners have the right to improve their property in a manner that they believe will be beneficial. A partner who improves a property for the benefit of the partnership has the status of *a yored bershus*, an authorized worker.[56] Even if the improvements are atypical for the property *(sadeh she'ein asuyah lita)*, the partner is entitled to full compensation.[57] This applies even if

55. *Choshen Mishpat* 375:7, *Rama*.

56. *Choshen Mishpat* 178:3.

57. *Rama* writes that if the improvement costs more than the value it created, the partner need only pay for the value of the improvements. *Beis Shmuel, Even HaEzer* 88:20 argues that a partner is entitled to recover his expenses even if they are greater than the value of the improvement.

This dispute applies only when the partner used personal money for the improvement. If, however, he used funds belonging to the partnership, he is not

the partner improved the property without notifying the other partner.

However, if the other partner objected to the proposed improvement and it was done against his wishes, he may demand that the improvement be removed, and need not pay for the expense.[58]

Bar Metzra

If a person buys a field and improves it, and then a *bar metzra* (A neighbor often has the first right to buy an adjacent property. He may force an outside buyer that violates this halachah to resell the property to him. This concept is discussed at length in Chapter Fourteen) claims it, he has the status of a *yored bershus,* an authorized worker.[59] At the time that he made the improvements, he believed that the field was his. He is entitled to full compensation for any improvement.

If he continues making improvements after he learns that the *bar metzra* is interested in the field, his status changes to a *yored shelo bershus,* an unauthorized worker.[60] At this point it should be clear that he is not the real owner of the field, and he is working on another person's property without a contract. His compensation for these new improvements will be governed by the regular laws of *yored.*

Mekach Ta'us

As explained in Chapter Two, a person who buys a defective item has the right to claim *mekach ta'us* and to void the sale. If the person improved the property before he discovered the

---

obligated to reimburse the partnership for the loss, unless he overstepped his authority when spending the money (*Nesivos* 178:2).

58. *Choshen Mishpat* 176:3; *Rama*. However, if the improvement was necessary, the partner must share in its cost.

59. *Choshen Mishpat* 175:6.

60. Ibid.

defect, he is entitled to reimbursement for the improvements that he made to the property. Because the improvements were made at a time when the sale was thought to be valid, he has the status of a *yored bershus* and is entitled to full compensation.[61]

Tenants

If a tenant makes improvements to the house for his own convenience, he has the status of a *yored shelo bershus*.[62] Improvements that were absolutely necessary will be completely reimbursed, while unnecessary improvements will be reimbursed as a *sadeh she'ein asuyah lita*.

61. Ibid. 232:14.

62. *Imrei Yosher* 2:200; *Chukos Chaim* 84; *Teshuvos V'Hanhagos* 469; *Pischei Choshen, Geneivah V'Ona'ah* 8:25.

See, however, *Nesivos* 158:8 and 236:7 based on *Shach* 391:2, and *Ramban* quoted in *Beis Yosef* 365, that a *yored* is entitled to compensation only if he intended to benefit the owner. A tenant makes the improvement for his own comfort and perhaps should not qualify for reimbursement.

Imrei Yosher 2:200 explains that a tenant recognizes that the improvement will benefit the landlord and is therefore considered having improved it for both of them. Therefore, he is entitled to be reimbursed. In contrast, the *Nesivos* refers to a case where the action was taken for himself and parenthetically benefited the other party.

See also *Chavatzeles HaSharon* 2:30.

See also *Ketzos* 356:3 who argues on *Nesivos*.

10 Timely Payments / Bal Talin

Introduction

The Arizal was exceptionally careful to pay his workers on time. Once, he realized that he didn't have funds available to pay his worker. Nightfall, which is the deadline for the mitzvah of b'yomo titein scharo, paying a worker the day he finishes his job, was quickly approaching. The Arizal chose to try to borrow money to pay his worker, even though it meant not davening Minchah on time.

According to many poskim,[1] *there is no obligation to borrow money to pay a worker. Nevertheless, the Arizal gave priority to raising funds to pay a worker over davening at the appropriate time. Why?*

When we daven, we stand before Hashem and declare that we are completely dependent on Hashem for all our needs. We beg Hashem to provide us with parnassah, health, and all of our other desires.

1. See "Lack of Funds," later in this chapter.

"Ki eilav hu nosei es nafsho" [2] *— our employees rely on us for their parnasah. They put in an honest day's work in order to be able to provide for themselves and their families.*

How can we daven to Hashem in good conscience, when we are letting down those who rely on us? If we do not provide for those who have served us well and deserve to be paid, how can we ask Hashem to provide us with what we have not earned and may not deserve?

There may be no technical obligation to borrow money to avoid the prohibition of bal talin. But perhaps the Arizal felt that he could not daven until he fulfilled his personal obligations. Only after he had provided for those who were dependent on him was he ready to daven for his own needs and requests.

For a Jew, paying workers on time is not just a question of good labor-management relationships. The Torah demands special sensitivity to the needs of workers. "*Ki eilav hu nosei es nafsho*" — the worker depends with all his heart on receiving his wages. A worker dedicates his entire day to his employer and may even risk his health in order to earn his paycheck. It is only right that he receives payment without delay.

Paying a worker is not simply an annoying obligation. It is a mitzvah that should be done with the same enthusiasm and joy as shaking a *lulav*.[3] In fact, *Pele Yoetz*[4] suggests that one should hire workers just to be able to fulfill the mitzvah of paying them on time. The *Chofetz Chaim*[5] writes that when paying a worker, a person should have in mind that he is fulfilling a *mitzvah d'Oraisa*, a Biblical commandment.

---

2. *Devarim* 24:15.

3. *Chofetz Chaim, Hakdamah* to ninth *Perek* of *Ahavas Chesed.*

4. *Schar Sachir.*

5. Introduction to the *Sefer HaMitzvos HaKatzar.*

This mitzvah is one of the most common mitzvos of *Choshen Mishpat*. Each time that one hires a handyman, takes a haircut, or visits a doctor, he is subject to *bal talin*. Yet, this mitzvah is also one of the least known. Many people are not even aware that they are doing a mitzvah, and are not familiar with the guidelines and time frame in which a worker must be paid.

What Is Bal Talin?

There is an obligation to pay all debts on time. However, certain debts are treated with special severity in halachah. There are two negative prohibitions and one positive commandment that specifically address paying Jewish workers in a timely fashion.[6] (Leases are also included in these mitzvos, as will be explained below.) These apply even though the worker is eventually paid. **Delaying** payment is prohibited.[7]

Time Frame

The Torah requires that a worker be paid by the end of the day or night that the work was completed.[8] If the job is completed

6. A positive mitzvah of *b'yomo titein scharo* (*Devarim* 24:15), and two negative prohibitions: *lo salin* (*Vayikra* 19:13) and *lo savo* (*Devarim* ibid.).

7. If a worker is not ultimately paid in full, the employer will violate five prohibitions (*Bava Metzia* 111a). According to *Rambam, Sechirus* 11:2, the employer will violate four prohibitions.

8. *Choshen Mishpat* 339:3.

The Gemara (*Bava Metzia* 110b) points out an apparent contradiction between the two prohibitions of delaying a worker's pay. One verse, *Lo savo alav hashemesh*, prohibits waiting past sunset to pay a worker. The other verse, *Lo salin peulas sachir ad boker*, prohibits delaying past daybreak. The Gemara explains that a worker is entitled to be paid only after he has completed the job. If he is a day laborer, he works the entire day, and the obligation to pay him begins at nightfall. The Torah allows the employer the entire night to arrange payment. If the worker is not paid by daybreak the next morning, the employer has violated *lo salin*. The wages of a worker who works throughout the night become due when he ends his work, at daybreak. Here too, the Torah allots the entire day for the employer to arrange payment. If the worker is not paid by sunset, the employer has violated *bal talin*.

The Gemara refers to instances where the job lasted throughout the day, and only during the night, payment must be made before dawn. If the worker finishes during the day, he must be paid before nightfall. Since the precise time of nightfall is unknown, one should pay before sunset (*sh'kiah*). Even if the job is completed just a few moments before sunset, the worker must be paid before the *sh'kiah* deadline. If the job is completed after *sh'kiah* but before *tzeis hakochavim* (the emergence of the stars), the worker should be paid immediately.[9]

Salaried employees must be paid on the last day of the agreed-upon pay period. Although the contract may be for an entire year, if the employment agreement calls for weekly payments, it will be subject to *bal talin* at the end of each and every week.[10]

Exact Change

A person that does not have exact change to pay a worker is obligated to find a way to break the large bills, even if it is inconvenient or entails a minor loss.[11]

Requesting Payment

Bal talin applies only when the employee asks for his wages. If he does not ask for his pay, he is demonstrating that he is not particular about his rights and *bal talin* would not apply.[12] Even

---

ended at nightfall. Because the payment became due at the beginning of the night, the employer has until the next morning to pay. However, a worker who completes his job while it was still daytime must be paid before nightfall.

Today, employees do not work the entire day or night. A typical 9-to-5 job would end during the night during the winter months. Accordingly, the employer would have until the next morning to pay the worker. During the summer months, 5 o'clock is still daytime. Accordingly, an employer will have only until nightfall to pay the worker.

9. *Ahavas Chesed* Part 1, Chapter 9, Halachah 2.

10. *Knesses HaGedolah, Hagahos HaTur* 339:7; *Tashbetz*.

11. *Ahavas Chesed, Nesiv HaChesed* 9:21.

12. *Choshen Mishpat* 339:10.

so, the *Zohar*[13] writes that one should pay on time even though the worker is willing to wait for his wages.

The *Chofetz Chaim*[14] adds that if the worker wants to be paid but is unable to contact his employer to ask for his salary, *bal talin* will apply. The worker is not waiving his right to timely payment; he is simply unable to ask for his wages.

After a Missed Payday

The laws of *bal talin* apply only to the day the work is completed, and can therefore only be violated only once per job.[15] If, after violating *bal talin*, the employer continues to procrastinate and delays paying the worker, he will not violate *bal talin* again for the continued delay. He will, however, violate *al tomar*, which will be explained later.

If, for any reason, one was exempt[16] from *bal talin* on the day the job was completed, one would not be subject to *bal talin* for future delays.[17]

After completing the paint job for which he was hired, Moshe noticed that the customer looked extremely preoccupied. Instead of disturbing him to ask for his pay, Moshe quietly left and returned the next morning. Since the correct time frame for payment has already passed, if the customer delays payment, he will not violate bal talin.

13. Quoted by *Shaar Mishpat, Pischei Teshuvah* 339, *Ahavas Chesed* introduction to Chapter 9.

14. *Ahavas Chesed, Nesiv HaChesed* 9:32.

15. *Choshen Mishpat* 339:8. Or each pay period for a salaried worker.

16. For example, if the worker did not request the money, one does not violate *bal talin*. If the worker requests payment the next day, there will be no *bal talin*.

17. *Choshen Mishpat* 339:9; *Nesiv HaChesed* 9:35.

Delaying Payment to Any Creditors

There is a separate prohibition of *Al tomar l'rei'acha lech va'shuv u'macher etein* that applies anytime a person denies payment to a creditor.[18] This prohibition will apply to any type of debt and will apply each time the creditor asks for payment.[19]

This prohibition has limitations. It applies only when the debtor deliberately delays paying his creditor. If he has a legitimate reason that prevents him from paying, he will not be in violation of this law.[20]

The Type of Payments that Are Included in the Mitzvah

Bal talin applies to any worker, whether he is a salaried employee, an independent contractor, or a craftsman.[21] It also applies to rentals of movable objects (*mitaltelin*) or real estate.[22] However, this mitzvah does not apply to purchases.[23] Accordingly, paying workers has precedence over paying for a purchase. If faced with a choice of paying either a worker or a vendor on time, the worker must be paid first. It must be stressed

18. *Mishlei* 3:28. This prohibition is *midivrei Kabbalah*.

19. *Choshen Mishpat* 339:8 (delaying payment to workers); 97:3 (delaying payment on a loan); *Imrei Binah, Eidus* 34 (refusing to return another's belongings).
See, however, *Toras Emes* 119 רצ"ע.

20. *Tosafos, Bava Metzia* 111a writes that if someone is preoccupied with another activity and is therefore unable to pay a worker, he will not violate *al tomar*. This defense is not valid for *bal talin*.

21. *Choshen Mishpat* 339:6.

22. Ibid. 339:1. *Shulchan Aruch* does not make a definitive ruling whether real estate leases are subject to *bal talin*. *Gaon, Shaar Mishpat, Aruch HaShulchan, Ahavas Chesed* 9:5 follow the stringent opinion.

23. A common scenario involves transactions that contain both labor and materials. The amount due for the labor is subject to *bal talin*, while the cost of the materials is considered a sale and would not be subject to *bal talin*.

Ketzos 306 (3) writes that if one pays part of the bill, the payment credited toward the amount is not subject to *bal talin*. The customer must therefore pay the entire amount in full to avoid a violation.

that this does not justify a late payment for a purchase. Paying the supplier late in this scenario is simply the lesser of two evils.

Real Estate Leases

According to halachah, payment for rentals is due at the **end** of a lease.[24] The halachos of *bal talin* apply only if payment is delayed past that time.

A typical lease agreement calls for rent to be paid in advance. The rent for the entire month is due at the beginning of that month. Although one is obligated to abide by the terms of the lease, paying the rent on the second or even the thirtieth of the month would not violate *bal talin*.[25] If, however, payment were delayed past the end of the month, *bal talin* would apply.[26]

Repairs

When an item is given to a craftsman for repair, *bal talin* will not apply until the item is actually returned to the owner.[27] Although the craftsman may have completed the work earlier, *bal talin* will not apply until the owner actually takes possession of the item.[28]

---

24. *Ein sechirus mishtalemes ela b'sof.*

25. This *psak* is based on conversations with various *gedolei haposkim*. See, however, *HaMesifta,* Iyar 5745/1985, p. 108.

26. If the landlord has a security deposit , there may be no *bal talin* as per footnote 28.

27. *Choshen Mishpat* 339:6.

28. *Sma* 10, *Shitah Mekubetzes, Bava Metzia* 112a quoting Rabbeinu Yehonasan, and *Shulchan Aruch HaRav* explain that an employer does not violate *bal talin* if he gives his employees collateral for the wages owed. Since the craftsman has possession of the item he repaired, his wages will not be subject to *bal talin*.

Levush suggests an alternate explanation. By not returning the item to the owner, the craftsman is demonstrating that he is willing to wait for his pay, and that he is waiving his rights to timely payment.

Pischei Teshuvah points out that according to *Levush*, one may violate *bal talin* even if he gives the worker collateral for his wages. *Aruch HaShulchan* explains that *bal talin* is predicated on the worker's need for the funds. Giving collateral will not help him feed his family.

This applies only to a craftsman who is repairing a client's item. However, wages owed to a craftsman for creating an item using his own raw materials will not be subject to *bal talin*. For example, if one orders a custom-made suit and the tailor provides the material, his payment will not be subject to *bal talin*.[29]

Priority

If a person owes wages to two workers, one of whom just completed his job, while the other was owed wages for an earlier job, the worker who just completed the job has priority in halachah. If the employer cannot afford to pay both workers, he must pay the worker who completed his work on that day.[30] The reason for this is that the *bal talin* deadline for the wages owed to the first worker has already passed. Once the deadline has passed, *bal talin* does not apply to future delays. If the second worker is not paid on time, the employer would violate *bal talin*. To avoid this violation, the second worker must be paid.[31]

Ketzos 72:23 suggests that wages are not due until the item is delivered. As such, *bal talin* will apply only after delivery.

Beur Halachah, Orach Chaim 242 suggests that if one cannot pay a craftsman, one should refuse to accept the item from him. As long as the owner does not take possession of the item, the wages are not due and *bal talin* will be avoided.

Aruch HaShulchan 339:8 argues that if the craftsman is prepared to return the item, one violates *bal talin* if he refuses to accept it.

29. *Toras Emes* 119. A tailor who alters a suit belonging to the customer is considered a worker and his wages are subject to *bal talin*. However, if the tailor creates a custom-made suit with his own materials, he is not considered an employee of the client. He is creating a suit and then selling it to the customer. There is a buyer-seller relationship as opposed to an employee-employer relationship, and therefore *bal talin* will not apply.

30. *Ahavas Chesed* 10:11.

31. Clearly, the employer has obligations to both workers. However, while the first worker has a claim against the employer for payment, the second employee has the additional severity of *bal talin*. Paying the second worker is the lesser of two evils.

Partial Payments

Bal talin applies to partial payments as well.[32] An employer who pays his worker most of his salary, but withholds a small amount, has violated *bal talin*.

Withholding Payments

Often, when a contractor finishes a job, the homeowner does not want to pay the entire bill immediately. The homeowner is concerned that if he pays the contractor completely, it may be difficult to get the contractor to stand behind his work. Withholding a portion of the bill gives the homeowner leverage and makes it easier for him to deal with the contractor if any issues arise.

This is a clear violation of *bal talin*. The worker has completed the entire job and is entitled to his entire pay. A homeowner is not permitted to gain leverage at the worker's expense.

If the homeowner intends to withhold money at the end of the job, he may stipulate this in advance, when he hires the worker. If the worker accepts these terms, *bal talin* will not apply.

These halachos apply after the job is completely finished. If, however, the job is not complete, there is no obligation to pay the worker.[33]

Lack of Funds

The *issur* of *bal talin* applies to an employer who **withholds** wages owed to a worker. If the employer does not have any

32. *Ahavas Chesed* 9:10.

33. In halachah, payment for a job is not due until the job is completed. In theory, if a worker completed 99 percent of the job, he is still not entitled to any pay whatsoever until the job is completely finished. However, if there is a clear *minhag* or custom to pay installments as the job progresses, one is obligated to follow the norm.

funds available to pay these wages, he will not violate *bal talin*.[34] This applies only to an employer who has absolutely no funds available. If he has money, he must pay his worker before paying other vendors or suppliers. In addition, if he has merchandise that is ready for sale, he must make every effort to sell the items in order to raise capital to pay the worker.[35] If the employer is able to collect a debt that is owed to him, he is obligated to do so to avoid *bal talin*.[36]

If the employer has some funds available, he is obligated to make a partial payment with whatever funds he has available.[37]

---

34. *Choshen Mishpat* 339:10.

35. *Chinuch* 588, *Ahavas Chesed* 9:7. The employer is obligated to sell merchandise in order to pay his workers on time, even if he will incur a small loss. However, he is not obligated to sell items at a significant loss in order to raise the funds needed to pay his worker.

This leads to an interesting question. A person is obligated to spend as much money as is necessary to avoid violating a negative prohibition. *Bal talin* is a negative prohibition. Yet, it is clear from the *Rishonim* that one is obligated to sell merchandise to raise capital only if it can be done with a minimal loss. What is the explanation for this limit?

R' Avraham Pam zt"l (*HaMesifta,* Iyar 5745/1985 page 108) writes that the *Ritva* states the halachah that if the employer has no funds with which to pay his worker, he is not in violation of *bal talin*. The *Ritva* then continues that if he has merchandise that can be readily sold without a loss, he is considered to have money and must liquidate the merchandise in order to avoid *bal talin.* The discussion is not what magnitude of loss is required to avoid *bal talin.* The discussion is whether having merchandise is considered having money available to pay a worker. The *Ritva* maintains that if the merchandise can be sold without a loss, it is the equivalent of cash, and one would be obligated to sell in order to avoid *bal talin*. If the merchandise is not readily sellable, it is not the equivalent of cash, and *bal talin* will not apply.

The requirement to spend money to avoid violating a prohibition applies only when the prohibition will in fact be violated. If, however, an employee only has merchandise that cannot readily be sold, he will qualify for the exemption of not having funds. Accordingly, he will not violate the prohibition and therefore has no reason to sell the merchandise at a loss.

If this interpretation is correct, then this exception would apply only when the employer has no money to pay the worker. However, if the employer has enough cash to pay the worker, but would rather pay his mortgage to avoid a penalty, there would be no justification to do so, since *bal talin* is a negative prohibition that must be avoided at all costs וצ"ע לדינא.

See also *R' Akiva Eiger* who refers *to Mutzal Mei'eish* (45) וצ"ע.

36. *Ahavas Chesed* 9:7.

37. Ibid. 9:10.

If one does not have funds available, one should try to borrow money in order to pay a worker.[38]

Stipulating in Advance

If an employer anticipates that he may have difficulty paying his workers on time, he should stipulate when he hires each worker that he has the right to pay him late. If the worker accepts the job under these terms, *bal talin* will not apply.[39]

In some industries, employees are paid at the beginning of a month for the work done in the previous month. Although in halachah wages are due at the end of each month, the parties may agree to any payment schedule that they choose. However, once the proper halachic time of payment has passed, *bal talin* will no longer apply. Even if the employer pays his worker much later, he will not violate *bal talin*.[40] He will, however, violate *al tomar l'rei'acha*, as discussed in "Delaying Payment to Other Creditors."

Hired by an Intermediary

Bal talin applies only when an employer personally hires a worker. If a worker was not hired directly by the employer, but rather through an agent, *bal talin* will not apply.[41] A businessman

38. *Shulchan Aruch HaRav, She'eilah* 18 quotes the *Arizal* that it is a *middas chassidus. Nesiv HaChesed* 9:21 writes that there may be an obligation to borrow money.

39. *Choshen Mishpat* 339, *Shach* (2) quoting *Sefer Chassidim* 1071. Nevertheless, one should strive to pay the worker on time.

40. *Choshen Mishpat* 339:9.

See however *Shevet HaLevi* 7:233, based on *Meiri* and *Ramach*, and *Teshuvos V'Hanhagos* 3:470 who maintain that if the parties set a later payday, the employer will violate *bal talin* if he delays past that day.

41. *Choshen Mishpat* 339:7. This appears to be inconsistent with the concept of *shaliach shel adam k'moso*, a person's agent may act on his behalf. *Meshech Chochmah* (*Vayikra* 19:13) suggests a novel interpretation of the verse *lo salin peulas sachir itcha*; only payment to a *sachir itcha*, a worker who was hired by you, is subject to these laws.

who delegates hiring to a human-resources department is not subject to the laws of *bal talin*.[42]

The Gemara[43] relates that Ameimar and Mar Zutra would hire workers for each other. They were so concerned that they might violate the laws of *bal talin* that they insisted on hiring workers through an intermediary to avoid any possible violation of *bal talin*.[44] This illustrates the severity that *Chazal* placed on violating these halachos.

Corporations

Corporations have an unusual halachic status concerning *bal talin*. Who is responsible to ensure that the employees are paid on time? Is the CEO or management of a company subject to *bal talin*, or is it the responsibility of the owners or shareholders of the company?

Shareholders

Shareholders of a corporation are not subject to *bal talin* since they do not hire the employees directly. The management of the company does the actual hiring. Although the management is working on behalf of the shareholders, because the employees were hired through an agent, *bal talin* will not apply.[45]

Tosafos Rid, Bava Metzia 111a suggests that when an employee is not hired directly by the employer, and is instead forced to deal with an intermediary, the worker is not confident that he will be paid on time. Accordingly, *bal talin* will not apply.

42. *Teshuras Shai* 2:86 makes an important distinction. If the agent has the discretion to choose whom to hire and to negotiate his wages, *bal talin* will not apply. If, however, the principal makes all of the decisions and the agent simply relays the information to the worker, the principal would be subject to the laws of *bal talin*.

43. *Bava Metzia* 111a.

44. However, the prohibition of *al tomar l'rei'acha* may still apply. See "Delaying Payment to Creditors."

45. See also Ch. 6 footnote 45.

Managers

There is a debate among the *poskim* whether the manager of a company has the obligation of *bal talin*. Although the manager hires the workers directly, he is not personally paying their salaries. The money comes from the company's account that is owned by the shareholders. *Mishnas R' Aharon*[46] suggests that *bal talin* applies only when an employer withholds wages for himself. In contrast, when a manager of a firm delays paying a worker, he is not keeping the salary for himself. The money belongs to the business that is completely owned by the shareholders. In addition, because the manager is only a hired hand and is not personally responsible for the worker's salary, he does not violate the laws of *bal talin*.

The *Chofetz Chaim*[47] seems to disagree. He writes that if a manager[48] hires workers, and it is understood that he is the one responsible to ensure that their salaries are paid in a timely fashion, *bal talin* will apply. However, it applies only when there are company funds available to pay the salaries. A manager does not have any obligation to use personal money to cover the payroll.

Prepayment

Some contemporary *poskim* maintain that one does not fulfill the positive mitzvah of paying a worker if he prepays for the job.[49] The mitzvah is *b'yomo titein scharo*, to pay a worker on the day the wages are due. By paying before the job is completed, the wages never become due, and there is no opportunity to fulfill the mitzvah.

46. Volume 2 responsa 73:3.

47. *Ahavas Chesed* 10:4.

48. The *Chofetz Chaim* is referring to an *apotropus*, someone appointed to manage the estate of orphans, or to a woman who is authorized to act on behalf of her husband.

49. *Kol HaTorah* Volume 41, p. 137 in the name of the *Chofetz Chaim*.

Teshuvos V'Hanhagos[50] disagrees. He maintains that the mitzvah is to ensure that a worker is paid before the Torah's deadline. Prepaying is certainly before that deadline.

Others agree in principle, that the payment must be made after the job is completed in order to fulfill the mitzvah. However, they argue that even when a worker is prepaid, he is not really entitled to the money until he completes the job. Only after the job is completed does the money become his. The mitzvah is fulfilled at that time.[51]

Acceptable Forms of Payment

According to halachah, workers must be paid in cash.[52] One may not pay a worker with merchandise or by assigning to the worker a debt that a third party owes the employer.

Checks

A check is not a form of currency and has no inherent value. It is simply an instrument that allows the bearer to collect payment from the account of the check writer. Theoretically, one can argue that a worker may insist that he be paid in cash and refuse to accept a check.

In most professions, the accepted custom is to pay with checks. A worker who accepts a job without stipulating that he wants to be paid specifically in cash is implicitly agreeing to the norm, and must accept a check. However, in a profession that does not have a clear custom of accepting checks, the worker may insist on

50. 3:470. See also *Derech Sichah, Parshas Ki Seitsei* from *R' Chaim Kanievsky.*

It should be noted that the *Chofetz Chaim* wrote extensively about the halachos of *bal talin.* If the *Chofetz Chaim* did indeed hold that one should not prepay a worker, he presumably would have mentioned it in *Ahavas Chesed.*

51. Based on *Chavos Daas* and *R' Akiva Eiger, Yoreh Deah* 160.

52. *Bava Metzia* 118a.

being paid with cash. Taxi drivers and babysitters are examples of workers who are generally paid with cash, and they are entitled to refuse to accept checks.

If a worker agrees to accept a check as payment, there is certainly no violation of *bal talin*. By agreeing to accept such payment, the worker has waived his right to cash payments. However, it is questionable whether one fulfills the mitzvah of *b'yomo titein scharo* when paying with a check.[53]

Mitzvah and Prohibition

There is a positive mitzvah to pay a worker on time. All of the above-mentioned exceptions to *bal talin* are instances in which one does not violate the prohibitions against late payment. However, the employer will lose a valuable opportunity to fulfill a mitzvah. One should strive to avoid these waivers and make an effort to fulfill this important mitzvah.

Chofetz Chaim's Business Advice

The *Chofetz Chaim* concludes his writings about *bal talin* with the following advice: Before allowing a worker to start a job, one should clarify all of the terms of the employment. This has many advantages. First, a worker has an incentive to be accommodating to his prospective employer in order to get the job. Once he has already been hired, he has little incentive to make further concessions. Therefore, it is in the employer's interest to negotiate the exact price and terms of the job before the employee actually begins working.

53. In places where third-party checks are readily accepted, many *poskim* consider checks to be the same as cash and one would fulfill the mitzvah of *b'yomo titein scharo*. However, large checks that must be cashed in a bank, or even smaller checks in communities where third-party checks are not readily cashed, may not be considered payment according to some *poskim* (*Mili D'Nizikin* in the name of *R' Moshe Feinstein zt"l*). Also see *Teshuvos V'Hanhagos* 3:470:3.

Anything that is not clarified in advance will need to be settled at the end of the job. At that time, the employer may either agree to the worker's demands, which may prove to be a very costly proposition, or he may refuse to pay the worker the full amount that he requests. The employer then runs the risk of violating the prohibitions both of cheating a worker and of *gezel*. It is extremely difficult for the employer to know precisely how much the worker is entitled to, and it is likely that the employer will err. Such situations can be avoided by clarifying everything in advance.

A nursing-home administrator hired a consultant to review certain operations. The parties did not discuss the costs in advance. After the job was completed, the consultant submitted his bill. The admistrator, who was well aware that the consultant had no way of forcing him to pay, began negotiating. He insisted on a 15-percent discount. Having no choice, the consultant reluctantly agreed to this below-market offer. The administrator has violated gezel, bal talin, and a number of other prohibitions.

11 Partnerships

Operating a Partnership

Managing partners have responsibilities toward their investors. They must operate the business in accordance with the accepted norms.[1] A partner may not make any unconventional business decisions without the unanimous consent of all of his partners.[2] If there is a disagreement between the partners, the partners must consult with other businessmen to determine the *derech hasochrim*, the normal course of action [of those in their industry].[3] If they can not determine *derech hasochrim*, they will either have to work out some form of compromise or dissolve the partnership. As such, it is strongly recommended to have an operating agreement that clarifies the decision-making process of the partnership.

1. *Choshen Mishpat* 176:10.

2. *Beur HaGra* 163:1 (9) implies that partnerships are like a *beis din*, and would follow majority rule וצ"ע.

3. *Aruch HaShulchan* 176:46.

See *Aruch HaShulchan* 176:30 and *Nesivos* 176:22 for a possible limitation to this concept.

It should be noted that there are various procedures and requirements necessary to create a valid partnership.[4] Simply agreeing to become partners or even executing an operating agreement will not necessarily create a halachically meaningful partnership. One should discuss partnership agreements with a Rav familiar with these areas of halachah to ensure that the agreement is drafted correctly.

Conflict of Interest

A managing partner may not be involved in other businesses, since that may interfere with his ability to effectively manage the partnership (although see footnote).[5]

Resigning

A managing partner may resign at any time. His obligation to his employer/partner is the same as that of any other worker, and is subject to the same limitations and conditions outlined in Chapter Nine, "Quitting a Job."[6] This applies to a partnership in which the managing partner is working for an investor. However,

4. These laws are discussed in the beginning of *Choshen Mishpat* 176.

See *Maharashdam, Choshen Mishpat* 168 that *Minhag HaSochrim* may create a binding partnership.

5. *Rambam, Shutfim* 5:1, *Choshen Mishpat* 176:10.

Beis Yosef, Choshen Mishpat 176:17 explains that partners "are expected [in the *Beis Yosef's* language] to devote their heart and soul to the partnership." If the partner is busy with other deals, he will be less vigilant with the partnership.

Taz (*Yoreh Deah* 177 [44]), *Shach* [67] limit this halachah to a partner who is managing a store, which requires his uninterrupted attention. A business venture that does not require full-time attention would not be subject to this limitation. (This approach is reflected in *Shulchan Aruch, Yoreh Deah* 177:39.)

See *Divrei Geonim, Klal* 99 concerning a partner who violates this rule and causes a loss.

6. *Choshen Mishpat* 176:23.

This right does not apply if it will cause the employer/partner a loss. In addition, if the partner is classified as a *kablan* (see Ch. 9 footnote 33), there may be a financial penalty imposed for resigning before the job is completed. See *Ketzos* 176:23 (8) and *Nesivos* 176:23(41).

if there are two or more active partners, neither has the right to quit before the partnership is dissolved.[7]

Dissolving a Partnership

It is almost inevitable that over time, partnerships may break up. The partners may have a disagreement over business strategies, making additional capital investments, or simply have a personality clash. If the parties come to a mutual agreement that the partnership should be dissolved, they may do so in any manner that they choose. If there is a disagreement over whether or how to dissolve a partnership, the following guidelines apply:

When a Partnership May Be Dissolved

Active investments — in which the parties pooled their funds together in order to buy and sell merchandise, to develop a property, or to take advantage of a business opportunity — have significant restrictions on withdrawals. Because the partners pooled their money together in order to accomplish a specific goal, there was an implied commitment to allow the funds to remain in the business until the goal was accomplished. Accordingly, the partners may not withdraw their funds until the objective has been met.[8] However, if it becomes clear that they cannot profitably achieve their original objective,[9] the partnership may be dissolved.

7. *Choshen Mishpat* 176:23. Partners are equals and neither is considered the other's servant. They do not qualify for the exemption of *Ki Li Bnei Yisrael Avadim* (*Sma* 176:58).

See *Nimukei Yosef, Bava Metzia* 105a and *Beis Yosef's* interpretation of *Rosh* and *Tosafos* in *Choshen Mishpat* 176 for a dissenting opinion.

See also *Machaneh Ephraim, Shutfim* 2 that maintains a partner has the right to quit his job, but may not withdraw his capital.

If there are two active partners and one silent partner, neither of the active partners may resign without the other's permission. However, if both active partners wish to resign, the silent partner can not stop them.

8. *Aruch HaShulchan* 176:43.

9. If they can make a profit, but one partner wants to withdraw his capital to take

If a partnership was created with the intention of continuing until a certain period of time, the partners have no withdrawal rights until then.[10] Even if the majority of partners wish to withdraw their funds and dissolve the partnership, they may not force the issue if any of the partners protest.[11]

If there was no preset timetable for the business venture, we must determine whether there is a particular season or time frame in which the merchandise that the partners own is typically sold. If there is, a partner may not force the liquidation of the business until that time.[12] For example, if partners buy seasonal merchandise, they may not force the dissolution of the partnership until the beginning of the selling season. Selling the merchandise earlier would cause the partners to lose out on the opportunity for which the business was created.

If there is no industry standard as to when the merchandise should be sold, any partner has the right to insist at any time that the assets be sold.[13]

How to Divide a Partnership

When the partners have the right to force the dissolution of a partnership, they must follow certain guidelines. There are numerous ways that a partnership can be dissolved, and there are many halachos governing the different methods.

The first option is to distribute the partnership's property equally among the partners. This option is practical only if the

advantage of a more lucrative opportunity, he may not do so (*Chazon Ish, Bava Basra* 9:4).

10. *Choshen Mishpat* 176:15. However, if it becomes clear that there will be no additional profit by prolonging the partnership, any partner may insist that the assets be sold and the partnership dissolved (*Chazon Ish, Bava Basra* 9:4; *Rif, Bava Metzia* 63a, *Dafei HaRif; Nesivos* 176:32; *Aruch HaShulchan* 176:40).

11. Unless there was either an operating agreement or a clear *minhag hamakom* that grants such a right.

12. *Choshen Mishpat* 176:17.

13. Ibid. 176:16. See *Aruch HaShulchan* 176:43 who writes that the minimum time frame for a store is one year.

partnership owns multiple items. If the items are all identical, the items are simply distributed among the partners. For example, if the partners own a number of similar vacant lots, they can simply distribute the lots to the partners.[14]

If the items are not identical or cannot be equally divided, the next option is to physically divide each property between the partners. Each property is divided into equal sections, and each partner receives a part of each property. This may only be done if the property can be divided without losing functionality[15] or value.[16]

For example, if a farm is being divided, each partner must receive enough land to be considered a farm. Each piece must be large enough to farm in a cost-effective manner.[17] Even the partner with the smallest share must receive this amount.[18]

If the property would lose value or function[19] if it were physically divided, the following options are available:

1. *Gud Agud* — One partner buys out the other partner. The party that initiates the *gud agud* sets a value for the partnership. The other partners are given a choice. They may either accept the buyout offer at the price that the first partner set, or they may buy the first partner's share of the business at the same price.[20]

The *gud agud* process has many conditions and limitations. For example, one can only initiate a *gud agud* if he can afford to buy

---

14. *Choshen Mishpat* 171:14. The items must both have the same functions. If one is more valuable than the other, see ibid. 171:13.

15. Ibid.171:5; *Rama*. Each partner must end up with all of the functionality that he enjoyed when they were partners.

16. *Rama* writes that the partners have the right to split the property as long as it will not cause a loss greater than ⅙ of its value.

Maharshach 3:122 writes that a property may be divided regardless of loss.

Chasam Sofer, Choshen Mishpat 12 agrees to *Maharshach* regarding a partnership created by an inheritance, but concurs with *Rama* regarding an ordinary partnership.

17. *Choshen Mishpat* 171:3.

18. Ibid.

19. *Rama*.

20. *Choshen Mishpat* 171:6.

out the other party.[21] A partner with limited financial means will be unable to force a *gud agud* since he cannot afford to buy the entire property.

Furthermore, the party who initiates the *gud agud* must have the cash on hand to immediately buy the entire property. If he does not have the cash available to buy the property, he may not initiate the *gud agud* process. However, when one party initiates a *gud agud*, the second party is given thirty days to raise the cash needed for the buyout.[22]

According to some opinions, a party may force a *gud agud* only if he intends to keep the entire property if he is successful in the *gud agud*. However, if his intention is to sell the property to an outsider, he may not force a *gud agud*.[23]

The price of a *gud agud* may not be below the true market value of the property.[24] It may, however, be priced above the property's true market value.[25]

2. *Sechirus*[26] — the property is rented out and the partners share the proceeds. If one partner wants to rent the entire property, he has the right to do so. If both partners want to rent the entire property, they can do a *gud agud* on the rental rights.

3. *Chalukas Hazman* — The partners alternate using the property.[27]

---

21. Ibid.

22. Ibid. 171; *Tur*, *Sma* 15(41)

23. Ibid. 171:6; *Rama*.

24. Ibid. Since any partner can initiate a *gud agud* and force the partner to buy or sell the property within thirty days, a person would be able to take advantage of a less affluent partner by setting a low price, knowing that his partner cannot raise cash and will be forced to sell at that price. By requiring that the *gud agud* price be at least market value, the partners are protected from a loss.

25. *Choshen Mishpat* 171:6.

26. Ibid. 171:8.

27. Ibid. Each party gets to use the entire property for a certain amount of time. The time period is determined by the typical use of the property. If a residential home is being divided, each partner lives in the house for the equivalent of a typical lease. A partner may not insist that they switch every month, since that is not a normal use of the property.

As the laws of dividing a partnership are quite complex, it is advisable to negotiate a mechanism for how the partnership will be dissolved before entering a partnership agreement. One should realize that virtually every partnership eventually sours and it is worthwhile to have an exit strategy in place from the beginning. The parties should consult with an experienced *dayan* or attorney to negotiate an agreement that will protect the two parties and allow for an orderly and mutually agreeable mechanism for dissolving the partnership.

Real Estate

12 Real Estate Brokers

Brokers

An agent's job is to facilitate a sale.[1] He is entitled to his commission even if he does not play an active roll in the negotiations.[2] Because an agent is not paid for his labor and may simply provide an idea or information, people sometimes have difficulty accepting the idea that the broker has earned his commission. They may try to avoid paying him by dealing directly with the principals. This is a violation of the prohibition of not paying a worker.[3]

1. An agent or *shadchan* that was hired by the principals is a *kablan* (*Igros Moshe* 49; *Mahari Ben Lev* 4:14). An agent who initiated a deal without being hired has the status of a *yored* (*Vilna Gaon* 185:13, 87:117).

2. *Shev Yaakov* 2:13; *Aruch HaShulchan* 185:12.

3. Neglecting to pay a worker is a violation of either four or five negative prohibitions and one positive mitzvah (*Choshen Mishpat* 339:2). These prohibitions all apply to an agent acting as a *kablan*. However, an agent acting as a *yored* (see footnotes 1 and 6) will not be subject to all of these prohibitions (*Pischei Teshuvah, Choshen Mishpat* 89:3).

Nonprofessional Agents

A person who facilitates a sale is entitled to a sales commission even if he is not a professional agent.[4] Even if the parties did not sign a listing agreement, and never discussed payment,[5] the "agent" is entitled to his fee.[6] However, depending on the *minhag*, a nonprofessional is not necessarily compensated the same amount as a professional agent.[7]

Unintended Deals

One is entitled to a commission only if at the time that he gave over the information, he did so with the intention of charging the recipient. If, a nonprofessional mentions a deal in passing without intending to charge a commission, he may not ask for reimbursement.[8]

An investor asks an associate for advice about a property on which he is doing due diligence. The associate thinks it is a good deal and recommends that he proceed with the transaction. The deal subsequently falls through. If the associate reopens negotiations and buys the property, he will have no liability to the investor. The investor did not intend to act as a broker, and is not entitled to a commission.

4. *Yaskil Avdi* 5; *Choshen Mishpat* 30.

5. *Choshen Mishpat* 264:7 regarding a *shadchan*.

6. A *yored* is entitled to compensation in spite of the fact that he was never formally hired by the owner. His services are typically the equivalent of a *sadeh ha'asuyah lita*, and the agent will be entitled to the customary commission.

Panim Me'iros 2:63 writes that by accepting the agent's actions/ advice, there is an implicit agreement to pay his fair wages.

7. *Mayim Rabbim, Choshen Mishpat* 27.

See, however, *Yaskil Avdi* 30:2 who entitles a nonprofessional to the full commission.

8. *Rama, Choshen Mishpat* 246:17 states that if a person provides a service without discussing payment, he may bill the recipient afterward. We do not assume that he intended to provide the service as a gift. If, however, the agent admits that he provided the lead without any intention of charging, he may not subsequently change his mind. See also *Rama* 363:10 and *Shach* (13).

Commissions on Future Deals

A broker is entitled to a commission solely on the property that he brought to the parties' attention. If the principals subsequently do other business together, the agent may not demand payment for these transactions.[9]

Agents and Brokerages

Real estate agents work under the supervision of a licensed broker. There is typically a commission split; a percentage of each commission goes to the broker, and the remainder goes to the agent who actually made the sale. An agent's employment contract typically states that any income generated from real estate related activity must be split with the broker. This would apply even to private deals that the agent arranges without using the broker's resources. An agent who makes a private sale without reporting it to his broker has violated his employment agreement and must share the profit with his employer.

Dividing a Commission

When more than one agent is involved in brokering a deal, the agents must split their portion of the commission between themselves. Typically, a listing agreement specifies how the commission will be split. What is the halachah in the absence of a listing agreement? If there are multiple agents involved in closing the deal, how is the commission divided?

These halachos are based on *minhag*, and are subject to change.[10] The parties are bound to follow the norms, unless a

9. Unless there is a clear *minhag* to the contrary.

10. *Aruch HaShulchan* 185:12.

specific agreement to do otherwise was made **before** the agent began the job.[11]

The current *minhag* is to divide the commission by giving the "starter" one-third and the "closer" two-thirds.[12]

The "starter" is the agent who introduced the parties to the deal. Even though the agent simply initiated the contact that leads to the sale and did not negotiate the details,[13] he is entitled to a third of the commission. The "closer," who negotiated and finalized the deal, is entitled to the remaining two-thirds of the commission.

To be entitled to part of the commission as a "starter," the agent must contribute to the ultimate sale. If the "starting" agent introduces the parties and the negotiations fail, and then at a later date, another agent successfully restarts the negotiations and closes the deal, we must examine whether the first agent contributed to the deal's ultimate success. For example, if the parties were more receptive to the offer because of the previous attempt, the original agent would be considered the starter.[14] If, however, the second agent had to redo the entire negotiations, and its ultimate success was not dependent in any way on the first agent's efforts, he would not have to share the commission.

There may be more than one agent doing each of these jobs. If there were two agents involved, one who persuaded the seller to proceed with the deal, while the other agent convinced the buyer, the two agents split the commission equally.[15]

---

11. See *Rama* 264:7 concerning an agent who was promised an unusually high commission.

12. *Dinei Mamanos* 3:8:2, *Pischei Choshen, Sechirus* 14:n10.

13. *Shev Yaakov* 2:13.

14. Ibid., *B'tzel HaChochmah* 3:10:1; *Igros Moshe, Choshen Mishpat* 1:49 writes that if the buyer responded to the advertisement because he had already looked at the property in the past, the original agent would be considered the starter.

15. *Shev Yaakov, Choshen Mishpat* 13.

Misrepresentation

Misrepresentation is prohibited even if there is no actual lie. If an agent makes a statement that is designed to give the client a false impression, it is *geneivas daas* even if the agent did not actually say anything false.[16] The prohibition applies to both Jews and non-Jews.[17]

"Puffing," exaggerating a claim, is also *geneivas daas*. Claiming that a neighborhood is the hottest area in town is permitted only if it is true.

Geneivas daas applies even if the client is getting his money's worth. Hiding a defect or misrepresenting the potential of an investment is wrong even if the property is fairly priced. See Section Two for more about the obligation to disclose defects. If the property is worth less because of the defect, the misrepresentation will fall under the category of *ona'ah* as well (see next paragraph).

Ona'ah

Anyone who assists a seller in overcharging a customer, or helps a buyer underpay the seller, is violating the laws of *ona'ah*. Although the agent is not a principal in the transaction, and the bulk of the profits of the *ona'ah* will go to the seller, the agent has violated a Biblical prohibition.[18] In addition, the broker will violate the prohibition of *lifnei eveir lo sitein michshol*, because he causes the seller to overcharge the buyer.[19] See Chapter One for a discussion of the laws of *ona'ah* and their application to real estate.[20]

16. *Choshen Mishpat* 228:6.

17. Ibid.; *Shulchan Aruch HaRav, Ona'ah* 12.

18. *Mishkanos Yaakov, Choshen Mishpat* 59 quoting *Ibn Ezra, Vayikra* 25:14.

19. *Vayikra* 19:14.

20. See Ch. 1 footnote 48 for a list of commentators who apply the prohibition of *ona'ah* to real estate.

Claiming There Are Higher Offers on a Property

A broker may not falsely claim that there are higher offers on a property in order to pressure a prospective buyer to raise his offer.[21] If it is clear that a buyer's higher offer was predicated on a fraudulent claim, the buyer will have the right to renege on the agreement.[22] In the absence of such proof, once the buyer closes on the property he may not void the sale because of the misrepresentation.[23]

Ribbis

One may not broker a deal that will call for *ribbis* payments. Doing so may be a violation of *lifnei eveir,* subject to the parameters discussed in Chapter Six footnote 6.[24]

If a buyer tells the broker that he needs the seller to provide a mortgage, the broker may not negotiate the loan if it will be done without a proper *heter iska.*

Ani Ha'mehapech

A broker encounters issues of *ani ha'mehapech* on a regular basis. It is important to realize that helping and encouraging a client to pursue a property on which another Jew has

---

21. *Sefer Chassidim* 388, 311 writes that this is a violation of *she'eiris Yisrael lo yedabru chazav.*

22. *Taz* 332:4; *Chavos Yair* 69; *Pischei Teshuvah* 207:9. The buyer must establish that the offer was in fact predicated on the false claim. *Taz* and *Chavos Yair* both concur that the burden of proof is on the buyer.

23. *Taz* 332:4; *Meiri, Bava Metzia* 76a. See also *Mishpat Shalom* 227:3.

If the buyer did not yet close on the property, but there is no clear evidence whether his offer was predicated on the broker's claim, *Chavos Yair* rules the buyer may back out of the deal. *Pischei Teshuvah* does not render a definitive *psak. Taz* and *Meiri* imply that the buyer must proceed with the deal.

24. *Rambam, Malveh V'Loveh* 4:2.

already finalized[25] a deal is a violation of *ani ha'mehapech.* Although the agent does not intend to purchase the property for himself, interfering with another's deal is a violation of *ani ha'mehapech.*[26]

Ani ha'mehapech is also germane when an agent is competing for a listing. If the seller has already decided to use a certain agent, one may not try to break the deal.[27] It is certainly forbidden to try to get a listing if the seller previously agreed to sell the property to someone else.

See Chapter Three for a discussion of *ani ha'mehapech.*

Mechusar Amana

One who reneges on a commitment to buy or sell a property is called *mechusar amana.*[28] This applies regardless of whether there was a legally binding contract. A broker may not facilitate or encourage such behavior. This topic is discussed in Chapter Four.[29]

Conflict of Interest

If a person sends an agent to buy a property, the agent may not buy the property for himself. If he does, he is considered a *ramai,* a dishonest person.[30]

---

25. See Ch. 3 footnote 2.

26. See Ch. 3 footnote 14.

27. *Aruch HaShulchan, Even HaEzer* 50:42.

28. *Choshen Mishpat* 204.

29. See also "Change in Price."

30. *Choshen Mishpat* 183:2.

Nesivos 183 interprets the restrictions on agents as an application of *ani ha'mehapech.* Accordingly, there would be an exception if the property represents a unique deal. (See also *Rambam, Ishus* 9:17 and *Chemdas Shlomo* 5:6,7.)

Yam Shel Shlomo, Kiddushin 3:1, *Imrei Yosher* 1:68 disagree and maintain that even in situations where the laws of *ani ha'mehapech* do not apply, an agent may not preempt the deal for himself.

If the owner refuses to sell the property to the principal, the agent may buy the property for himself.[31] However, he must first notify the principal that he is unable to purchase the property on his behalf.[32] If the agent is afraid that he will lose the deal if he waits to notify the principal, he may buy it for himself and notify the principal afterwards.[33]

Inappropriate Advice

Making an inappropriate recommendation[34] is a violation of *lifnei eveir lo sitein michshol*[35] and *arrur mashgeh eveir badarech.*[36] This halachah is very relevant to agents.[37] Because they are only paid when they successfully close a deal, they have a strong incentive to push a deal through, regardless of whether it is in their clients' best interest. An agent may be tempted to convince a client to buy or sell a property even though the agent recognizes that it is not the client's best option. Doing so would be a violation of *lifnei eveir.*

Lifnei eveir is different than *geneivas daas. Geneivas daas* is misleading a client. Misrepresenting a particular neighborhood

31. *Choshen Mishpat* 183: 2.

32. Ibid. 183:2. *Rashi, Kiddushin* 59a explains that the purpose of notifying the principal is so that he should understand that the agent acted appropriately.

33. *Choshen Mishpat* 183: 2.

34. The *Acharonim* debate whether one violates *lifnei eveir* immediately upon placing the stumbling block in front of the blind person, or only when the person actually stumbles. (See *Sdei Chemed*, Volume 2, *Maareches vuv Siman* 26 1:18; *R' Yeruchem Perlow* on *Sefer HaMitzvos L'Rav Saadiah Gaon, Lo Saaseh* 55.) According to the first interpretation, one may violate *lifnei eveir* by giving bad advice even if the person ignores that advice.

35. *Vayikra* 19:14; *Chinuch* 232; *Rambam, Mitzvah* 299, *Rotze'ach* 12:12-14; *S'mag* 168.

Rashi (*Vayikra* 25:17) based on *Sifra* (*Behar* 4), *Sforno*, write that giving inappropriate advice is a violation of *ona'as devarim* (although see *Be'er BaSadeh* and *Maskil L'Dovid*).

36. *Devarim* 27:18; *Chofetz Chaim, Be'er Mayim Chaim, Arurin* 2.

37. *Be'er Mayim Chaim, Arurin* 2.

as exclusive and "up and coming" would be a violation of *geneivas daas*. *Lifnei eveir* applies even when there are no factual misrepresentations. Urging a client to purchase a property in a truly exclusive neighborhood is a violation of *lifnei eveir* if the agent knows that the buyer will not be able to afford the high mortgage payments. Although the agent made no factual misrepresentations, he is guilty of giving bad advice and has violated *lifnei eveir*.

The literal meaning of *lifnei eveir lo sitein michshol* is that you shall not place a stumbling block in front of a blind person. The *Sifra* interprets this to mean giving bad advice to a person who is "blind in the matter." This applies any time a person asks for advice in an area with which he is unfamiliar. Some commentators apply this prohibition to an *akum* as well.[38]

This prohibition applies whether or not the advice-giver stands to benefit from his ill-intentioned advice.[39]

Subjective Issues

Lifnei eveir applies to subjective issues as well. Although there may be no clear right or wrong answer, one is obligated to give the advice that he believes is truly best for the person seeking his counsel.

Clients may ask an agent for his advice or opinion about a deal. Although the client understands that the agent will be biased, the agent must try to give an honest opinion to the client. If the agent feels that he is unable to be completely honest, he should not

38. *Minchas Chinuch* 232.

Although see *Chinuch* 232; *Shaarei Teshuvah, Shaar* 3:53; and *Kovetz Shiurim, Pesachim* 95.

39. *Mesillas Yesharim*, Chapter 11. The examples mentioned in *Toras Kohanim* include encouraging a person to sell an item, with the intention of buying it (the advice-giver has ulterior motives), or giving advice about a *shidduch* (the advice-giver has no personal benefit).

offer his opinion. A disclaimer that one is biased does not give the agent a license to willfully give bad advice.

Gray Areas

Often, it is difficult to discern whether advice was given sincerely or not. There are many gray areas in which one could justify giving certain advice although it may be inappropriate. For these situations, the Torah writes (*Vayikra* 19:14), *V'yareisa me'Elokecha,* "And you should fear Hashem." Rashi explains that the prohibition depends on the person's true intentions. Although we are unable to determine whether the advice-giver was sincere, Hashem, who is privy to all of our thoughts, will determine the real motivation for the advice and judge the adviser. When one gives advice, he must give the advice that he would want if he were in the other person's shoes.[40]

Appropriate Advice

Aside from the prohibition against giving inappropriate advice, there is a positive obligation to offer beneficial advice.[41] Giving appropriate advice is one of the highest forms of *chesed.*[42] It costs nothing, but can be of tremendous value to the recipient.

A homeowner is looking for a larger house. He contacts a broker

40. *Mesillas Yesharim*, Chapter 11.

41. *Choshen Mishpat* 97:1, *Shaarei Teshuvah* 3:54. See *Beur HaGra* (4) , *Taz* and *Shaarei Teshuvah* for the source of this obligation.

42. *Shaarei Teshuvah* 3:54.

who shows him a very appropriate and reasonably priced home. The broker (who is also the listing agent) informs the buyer that there are four other people interested in the home, and that a bidding war is about to begin. The broker makes the following proposal: "If you give me the listing to sell the house that you own, I'll push your bid through." The buyer, who has already offered the listing of his home to another agent, has no choice but to accept. The agent then goes ahead and convinces the seller to sign the contract.

There are a number of problems with this behavior. First, one may not give someone bad advice. The agent knows that the seller could get a higher price for the house if he waits for the other potential buyers to submit their offers; the agent convinced the seller to sign the contract with this particular buyer simply because he wants to get the buyer's listing.

Second, this may be a case of ani ha'mehapech. The buyer has already made a final decision to use the services of another broker to list his home. The second broker interferes with that deal by linking the purchase to the listing.

Another issue is the fact that the agent is a "selling agent." The agent is paid by the seller and has a responsibility to protect his interests. Demanding payment from the buyer to work against the seller's interests is clearly a violation of this agreement.[43] *Depending*

43. This issue applies whenever kickbacks or gifts are given to a manager or purchasing agent to induce him to steer business toward a particular company. The manager is paid by his employer to try to get the best deal for the company. If the employer knew that his manager was compromised and had a different agenda, he perhaps would not agree to pay him his salary.

In practice, employers are aware that suppliers typically give gifts before holidays and offer promotions to purchasing managers. One may accept gifts that conform with the norm, and that his employer is aware of. However, if there is a direct kickback, or if an unusually excessive gift is given, it would be problematic.

As a general rule, if one is reluctant to tell his boss about a particular gift, it is probably inappropriate.

on the exact circumstances, there are a number of monetary claims that the seller may have against the agent.[44]

44. 1) A refund on the commission. The seller agreed to pay the agent a commission to represent him. Presumably, the market value for an agent who has a conflict of interest would be lower than the commission the seller had agreed to pay.

2) Damages. If the seller relied exclusively on the agent's advice, and the agent caused him to sell the property at below-market value, he may be liable for the monetary loss that he caused. The specific parameters of this concept are beyond the scope of this work.

3) A share in the value of the listing. The seller may be entitled to a portion of the value of the listing that the agent received from the buyer, based on the following argument.

Shulchan Aruch, Choshen Mishpat 183:6 states that if an agent buys an item on behalf of another party, and receives a present from the seller, he may not keep it for himself. The agent is obligated to share the present with the buyer.

There are two interpretations of this halachah.

According to *Rashi* (*Kesubos* 98b), the agent shares the gift with the buyer because it is unclear for whom the gift was intended. Was it intended for the principal of the deal or for the agent? Because it is unclear, the parties split the gift between them (*Rama* accepts this reasoning).

Rif (*Kesubos* 57b, *Dafei HaRif*) offers another explanation. The gift is shared because it was engendered by both parties. The agent would not have received the gift had the buyer not been willing to purchase the item, and the buyer would not have received the gift if not for the agent's contact with the seller. Accordingly, the parties split the gift (*Taz, Nesivos Chiddushim* accept this ruling).

In our scenario, the buyer did not just pay a cash price for the house. He also "paid" by providing a listing agreement on his house. Such a listing has value. As such, the seller may be entitled to a share in the value of the listing. This will depend on which interpretation of this halachah we follow.

If we follow the first explanation, the agent would not be required to share the value of the listing. It is clear that the buyer intended to give the listing to the agent, and not to the seller.

If, however, we follow the explanation of the *Rif*, as long as the gift was generated from the principal's money/assets, the agent would be obligated to share the gift with the principal. In our scenario, the seller's house was used to extort the listing, and the seller would be entitled to a share of the value.

13 Real Estate Management

Landlord –Tenant Disputes

Landlords and tenants often have disagreements over the responsibility to maintain and repair a rental unit. Tenants often assume that the landlord is responsible for all repairs, while landlords may feel that they are not responsible for minor repairs. As a rule, in these matters we follow the *minhag hamakom*,[1] the accepted norm. Anyone signing a lease is assumed to be agreeing to the accepted norm, unless the parties stipulate otherwise in the contract.

1. *Choshen Mishpat* 314:2; *Rama*.

Mishnah, *Bava Metzia* 116b states that the landlord is responsible for repairs that require a professional. The tenant is responsible for repairs that do not require a professional. However, *Rama* 314:1 makes it clear that these guidelines apply only if the unit needed repairs at the time of the lease (or if the lease is not on a specific unit. This scenario is virtually unheard of today). However, if at the time of the lease, the unit was in good condition, and the repair became necessary later, it would be the tenant's responsibility regardless of whether it required a professional (although see *Shulchan Aruch* 312:17, *Ketzos* 314:1, *Minchas Pitim* 314).

The examples discussed are repairs that are necessary. Cosmetic improvements would not be covered.

As a matter of halachah, we follow the *minhag hamakom* as per the *psak* of *Rambam* and *Rama*.

If the tenant lays out money for a repair that is the landlord's responsibility, he may deduct it from his rent.[2] However, he should get approval from the landlord before he makes the repair.[3]

To avoid misunderstandings, it is important to write a lease that clearly stipulates the obligations of each party. The more detailed the lease agreement is, the less likely it is for there to be disagreements later.

Subletting

In the absence of any *minhag* to the contrary, halachah typically allows a tenant to sublet his unit to a third party.[4] However, this right is limited. The tenant may not sublet the unit to a larger family[5] or to someone who may do damage to the unit.[6]

If there is a clear practice or *minhag hamakom* regarding subletting, it must be followed. However, for a *minhag* to be meaningful, it must be common and widespread.[7] It can only override halachah when it becomes the accepted norm that both parties implicitly agree to when they sign an agreement.

If the lease agreement specifies whether or under what conditions the tenant may sublet the unit, the contract must be followed. An agreement between the parties will override both halachah and *minhag*.

---

2. The tenant has the status of a *yored b'reshus*.

3. See *Kesef HaKadoshim* 314:1.

4. *Choshen Mishpat* 316:1.

This applies only to real estate that cannot be stolen or removed. In contrast, one who rents a movable object may not sublet it to another party unless the owner gives specific permission (*Rambam, Sechirus* 5:5).

5. *Choshen Mishpat* 316. A larger family is more likely to damage the unit. See also *Aruch HaShulchan* 316:2.

6. *Choshen Mishpat* 312:7; *Rama; Aruch HaShulchan* 316:2. This applies only to someone known to be problematic. The landlord may not unilaterally decide he does not like or trust someone.

7. *Choshen Mishpat* 331:1.

Breaking a Lease

A tenant or landlord is not allowed to leave/evict during the term of the lease. If a tenant leaves during the lease period, he will be responsible to pay rent until the end of the term.[8] However, if the landlord[9] finds a replacement for the tenant, he may not charge rent to both the tenant and the replacement.[10]

Eviction Notice

If a lease contract has an ending date, the parties are not required by halachah to give any prior notice that they do not intend to renew the lease. It should be clear to the parties that their obligations to each other end on the date specified in the lease[11]. If, however, there is a *minhag* to give notice in advance, or if the contract stipulates that the parties must give notice, the parties will be bound by such terms.

If the lease does not have a specific ending date, halachah requires a landlord and tenant to give each other enough notice before evicting/leaving so that the other party is able to find another rental/tenant unit. If there is no clear *minhag*, we follow

---

8. Ibid. 311:6; *Mordechei, Bava Basra* 529. See Ch. 9 footnote 11.

9. *Nesivos* 316:2 writes that if suitable tenants are available, the tenant is not responsible to pay the rent, even if the landlord neglects to find a replacement tenant.

Chazon Ish, Bava Kamma 23:7, based on *Rama* 312:7 writes that it is the tenant's responsibility to actually find a replacement.

10. *Sma* 316:2 (3), *Ketzos* 316(2); *Nesivos* 316(2); *Pischei Teshuvah* 316(2); *Aruch HaShulchan* 316:5.

Nesivos limits this halachah to instances in which the tenant has the right to sublet. Because he can sublet the unit, he is entitled to its rental income. Thus, the rental income that the replacement tenant pays relieves the original tenant of his obligations to the landlord. However, if the lease contract or accepted *minhag* preclude the tenant from subletting the unit, the landlord may keep any rental income he receives from a replacement tenant, in addition to the rent he receives from the original tenant (although *Ketzos* disagrees).

See also *Pischei Teshuvah* (2).

11. *Choshen Mishpat* 312:8.

the guidelines given in *Shulchan Aruch.*[12] *Shulchan Aruch* differentiates between the type of property, and where it is located.

A resident of a small city requires thirty days to find a replacement unit/tenant. However, the thirty days must be completed before the beginning of the winter.[13] During winter it was unusual for people to move and therefore difficult to find a vacancy.

A resident of a larger city requires twelve months' notice in order to find a suitable replacement.[14]

A store requires twelve months regardless of the size of the city.[15] Shopkeepers often extend credit, and they need time to collect their debts.

These distinctions are clearly subject to change based on the local market conditions, and a *beis din* will have to decide how to apply these halachos.

If the tenant moves out without giving proper notice, he is responsible to pay rent for the duration of the notice period.[16]

Extending a Lease

If a tenant remains in the property after the end of the lease without discussing or renegotiating the terms of the lease, the original agreement remains in force.[17]

12. Ibid. 312:5.

13. The thirty days' notice must end before Succos.

14. *Sma* (9) explains that larger cities are more crowded and it is harder to find appropriate housing.

15. *Choshen Mishpat* 312:6.
Bakeries require three years' notice.

16. Ibid. 312:7. *Shaar Mishpat* 2 explains that this obligation is not actionable in *beis din*. It is *latzeis yedei Shamayim – to discharge his obligation to heaven.*
Nachalas Tzvi argues that the tenant has a monetary obligation to pay rent until the notice period ends. This applies only if the landlord is unable to find a suitable replacement tenant.

17. *Rivash* 475; *Shach* 312 (10), 333(44).

Landlord–Tenant Court

When a dispute arises between a landlord and a tenant, they must resolve the dispute in a *beis din*. Neither party has the right to initiate legal action in any form of secular court. Even if the lease sanctions certain legal action, the parties are obligated to submit all disputes to *beis din*. See Chapter Fifteen for a description of the *beis din* process.

Tenants have special protections under law. There are various rent-control laws and limits on a landlord's ability to evict a tenant. A *beis din* will take these laws into account when adjudicating a landlord–tenant dispute, and make a determination if and how to apply the various governing laws.[18] Even when the dispute hinges upon the interpretation of a secular law, one is obligated to submit the dispute to a *beis din*.

Ribbis

There are numeous important ribbis-related concerns that commonly arise when managing real estate. These issues are discussed in Chapter Eight, in the section "Real Estate-Related Issues"

18. *Dina d'malchusa dina* is a complex topic that is beyond the scope of this work. It should be noted that the concept has significant limitations and a *beis din* must decide if and how to apply secular law.

14 Neighbors' Rights / Bar Metzra

Introduction

The pasuk tells us, "V'asisa hayashar v'hatov,"[1] "And you shall do that which is right and good." The Ramban explains that it would be impossible for the Torah to specify how to deal with a fellow neighbor or friend in each situation that may arise. Rather, the Torah prohibits a few specific behaviors such as gossip and revenge, and then states a general rule of v'asisa hayashar v'hatov, you shall do that which is right and good.

Our mission is not simply to comply with the rules of the Torah. We are expected to internalize the values reflected by mitzvos bein adam l'chaveiro, and extend them to our everyday lives. It is not enough to ensure that we do not openly violate the mitzvos; we must ensure that every action that we take measures up to the ideals of yashar v'tov.

Yashar v'tov is generally not actionable in beis din. Beis din does not judge every action a person takes

1. *Devarim* 6:18.

to decide whether it measures up to these standards. However, there is one instance where Chazal felt that the imperative of yashar v'tov is so strong that they enacted guidelines whereby beis din may actually step in and force the parties to act in the appropriate manner.[2] *These are the laws of bar metzra.*

The Concept

The laws of *bar metzra* give a neighbor priority to purchase an adjacent property when it is offered for sale. If an outside buyer purchases the property without following the appropriate procedure, the neighbor may claim *bar metzra* and force the buyer to resell the property to him.

Rashi[3] explains that there is an advantage in owning adjacent properties. In the case of a farm, being able to combine two fields together makes it easier to plant and plow the fields. Similarly, owning two neighboring lots enables one to combine them and build a larger house. For the neighbor, this particular property offers a tremendous benefit. For an outside buyer, there is nothing special about this particular property. He can just as well purchase an equivalent property elsewhere. Therefore *v'asisa hayashar v'hatov* instructs the outsider to allow the neighbor to purchase the adjacent property.

A Bar Metzra's Rights

When a property is offered for sale, the *bar metzra* should be given the first opportunity to purchase it.[4] If an outside buy-

2. *Maggid Mishneh, Shecheinim* 14:5.

3. *Bava Metzia* 108a.

4. *Aruch HaShulchan* 175: 7 implies that the seller has an obligation of *yashar v'tov* to offer it to the *bar metzra*.

Sma 175 :36 (63) writes that although the seller has no obligation to offer it to the

er purchases the property, a *bar metzra* has the right to force the buyer to resell the property to him at the exact price the buyer paid. The buyer is viewed as an agent for the neighbor.[5] Even if the buyer was unaware that the neighbor was interested in the property, he is obligated to transfer the land to the *bar metzra*.[6]

Occasionally, a neighbor will use the laws of *bar metzra* to discourage other parties from bidding on a property. His intention is to drive away potential bidders and to force the seller to accept a below-market price. This is completely inappropriate.[7] These halachos are based on *yashar v'tov*. Taking advantage of the seller under the pretext of *yashar v'tov* is an affront to the very ideals on which this halachah is based.

It should be noted that the laws of *bar metzra* are fairly complex. It is uncommon for a neighbor to actually meet all of the necessary criteria to qualify for the rights of a *bar metzra*. As such, it is especially inappropriate for a neighbor to harrass a potential buyer and to pressure him not to pursue a property before verifying that he actually qualifies as a *bar metzra*.

Parameters

For *bar metzra* to apply, the properties must be contiguous and the neighbor must be able to combine the two properties and use them together.[8] If the two properties cannot be used together,

neighbor, it is advisable for him to do so. Otherwise, outside buyers may be reluctant to become involved in a property that the *bar metzra* may ultimately claim.

5. *Choshen Mishpat* 175:6.

6. This can be inferred from *Bava Metzia* 108a. Even if the neighbor tells the buyer that he is not interested in the property, he may later claim b*ar metzra* (provided he never made a *kinyan*). Although the buyer thought that the neighbor was not interested, the laws of *bar metzra* still apply. See also *She'aris Yosef* 17.

7. See *Kesef HaKadoshim* 17:9 that if a *bar metzra* is harassing potential buyers and making it difficult for the owner to sell his property, one may advise the owner how to circumvent the laws of *bar metzra*.

8. *Sh"ut HaMeyuchas L'Ramban* 26, *Rivash* 397 (quoted by *Hagahos HaSma* 175 [99]); *Taz* (53); *Aruch HaShulchan* 175:56.

The classic example is two fields that can be plowed together. If a barrier separates the two fields, as long as there is an opening large enough for a plow to fit through, *bar metzra* will not apply. For example, if a stream separates two farms, they cannot be plowed together and *yashar v'tov* will not apply.[9]

Often, the neighbor wants the property as an investment. His intention is to buy the property, develop it, and then sell it. He will not use the properties together, and does not intend to combine the two lots in any way. In such cases, there is no real advantage in their being adjacent and the neighbor does not have priority in halachah.[10]

A Bar Metzra's Obligations

A *bar metzra* must act immediately to preserve his rights. He must bring the necessary funds to purchase the property as soon as he hears that the property was sold.[11] If he does not have the funds available,[12] or if he delays before bringing his claim, he loses his rights.[13]

---

the neighbor may claim *bar metzra* since he would be able to plow at least part of the fields together. *Rishonim* extend this concept to adjacent houses that can be encircled by a fence and used together.

In all of these instances, the advantage comes from being immediately adjacent, and being able to use the two properties **together.** If they cannot be combined and used together, there is no claim of *bar metzra*. Being near the other property is not enough to create a *bar metzra*.

If a neighbor wants an adjacent property for his children, he may claim *bar metzra* (*Igros Moshe, Choshen Mishpat* 1:44. See also *Aruch HaShulchan* 175:60).

9. *Choshen Mishpat* 175:27. This limitation applies only if the barrier is significant and typically is not removed. A shallow gully between two properties that can easily be filled will not disallow a *bar metzra* (*Sma* [45]).

10. *Maharik* 132; *Shoel U'Meishiv Mahadura* 2 *Chelek* 1:83.

See, however, *Aruch HaShulchan* 175:60 who implies that if the properties could be used together, the neighbor has priority even though he does not intend any actual joint use וצ"ע.

11. *Choshen Mishpat* 175:32. Any delay will be interpreted as an indication that the *bar metzra* is waiving his rights (*Sma* [57]).

12. *Choshen Mishpat* 175:25.

13. The *bar metzra* must exercise his rights immediately *after* the sale. However, he may wait until the property is actually sold. He has no obligation to approach the seller, even if he was aware of the pending sale. See also "Loss to Seller" and "How to Deal With a *Bar Metzra.*"

If the *bar metzra* is away or sick at the time of the sale, and was unable to claim the property, he will not be able to claim *bar metzra* when he returns or recovers.[14] However, the seller should inform *beis din* of the pending sale to enable a relative of the *bar metzra* to purchase the property on his behalf.[15]

Contracts

To claim *bar metzra*, the neighbor must actually own the property. An investor who has a contract on a property cannot claim *bar metzra* on an adjacent property until he actually closes.[16]

Land Use

Beis din will consider what the parties intend to do with the property in determining whether *bar metzra* applies.[17] If the outside bidder intends to use the land in a manner that halachah considers more beneficial than the neighbor's intended use, *bar metzra* will not apply.[18] For example, if the neighbor wants to leave the land vacant, and the outside bidder wants to build houses on

---

See also *Divrei Geonim* 60:34, *Minchas Pitim* 175:32, and *Teshuvos She'eilas Shalom* 36 that even if the buyer gave a deposit to the seller, the *bar metzra* has no obligation to protest until the sale is actually consummated. See also *Yarkesei HaEphod* who disagrees.

14. *Choshen Mishpat* 175:34; *Meiri, Bava Metzia* 108. Allowing such claims would complicate all sales since every buyer would be concerned that a neighbor may surface months later and demand the property.

See 175:32 and *Nesivos* 29 who limit this halachah.

15. *Rama* 175:34.

16. *Sh"ut Moznei Tzedek* 2: *Choshen Mishpat* 7.

17. *Choshen Mishpat* 175:26.

18. *Aruch HaShulchan* 175:55 explains that building houses or planting fruit trees is *yishuv haaretz* and benefits the public. *Yasher v'tov* may not be applied to the detriment of others.

Beis Yosef writes that this concept is not limited to Eretz Yisrael.

the property, the neighbor will not have priority. Building houses is considered a better use of the land.[19]

Gifts

The laws of *bar metzra* are limited to sales. If the property was given away as a present, the neighbor has no claim on it.[20]

Reimbursing the Buyer

Bargain

The *bar metzra* has the right to repurchase the property at the exact price that the outside buyer paid. Even if the property was sold for less than its true value, the *bar metzra* pays only the purchase price.[21]

Overpaid

When the *bar metzra* forces the buyer to resell the property, he must pay the full purchase price. If the buyer overpaid for the property, the *bar metzra* must either reimburse him completely or forfeit his rights to the property.[22]

19. See *Perach Mateh Aharon* 53 that an outside buyer intending to build a house on a property has precedence over a neighbor using it as a courtyard.

20. *Choshen Mishpat* 175:54.

21. Ibid. 175:7. This applies when the property was offered to the general public at the discounted price. However, if the seller gave a discount specifically for the buyer, the *bar metzra* must pay the full value of the property.

22. Ibid. 175:9.

Change in Value

If the property appreciates in value after the sale and becomes worth more than what the buyer actually paid for it, the *bar metzra* is not required to pay the current value of the property. The *bar metzra* must reimburse the buyer only for the amount that he actually spent.[23]

If the property decreases in value, the *bar metzra* must either pay the buyer the full purchase price or forfeit his rights to the property.[24]

Improvements to the Property

If the buyer improved the property before the *bar metzra* made his claim, he is entitled to reimbursement.[25] He has the status of a *yored bershus*, and the *bar metzra* must pay the full price for the work.

However, if the buyer continued making improvements after the *bar metzra* claims the property, he has the status of a *yored shelo bershus*[26] and will not necessarily be completely reimbursed. The parameters of *yored* are discussed in Chapter Nine.

Expenses

When a *bar metzra* claims a property, he must reimburse the buyer for his expenses.[27] It should be noted that if the buyer

23. Ibid. 175:6. This is uncommon because of the limited time frame in which the neighbor has the right to claim *bar metzra*.

24. Ibid.

25. Ibid.

26. Ibid.

27. *Chemdas Shlomo, Choshen Mishpat* 8. *Yasher v'tov* requires that the buyer be reimbursed for his expenses and not suffer a loss.

It should be noted that *Chemdas Shlomo* refers to a case where the outside buyer was unaware that a *bar metzra* was interested in the property. Perhaps the concept of *yashar v'tov* would not apply if the buyer was making a conscious attempt to

incurs unusual or indirect costs, he might not be able to pass them along to the *bar metzra.*[28] It is therefore advisable to determine if there is a *bar metzra* who is interested in the property before incurring any expenses.

Damage

The buyer is responsible for any damage that he causes to the property. The *bar metzra* may deduct the cost of damage from the sale price.[29]

If the buyer collected rent before the *bar metzra* made his claim, he does not have to return the rent to the *bar metzra.*[30]

Fraudulent Bar Metzra

If a *bar metzra* forces the buyer to resell a property, and then it is discovered that the *bar metzra* was not entitled to these rights,

undermine the rights of the neighbor ונ"ע. See following note.

28. *Pischei Teshuvah* 175:31 (11) questions why the *Chemdas Shlomo* needs to invoke the concept of *yashar v'tov* to justify reimbursing the buyer. If the buyer is considered an agent of the *bar metzra*, he should be entitled to be reimbursed for expenses incurred while acting on behalf of the *bar metzra*, even without the concept of *yashar v'tov.*

Pischei Teshuvah explains that an agent is normally entitled to reimbursement only for usual and customary expenses. If an agent incurs additional expenses that he was not authorized to make, he will not be reimbursed. *Pischei Teshuvah* suggests perhaps *bar metzra* is different. Even if the outside buyer incurred unusual expenses while purchasing the property, *yasher v'tov* requires the *bar metzra* to reimburse him.

The *Pischei Teshuvah* does not make a definitive ruling.

29. *Choshen Mishpat* 175:6.

30. *Choshen Mishpat* 175:6 rules that if the buyer harvests and eats produce of a field before the *bar metzra* makes his claim, he need not reimburse the *bar metzra*. *Sma* (11) explains that harvesting a field is a normal use, and the buyer need not reimburse the *bar metzra*. Collecting rent is similar to harvesting fruits.

Divrei Geonim 60:33 writes that the *bar metzra* is entitled to charge the buyer rent for occupying the premises. *Yarkesei HaEphod* 14 explains that this applies only if the *bar metzra* attempted to claim the property, and the buyer refused to submit to *beis din*. However, if the buyer complies with *beis din*'s rulings, he is not liable for any rent that accrued before the *bar metzra* made his claim.

See also *Teshuvas HaRi Migash* quoted by *Shitah Mekubetzes, Bava Metzia* 108b and *Mishpat Shalom* 175:6.

the original buyer has two options.[31] He may take the property back and refund the fraudulent *bar metzra*'s purchase price, or he may allow the sale to remain in effect. If the value of the property went down, he will likely choose to allow the fraudulent *bar metzra* to keep the field. If the property value increased, he may take the property back and refund the "*bar metzra's*" money.

Multiple Bar Metzra

If more than one neighbor claims their rights of *bar metzra*, they must divide the property equally.[32] Each *bar metzra* is entitled to receive a piece of the property that borders on his field.[33] However, if one neighbor preempts the others and buys the entire property, the other neighbors cannot force him to share it with them.[34]

31. *Choshen Mishpat* 175:46.

32. Ibid. 175:11. This refers to instances where the neighbors claim *bar metzra* after the sale, and are forcing the outside buyer to resell the property to them.

If, however, the neighbors approach the owner of the property before the sale, the *poskim* disagree whether the seller may choose to sell the entire property to one neighbor, or if they must divide the property among themselves (*Rama*).

33. If there are four *bar metzras* who claim the property, each *bar metzra* receives a triangular-shaped field, as in the diagram.

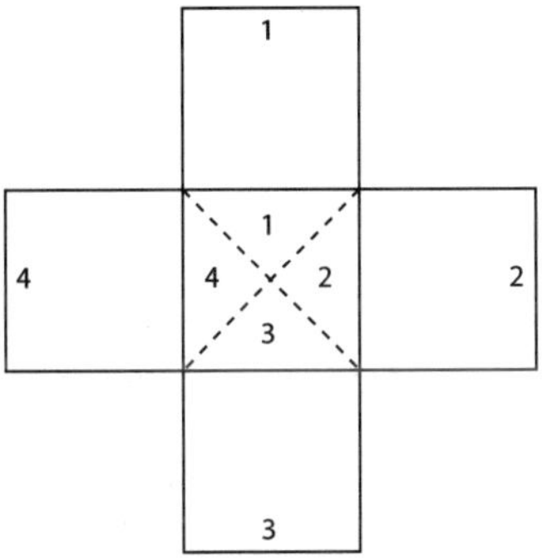

The center box represents the field that is being sold. The surrounding boxes #1-4 represent four *bar metzras* that claim the field.

34. *Choshen Mishpat* 175:11. See also *Nesivos* (2).

Auctions

The rights of a *bar metzra* will apply to property sold at a public auction. A neighbor may force the winning bidder to sell him the property.[35]

Loss to Seller

Because the concept of *bar metzra* is predicated on *yashar v'tov, Chazal* did not institute these laws if they would cause a loss to the seller.[36] Therefore, the *bar metzra* must match the buyer's offer completely. If he is not willing to meet the price or any other terms of the deal, he cannot force the seller to accept his offer.[37] For example, if the *bar metzra* insists on a mortgage contingency, and the original buyer was willing to accept the contract without any condition, the laws of *bar metzra* will not apply.

If the *bar metzra* is not ready to close on the property by the date that the other buyer is able to, the seller is not obligated to hold it for him.[38]

35. *Teshuras Shai* 2:120.

Although the *bar metzra* had the opportunity to purchase the property at the auction, he may nevertheless claim the property afterward. A similar case can be found in *Tosafos, Bava Metzia* 108a.

See, however, *Chiddushim U'Veurim, Bava Metzia* 108; *Chaim Shel Shalom* 2:99.

36. *Rama* 23.

37. *Choshen Mishpat* 175:23.

38. Ibid. 175:23,25.

When the Seller Is Under Pressure

If the seller is under pressure to sell his assets quickly[39] in order to pay taxes,[40] avoid foreclosure, or to feed his family,[41] anyone is allowed to buy the property. Giving the *bar metzra* rights would slow down the process at the seller's expense, so *yashar v'tov* will not apply. Still, if the *bar metzra* approaches the seller before the sale takes place and offers to purchase the property, there are *poskim* who argue that he should be given preference.[42]

Multiple Properties

If the seller is trying to sell multiple properties in one package deal, the laws of *bar metzra* do not apply.[43] Finding a buyer for a large package is difficult, and *Chazal* did not want to complicate the process and put the seller at risk of losing the opportunity.

If the Seller Prefers an Outside Buyer

The rights of a *bar metzra* are not dependent on the good will of the seller. Even if the seller prefers to sell the property to another party, the *bar metzra* has the right to force the buyer to transfer the property to him. Even if the seller claims that he would not have sold the property had he known that the *bar*

39. *Meiri, Bava Metzia* 108b applies this to any pressing situation, not just the examples enumerated in the Gemara. If the owner needs to raise cash to take advantage of an opportunity for an extraordinary profit, he may claim this exemption.

40. *Choshen Mishpat* 175:43.

41. Ibid.

42. *Rama.*

43. *Choshen Mishpat* 175:36. *Taz* 36 and *Chasam Sofer* 95 apply this concept if at least two properties are being sold. See *Shach* (12) , *Nesivos* 175:13, 175:33 who disagree and require a larger package.

metzra was going to claim it, the sale is valid and the *bar metzra* is entitled to the property.[44]

Har'amah — Subterfuge

Any time that *beis din* determines that a *har'amah* is taking place in order to circumvent the laws of *bar metzra, beis din* will ignore the *har'amah* and allow the neighbor to purchase the property.[45] *Teshuvas Maimoni*[46] writes that the source of *bar metzra* is *v'asisa hayashar v'hatov*, and is similar to a Biblical mitzvah. It is forbidden to use a *har'amah* (subterfuge) to avoid doing *yashar v'tov*.

Yashar V'tov

There are circumstances in which applying the laws of *bar metzra* will not result in the *yashar v'tov* that these laws were designed to foster. *Beis din* will make such considerations and will not apply the laws of *bar metzra* to such scenarios.[47]

44. *Choshen Mishpat* 175:6.
See, however, *Minchas Yitzchak* 10:148 who quotes *Divrei Chaim* 2:19 and *Choshen V'Ephod* that if the seller has a legitimate reason to sell to the outside buyer he may do so, since *bar metzra* does not apply if it would cause a loss to the seller. See also footnote 61.
See also *Mishpat Shalom* 175:6, *Karnei Re'eim* 137.

45. *Choshen Mishpat* 175:24.

46. *Kinyan* 16.

47. *Teshuvas HaRif* in *Shitah Mekubetzes* 108b, *Chasam Sofer, Choshen Mishpat* 11.
Sma(99) rules that if applying *bar metzra* will not result in *yashar v'tov, beis din* may rely on a halachic opinion that is otherwise rejected by halachah. *Sma* implies that *beis din* may not reject *bar metzra* on grounds of *yashar v'tov* alone; there must also be at least some halachic basis for disqualifying the claim.

If the Buyer Cannot Find Another Property

If a person who does not own a house bids on a property, a *bar metzra* who already owns a home does not have priority.[48] This applies only if the buyer already lives in the city, and cannot find another house. If other houses are available, or if the buyer is from another city, the laws of *bar metzra* will apply.[49]

Selling to One's Child

If the owner wants to sell the property to his child,[50] it is a greater *yashar v'tov* to allow the sale, and *bar metzra* will not apply.[51]

Undesirable Neighbors

If someone undesirable, who will not listen to *beis din* and may cause damage to his neighbors, sells his property,[52] *bar metzra* will not apply. Anyone who convinces the objectionable neighbor to sell his property and to move out of the neighborhood is doing the *bar metzra* a great service,[53] and may buy the property for himself.

---

48. *Choshen Mishpat* 175:49.

49. *Rama* 175:49; *Mahari Vall* 99.

50. See *Nachalas Tzvi* that discusses grandchildren.

51. *Teshuvas HaRif* (*Shitah Mekubetzes, Bava Metzia* 108); *Pischei Teshuvah* 37(13). See *Teshuvas Maimoni, Kinyan* 33 who objects.

52. *Choshen Mishpat* 175:38. See *Ranach* 125 that this applies to anyone who will not listen to *beis din*, regardless of whether or not they are an *akum*.

53. *Knesses HaGedolah* points out that when it is clear that the property would have been sold to a suitable buyer even had the outside buyer not been involved, the *bar metzra* may claim the property. However, if the owner may have sold it to another unsuitable neighbor (*Nimukei Yosef, Bava Metzia* 108b), or if he may have changed his mind and decided to keep the property for himself (*Terumas HaDeshen* 338), the laws of *bar metzra* will not apply. (See *Divrei Malkiel* 1:98:11 who entertains the possibility of *lo plug* concerning buying from an *akum*.)

Disadvantaged Buyer

If a disadvantaged buyer manages to find a property in which to invest,[54] *bar metzra* will not apply. Because it is difficult for him to successfully purchase a property, it would not be *yashar v'tov* to take it away from him. Some examples of disadvantaged buyers are:

- an orphan under bar/ bas mitzvah;[55]
- a woman who buys property with her own (not her husband's) money;[56]
- a *tzedakah* organization.[57]

Other Situations that Have Bar Metzra Rights

Tenants

A tenant has first rights to buy the property in which he is living.[58] This right applies before the landlord actually sells the

54. See *Choshen Mishpat* 175:47 for a discussion of whether *bar metzra* applies to such people who *sell* a property.

55. Ibid.

56. *Rama* limits this to an unmarried woman or to a woman who is known to have private assets. Otherwise, *beis din* assumes that the husband is buying it and putting it under his wife's name to avoid *hilchos bar metzra*.

R' Akiva Eiger quotes *Teshuvas Ranach* 125 who extends this exception from the rules of *bar metzra* to a person buying a property for his daughter's dowry.

57. *Choshen Mishpat* 175:55 says that a *donation* to the poor, *hekdesh aniyim*, is not subject to the laws of *bar metzra*. *Minchas Yitzchak* 10:148 (based on *Beur HaGra* 137) explains that the charity is like a disadvantaged buyer. Accordingly, this exception will apply to *sales* as well.

Divrei Geonim 60:27, *Bnei Aharon* 28, and *Minchas Yitzchak* extend this exception to a shul.

Divrei Chaim, Choshen Mishpat 2:18 suggests another reason. He writes that a yeshivah is a more desirable use of the land. As such, it is exempted from *bar metzra* as explained in section "Use of Land."

58. There is significant debate about the rights of a tenant. This *psak* is based on the

property. However, if the landlord disregards this halachah and sells the property to another party, the tenant may not force the buyer to resell it to him.[59]

This priority applies to future leases as well. If a landlord chooses to rent the property to a different tenant, the current tenant may claim *bar metzra* and remain in the house,[60] provided he is willing to match the terms of the new lease.

If there is an advantage for the landlord to lease the property to someone else, the current tenant may not claim *bar metzra*.[61]

Collateral and Liens

A lender who takes a property as collateral (*mashkon*)[62] has the rights of a *bar metzra*.[63] The status of a lien on a property is questionable.[64]

---

verdict of *Rama* (according to *Sma* [116]), *Shevus Yaakov* 3:165, *Aruch HaShulchan* 41.

59. *Pischei Teshuvah* 28 from *Maharshal* 43; *Shaar Mishpat, Sh"ut Bach* 69; *Shevus Yaakov* 3:165; *Beis Shlomo, Choshen Mishpat* 98.

60. *Taz* 58; *Nesivos* (65).

61. *Pischei Teshuvah* 27 quotes *Shevus Yaakov* 3:165 that maintains that if the seller prefers to rent to the second party, *bar metzra* will not apply. (See also *Teshuras Shai* 1:121, *Beis Yitzchak, Choshen Mishpat* 46.)

Ketzos 3 disallows the claim of *bar metzra* if the prospective tenant has a smaller family. Since it is to the landlord's advantage to have fewer people occupying his unit, *bar metzra* does not apply.

Beis Yosef (and *Nesivos Chiddushim*) writes that once the current tenant's lease expires, there is no claim of *bar metzra* even if they continue to live on the premises. The rights of a tenant apply only if the landlord signs a new contract during the term of a lease.

62. *Mordechai, Bava Metzia* 394 writes that the lender must actually live in the property that is taken as collateral. *Beis Yosef, Bedek HaBayis* 91 argues that this is unnecessary.

63. *Choshen Mishpat* 175:57.

64. *Chasam Sofer, Choshen Mishpat* 11 writes that a recorded mortgage, "*tabilatzion*" is like collateral and is not subject to *bar metzra*. *Erech Shai* 175:57 and *Minchas Pitim* argue that according to halachah, every lender has the equivalent of a lien against the assets of the borrower (provided a proper contract was executed). Since it is clear that not every lender has the rights of *bar metzra*, a mortgage cannot confer the status of a *bar metzra*. Only collateral, over which the lender has a much stronger

Partners

Properties that Are Jointly Owned

A partner has the status of a *bar metzra*. If a partner sells his share of a property, his partners have first rights to it.[65] Even if a neighbor who is a *bar metzra* buys the property, the partner may force him to resell it to him. This applies only to a property that is jointly owned by the partnership.

Properties that Are Not Jointly Owned

A partner has priority even if he is not a partner in this particular property. For example, if two people own a hardware store and one of them decides to sell his house, he should first offer it to his business partner. However, this halachah only creates a preference. If the property was already sold to an outsider, the business partner may not claim it.[66]

If both a business partner (who does not own a share of this particular property) and a *bar metzra* are interested in the prop-

---

level of control, will grant such rights.

A close reading of the *Chasam Sofer* indicates that the mortgaged property could not be sold until the debt was paid. In contrast, a property with a regular halachic lien may be sold. While the lien will survive the closing and the lender may foreclose on the property from the buyer, the sale itself is allowed. Accordingly, perhaps the *Chasam Sofer* applies the rights of *bar metzra* whenever the lien is strong enough to prevent a sale. The recorded mortgages of his time gave such rights to the lender, in contrast to the rights of a standard halachic lienholder.

Historically, a mortgage note gave immediate title to the lender, subject to the borrowers right to "redeem" the property by paying the debt by a certain time. (Certain states still operate under the title-theory when dealing with mortgages.) Perhaps the *Chasam Sofer* recognized these instruments as collateral. In contrast, a modern-day lien, which does not grant the lender such rights, and in fact requires a lengthy foreclosure process to actually take title, would not have such status even according to *Chasam Sofer.*

65. *Choshen Mishpat* 175:5.

66. Ibid. 175:49.

erty, one should sell to the *bar metzra*.[67] However, if one sells the property to his business associate, the *bar metzra* may not force the buyer to resell it to him.[68]

Mitaltelin — Movable Objects

These laws apply only to real estate and do not govern *mitaltelin*, movable objects. However, if *beis din* determines in a particular case that selling merchandise to an outside buyer will cause a loss to existing partners, the partners will be able to claim *bar metzra*.[69]

A Buyer's Responsibilities

While it is appropriate to afford the neighbor the first opportunity to purchase a property, there is no prohibition against buying the property.[70] One may purchase a property, and then if the neighbor claims *bar metzra*, go to *beis din* to determine his rights. There is no obligation to canvass the neighborhood and ask all the neighbors if they intend to exercise their rights as *bar metzra* before making a purchase.

After the purchase, the neighbors may summon the buyer to *beis din* to determine whether they are entitled to the property.[71] Even though the neighbor had an opportunity to purchase the property, he may still be entitled to force the buyer to resell it to him.[72]

67. *Aruch HaShulchan* 175:33.
68. *Choshen Mishpat* 175:49.
69. Ibid. 175:53; *Rama*.
70. *Divrei Malkiel* 1:98:10. *Bar metzra* is a right to buy the field, not a prohibition.
71. See "Expenses."
72. See the following section.

If the seller rejects the offer that the *bar metzra* makes, another party may make a higher offer.[73]

How to Deal with a Bar Metzra

To avoid a conflict with a *bar metzra*, the seller[74] should offer the property to the *bar metzra*. This is *yashar v'tov*, giving the neighbor an opportunity to buy the property. If the *bar metzra* tells the owner[75] that he is not interested in the property and he should sell it to someone else, he forfeits his right to claim *bar metzra*[76] in the future.

However, the property must be offered to the *bar metzra* with the same terms that the buyer would ultimately pay. Informing the *bar metzra* that the property is for sale will not suffice.[77] The *bar metzra* must be given the exact terms of the sale.

If the buyer negotiates a better deal from the seller, this new deal must be offered to the *bar metzra*. Otherwise, the *bar metzra* may claim that he only waived his right to purchase the property

73. *Machazeh Avraham* 16 argues that one may not bid up the price if the *bar metzra* is interested. One may submit a higher offer only if the seller rejects the neighbor's bid.

74. Although the laws of *bar metzra* apply primarily to the buyer and not to the seller (*Bava Metzia* 108b), it is appropriate and *yashar v'tov* for the seller to give the neighbor the first chance to buy the property (see *Aruch HaShulchan* 175:7). See also footnote 4.

75. The seller must offer the property to the *bar metzra*. If the prospective buyer offers the property to the neighbor, the neighbor must make a formal *kinyan* for his waiver to be effective (*Choshen Mishpat* 175:29; see *Chemdas Shlomo, Choshen Mishpat* 8 for an explanation).

See *Ginas Veradim* 6:6 who requires that both the seller and buyer offer the *bar metzra* the property.

76. *Choshen Mishpat* 175:31. A *bar metzra's* right to force the buyer to transfer the property to him is predicated on the halachah that the buyer is considered an agent for the *bar metzra*. When the *bar metzra* indicates that he is not interested in purchasing the property, he is notifying the outside buyer not to act as his agent.

77. *Sma* (56). A *bar* metzra may claim that he was afraid that if he indicated interest in the property, the seller would raise the price. If he is offered the actual price and declines, he has no claim.

Igros Moshe, Choshen Mishpat 2 21:2 indicates that some opinions maintain that the *bar metzra* will lose his rights even if he was not offered the specific price.

at the higher price. He did not agree to waive his rights to buy it at the reduced price.

Ani Ha'mehapech and Bar Metzra

Even in situations where *Chazal* exempt the parties from the obligations of *bar metzra*,[78] *Chazal* recognize the unique value that a property has for a neighbor. If the owner reaches an agreement to sell the property to another party, according to many opinions the *bar metzra* may still try to get the deal. Even though this is normally prohibited because of the rules of *ani ha'mehapech*, the property is considered a "windfall" to the *bar metzra* and he is allowed to pursue the deal. See Chapter Three for a more detailed discussion of the laws of *ani ha'mehapech* and for dissenting opinions.

Doubts

For a *bar metzra* to force an outside buyer to transfer the property to him, he must be able to establish without any doubt that he is entitled to the rights of a *bar metzra*. If there are any unclear issues[79] regarding the *bar metzra's* rights, the outside buyer may keep the property.[80]

---

78. See "*Yasher V'tov.*"

79. If zoning variances are needed and it is unclear that the *bar metzra* will be able to obtain them, one could argue that this would be classified as a "doubt" and the laws of *bar metzra* would not apply.

80. *Choshen Mishpat* 175:45. This applies after the outside buyer purchased the property. If the "doubtful *bar metzra*" comes before the sale takes place, the seller should sell to him.

This applies both to doubts arising from unknown facts or if the halachah is in doubt (*Aruch HaShulchan* 175:62).

When There Is No Bar Metzra

If two parties are interested in a property, and neither qualifies as a *bar metzra*, one should give priority in the following order:[81]

- a *talmid chacham;*
- a neighbor;[82]
- a relative.

These guidelines are recommendations and are not enforceable.[83]

Bar metzra is another halachah that is not based on standard legal monetary rights. A person does not own an option on his neighbor's field. Yet we are all expected to politely step aside and allow the neighbor to purchase the property if he chooses. Why? Because the property means more to him than it does to us. Not only are we expected to live up to these lofty standards, beis din will enforce them as well. Understanding how much we are responsible to worry about another Jew's success should inspire us to change our self-centered mentality and act for the benefit of all of Klal Yisrael.

81. *Choshen Mishpat* 175:50.

82. The *Rama* points out that we are referring to a neighbor with whom the owner is friendly.

83. *Rashi, Bava Metzia* 108b; *Ri; Meiri; Rambam, Shecheinim* 14.

15 Beis Din

Introduction

"Adam nikur b'kiso, b'kaaso, u'v'koso."[1]

A person's true character can be seen through his wallet (financial matters), his anger, and in his cup, i.e, when he is drunk.

Financial disputes have two of these ingredients, kiso (wallet) and kaaso (anger), and tend to bring out the worst in people.

When involved in a dispute, people often become emotional about the issue. Each party has a natural bias, and there is a need for an objective third party to resolve the dispute. That is the function of a beis din. The dayanim (judges) are knowledgable in the laws of Choshen Mishpat, and, as objective"outsiders," are able to reach an appropriate verdict and resolve the dispute.

Yet, people are often reluctant to resolve their disputes in a beis din because they are unfamiliar with the beis din process. The secular legal system, with all

1. *Eruvin* 65b.

of its problems, is a known entity. People understand the process, are familiar with the laws and guidelines, and have a general idea of what to expect. In contrast, most people have never been to beis din before. They are unfamiliar with how a beis din operates, and do not know what to expect. Submitting a dispute that involves large sums of money, and about which they have very strong feelings, is extremely difficult. This chapter will outline the basic procedures of a din Torah, and will offer guidance as to how to make the process as pleasant and effective as possible.

Beis Din and Secular Courts

Jews may not litigate a dispute in a secular court. One who litigates in a secular court is called a *rasha*, and is comparable to a blasphemer,[2] and to one who lifts his hands against the Torah.[3] *Beis din* is obligated to put him in excommunication (*cherem*) until he withdraws the case from the court.[4] This prohibition applies even if both parties prefer to litigate in a secular court over a *din Torah*.[5] Even in situations where the secular court will rule according to the laws of the Torah, submitting a dispute to the secular court is prohibited.[6] *Beis din* is the proper venue for Jews to settle all their disputes.

Unfortunately, it is not uncommon to see observant Jews litigating their disputes in civil court. Some people do so out of ignorance. Others do so because they believe that a secular court will be more sympathetic to their claims. Regardless of the reason, it is unacceptable. Any money that a secular court awards

2.*Choshen Mishpat* 26:1.

3. *Sma* 26:4 explains that by choosing secular courts over *din Torah*, one indicates his belief that the Torah and its laws are untrue.

4. *Choshen Mishpat* 26:1; *Rama*.

5. *Choshen Mishpat* 26:1.

6. Ibid.

a person that is in excess of what he is entitled to according to halachah is considered stolen.[7]

Accepting Jurisdiction of Secular Courts

One may incorporate into a contract a clause stating that the contract may be enforced in a secular court.[8] Such clauses are understood to mean that, in the event that one of the parties refuses to listen to *beis din*, the contract may be enforced in a secular court.[9] However, such clauses usually do not give either party the right to circumvent *beis din* and go directly to court.[10]

The Din Torah Process

Initiating a Din Torah

When a dispute arises, the parties should make every attempt to resolve the issue themselves. Even if a person

---

7. *Tashbatz* 2:290, quoted by *R' Akiva Eiger* 26:1.

8. *Teshuvos HaRosh* 18:5.

Sma 26:11, 61:14 writes that such clauses grant the parties the rights that they would have under secular law.

Taz 26 (3) (based on *Shulchan Aruch*), *Aruch HaShulchan* 26:4 disagree.

9. The literal meaning of the clause is that any dispute regarding the contract should be litigated in a secular court. However, such an agreement would violate the prohibition against litigating in a secular court. *Teshuvos HaRosh* explains that we interpret the clause in a manner that is consistent with halachah. Therefore, it is understood to be referring to a case where one of the parties will not come to *beis din*. In such circumstances, *beis din* may grant permission to litigate in a secular court.

10. *Yam Shel Shlomo, Bava Kamma Perek* 8:65 writes that this clause allows one to bypass *beis din* and litigate in a secular court if the borrower is a לא צייה דינא, a person who will not listen to *beis din*. In contrast, if such a clause is not inserted in the contract, the lender would be required to get permission from *beis din* to initiate legal action regardless of the borrower's behavior.

Aruch HaShulchan 26:5 argues with *Yam Shel Shlomo* and writes that one needs permission from *beis din* to initiate legal action even when such a clause was included in the contract.

is convinced that he is completely right, it is worthwhile to bend over backward and make some sort of compromise to settle the dispute. *"Lo charvah Yerushalayim elah mipnei she'he'emidu dineihem al din Torah* — Jerusalem was destroyed only because people demanded the exact letter of the law."[11] The *Nesivos*[12] cautioned his descendants never to be involved in a *din Torah.* Rather, they should be willing to compromise in order to resolve any dispute in a peaceful manner.[13]

If compromise is impossible, one should call the other party to a *din Torah.* It is better to go to *beis din* and resolve the dispute than to have an ongoing feud with the other party. A *din Torah* brings closure to the issue; once *beis din* issues their ruling and the parties comply, the parties have fulfilled their obligations and the feud should end.

If the two parties can agree on a specific *beis din*, they simply make an appointment. However, if one of the parties refuses to come to a *beis din*, the other party will initiate the *hazmanah* process.

Hazmanah – Summons

A *hazmanah*, or summons, is sent to call a party to a *din Torah.*[14] A person is obligated to respond to any summons that he receives. Even if one believes that the claim is frivolous, the other party has the right to present his claim before a *beis din* that will adjudicate the matter. A *psak* from one's Rav that he is completely right does not release a person from his obligation to go to *beis*

---

11. *Bava Metzia* 30b.

12. *Tzava'ah,* paragraph 23.

13. *Rav Pam zt"l* in *Atarah L'Melech*, p. 152 points out that *hiddur mitzvah ad shelish,* one is obligated to spend up to one-third extra in order to beautify a mitzvah. Our obligations *bein adam l'chaveiro* are also mitzvos, and one should not hesitate to spend money to avoid a dispute, even when one is convinced he is right. R' Pam concludes that one can be confident that any money spent to avoid disputes will be repaid in both this world and the next.

14. *Choshen Mishpat* 11:1.

din. Only a *beis din* that was accepted by both parties and heard both parties' claims may issue a *psak*.

Responding to a Summons – Choosing a Venue

A person is obligated to answer the first summons that he receives.[15] However, he may not be obligated to submit the dispute to the particular *beis din* that sent the summons. The defendant may have the option of responding that he wants a different *beis din* to adjudicate the dispute.[16] The two parties will have to come to an agreement over which *beis din* to use.

One should carefully research a *beis din* before submitting to its jurisdiction. There are many professional *batei din* that adjudicate disputes in a fair, efficient, and halachically preferable manner. However, *batei din* have different strengths, and the parties should ensure that they choose a *beis din* that will be appropriate for their particular dispute.

Types of Batei Din

There are two basic types of *batei din*. The first class consists of regular, "professional" *batei din*. The *beis din* will consist of three independent impartial judges. However, if the parties cannot agree on a regular *beis din*, they may opt for the second type of *beis din* and create a *zabla beis din*.

---

15. *Beis din* can issue a *siruv* (see section *Ksav Siruv* — Writ of Contempt) against a party that ignores even one *hazmanah*, if the person was available to come to the *din Torah* (*Choshen Mishpat* 11:1). In practice the *minhag* is not to issue a *siruv* until three *hazmanos* are ignored. This does not justify ignoring any *hazmanah*; it simply means that *beis din* will not punish someone for not answering the first two.

One may not drag out the process in order to force the other party to either drop the case or agree to a settlement (*Choshen Mishpat* 12:6).

16. Ibid. 14 :1.

A *zabla*[17] *beis din* consists of three judges. However, these judges are not completely independent. Each party chooses one judge or *borer* to be a part of the *beis din*. The two *borerim* then[18] choose a *shalish,* a third independent judge, to complete the *beis din*.

The concept behind a *zabla beis din* is that if each party has the right to choose one of the *dayanim*, the parties will be more willing to accept the ultimate verdict of the *beis din*.[19] Each party assumes that the *dayan* that they choose will represent their interests. The *dayanim*, as well, will be motivated to find any arguments that will help their clients. As a result no legal arguments will be overlooked and a proper verdict will emerge.[20]

The role of a *borer* is complex. He is allowed to seek legitimate halachic sources and arguments that support his side's claim.[21] However, he is still a *dayan*. He may not make any false claims or try to subvert the *din Torah* process. In addition, according to many *poskim*, the prohibition against hearing one party's claims or testimony in the absence of the other party applies to a *borer* as well.[22] However, in practice, many modern-day *borerim* maintain contact with their respective parties, and privately discuss the case with their party.[23] As a result, the *shalish*, who is the

17. The word *zabla* is an abbreviation of *zeh borer lo echad, v'zeh borer lo echad,* "This [party] chooses one [judge], and this [party] chooses one [judge]."

18. *Choshen Mishpat* 13:1. In practice the *borrerim* consult with their clients before choosing a *shalish*. See also *Pischei Teshuvah* 13:1 (2).

19. *Rashi, Sanhedrin* 23a.

20. *Taz* 13 explaining *Rashi*.

21. *Choshen Mishpat* 13:1. There is considerable discussion among the *poskim* as to what extent a *borer* may advocate for his client. See *Tur* 13 and *Pischei Teshuvah* (3).

22. *Panim Me'iros* 2:159.

23. *Aruch HaShulchan* 13:4 justifies this practice by arguing that the parties to the *din Torah* expect the *borerim* to speak to their clients. As such, there is an implied acceptance by both litigants for this to occur.

Based on this reasoning, it would seem that either party can insist, before accepting the authority of the *beis din*, that neither party speak to his *borer* without the other party being present.

See also *Panim Me'iros* 2:159 that takes strong issue with the practice of *borerim* speaking privately with their clients.

independent judge on the *beis din*, has the primary responsibility for the case.

When the *beis din* is ready to issue a verdict, each *borer* is obligated to opine according to halachah, regardless of which side he is representing. However, it is natural for a *borer* to be biased toward his client. As a result, in fact it is the *shalish*, who, as the independent *dayan*, has a greater responsibility to ensure that the ruling is fair. Consequently, it is critical to ensure that the *shalish* is a reputable and competent *dayan*.

Using a *zabla beis din* typically takes significantly longer then a regular *beis din* since the system is unstructured. The *dayanim*, who do not work together on any formal *beis din*, must coordinate their different schedules. If there is a need for one of the parties to communicate with the *beis din*, he must contact his *borer*, who will then contact the *shalish*, who will pass the message to the other party's *borer*. Such exchanges are time consuming and add significantly to the duration and cost of the *din Torah*.

The system also lends itself to abuse. *Borerim* have differing views on how far they will go to protect their clients. If one is going to use a *zabla beis din*, he must be extremely careful about who all the judges will be.

Mesareiv L'din — Refusal to Submit to the Authority of Beis Din

If a party does not respond to the first summons, the *beis din* issues a second, and then a third summons.[24] If the party still refuses to come to *beis din*, the *beis din* will issue a *hasraos siruv*, warning the party that he will be considered a *mesareiv l'din*, "in contempt" of *beis din*. If the party ignores the warning, the *beis din* will issue a *ksav siruv*, a "writ of contempt."

---

24. *Choshen Mishpat* 11:1, *Nesivos Chiddushim* 4, *Pischei Teshuvah* quoting *Urim* (4). A *hazmanah* typically gives the defendant one week to schedule a session.

Ksav Siruv — "Writ of Contempt"

A *ksav siruv* is a document that declares that *beis din* considers the party worthy of a *nidui* (a form of excommunication). *Shulchan Aruch*[25] describes the laws that govern the community's behavior toward a person in *nidui.* He may not be counted for a *minyan,*[26] may not be called to the Torah for an *aliyah*, and people[27] may not enter his house or stand within four *amos* (cubits) of him.

If necessary, *beis din* has the right to order that the person's children not be allowed into school.[28]

Heter Arkaos — Permission to Litigate in Secular Court

Beis din may also issue a *heter arkaos*, allowing the other party to initiate legal proceedings against the offending party.[29] This *heter* is typically limited to civil action, as opposed to criminal proceedings. If the offending party does *teshuvah* and agrees to come to *beis din*, the *beis din* will typically retract the *heter arkaos.*[30]

If a person is *mesareiv l'din*, and *beis din* allows the other party to initiate legal action, the offending party may be held responsible for legal costs.[31]

25. *Yoreh Deah* 334:2.

26. Although see *Yoreh Deah* 334, *Shach* 21 who limits this halachah.

27. Other than immediate family.

28. *Rama, Yoreh Deah* 334:6. *Taz* limits this to children who are minors.
Maharshal argues with this halachah and maintains that children can not be penalized for their father's wrongdoing.

29. *Choshen Mishpat* 26:2.

30. Ibid. 26:1. This applies when the offending party recognizes their mistake, and does *teshuvah* prior to the legal proceedings. However, if he loses the court case, and then asks *beis din* to retry the case, *beis din* will refuse.

31. *Rama, Choshen Mishpat* 14:5. See *Nesivos* (5) who limits this halachah. See also *Igros Moshe, Choshen Mishpat* 2:26.

It is important to realize that a *heter arkaos* must be granted by a *beis din*.[32] Suing a Jew in a secular court on the advice of a friend or Rav without calling the party to a *din Torah* is not acceptable.

Shtar Berurin and Arbitration Agreements

Before the actual *din Torah* begins, the parties are typically asked to sign two documents, a *shtar berurin* and an arbitration agreement.

A *shtar berurin* is a halachic document in which the parties accept the particular *beis din*. A *kinyan suddar* is typically made to formalize their acceptance of the *beis din* and their agreement to abide by the ultimate *psak*. It is extremely important that a *kinyan suddar* and a *shtar* be executed. Otherwise, it will be difficult to enforce the final verdict.

The second document is an arbitration agreement that gives the *beis din* legal jurisdiction over the dispute. By signing such a document, the parties bind themselves to arbitrate the matter, and the ruling of the *beis din* will be legally enforceable. If executed correctly, this document will prevent either party from overturning the *beis din's* ruling.

The documents often give additional protections and powers to the *beis din*. Some of the clauses may:

- allow the *beis din* to subpoena documents or witnesses;
- grant the *beis din* the right to continue proceedings in the absence of one of the parties if they refuse to come to *beis din*;

32. *Shulchan Aruch, Choshen Mishpat* 26:2. *Yam Shel Shlomo, Bava Kamma* 8:65 writes that the necessity to get permission from *beis din* is a Rabbinic *takanah* (regulation).

- allow the *beis din* to issue intermediate decisions;
- grant the *beis din* the authority to issue a ruling based on *pesher* (compromise) or *pesher karov l'din* (see below);
- allow the *beis din* to issue a ruling or compromise (*pesharah*) with only two judges;[33]
- indemnify the *beis din* from any legal proceedings that the parties may initiate;
- waive certain legal rights that are not required by halachah.

Pesher — Compromise

The *dayanim* are obligated to offer the litigants the option of receiving a verdict based on *pesher*, compromise, rather than strict *din*.[34] This allows *beis din* to take factors other than strict halachah into account when they issue their ruling. *Beis din* will examine the fairness of the situation and adjust the verdict accordingly. Halachah favors verdicts based on compromise [35] for a number of reasons.

First, under any circumstances, the Torah prefers *pesharah* as a way of promoting peace.[36] Secondly, because the laws of *Choshen Mishpat* are very complex, a *dayan* should try to avoid undertaking to issue a verdict in which he commits to determine

33. *Choshen Mishpat* 18:1. According to halachah, the case is decided by the majority of *dayanim*. However, a compromise requires a unanimous decision. *Choshen Mishpat* 12:18, *Bach* 12 (9), *Sma* 13 (20). See also *Pischei Teshuvah* 13 (10). Most arbitration agreements give the *beis din* the authority to issue a compromise ruling based on the majority of *dayanim*.

34. *Choshen Mishpat* 12:2. *Sma* 6 and *Aruch HaShulchan* 12:2 write that there is an obligation for the *dayanim* to try to persuade the litigants to agree to *pesher*. *Taz* writes that the *beis din* must offer, but not necessarily encourage, the option of *pesher*.

35. *Choshen Mishpat* 12:2.

36. *Sanhedrin* 6b, *Shevus Yaakov* 2:145.

absolute *din*.[37] In addition, many situations require one of the parties to take an oath. Because of the severity of making a false oath, *beis din* generally does not administer such oaths. This necessitates a compromise in lieu of oath-taking.[38]

Compromise is also appropriate if there is no clearly accepted halachah or if there is a factual issue that the *dayanim* cannot resolve.[39]

Levels of Pesher — Pesher and Pesher Karov L'din

There are two levels of authority for *pesharah* that a *beis din* may be given.

Pesharah gives the *beis din* broad authority to issue a ruling based on its discretion of what is appropriate.[40] They may take into account ethical or *yashrus* issues, that would not necessarily be relevant to a ruling based strictly on *din*.

Pesher karov l'din, or a compromise that is close to the clear halachah, limits the *beis din*'s authority. They will first determine who is right according to strict halachah. The *beis din* may then adjust the award by up to one-third.[41]

The litigating parties must come to a mutual agreement to grant the *beis din* such discretion. Either party has the right to insist that the *beis din*'s authority be limited to *pesher karov l'din*.

It should be noted that *beis din* will not necessarily use its

37. *Choshen Mishpat* 12:20.

38. Ibid. 12:2; *Igros Moshe, Choshen Mishpat* 1:32. See footnote 41.

39. *Choshen Mishpat* 12:5. In these circumstances, *beis din* has the authority to impose a compromise even if the parties insisted on receiving a verdict based on *din* and did not voluntarily grant the *beis din* any additional powers (*Sma* 12:12; *Teshuvos HaRosh* 107:6).

40. *Shevus Yaakov* 2:145.

41. Ibid. *Divrei Malkiel* 2:133, *Igros Moshe, Choshen Mishpat* 1:32 write that if one of the parties is obligated to make an oath, *beis din* may adjust the *din* by more than one-third in order to "buy out" the obligation to make the oath.

authority for compromise. If *beis din* feels that the strict *din* can be easily ascertained, and there are no mitigating factors that justify adjusting the strict *din*, they will issue a ruling based on strict *din*. While the *beis din* will ask for the right to compromise, they are under no obligation to use that authority.

Trial Proceedings

The judges will hear the plaintiff's claims first.[42] After the plaintiff presents his claims, the defendant is given the opportunity to present his arguments and counterclaims. The case moves from one party to the other, with the *dayanim* questioning both parties until they have gathered all the information they need. If the case involves legal or technical issues with which the *dayanim* are unfamiliar, the *dayanim* will typically consult with professionals in order to familiarize themselves with the topic being contested.

Fifth Amendment Rights

Halachah does not recognize the right to remain silent.[43] While *beis din* cannot force a party to answer questions against his will, his refusal to answer questions can be held against him.[44] The parties do not have the right to cross-examine witnesses. Questions to witnesses are usually posed by the *dayanim*, and not by any of the other parties. For legal purposes, many arbitration agreements specify that the parties waive their right to cross-examination.

42. *Choshen Mishpat* 24:1.

43. It should be noted that secular law does not extend Fifth Amendment rights to civil cases. A person's refusal to testify against himself can be used against him in civil proceedings. The protection is limited to criminal proceedings.

44. *Rama, Choshen Mishpat* 75:1. *Beis din* may conclude that a party is trying to hide the truth if he does not answer questions.

Ex Parte Communication

During a *din Torah*, the *dayanim*[45] may not hear testimony or claims from one party unless the other party is present.[46] This is not only a procedural issue. Doing so is a violation of *shemo'a bein acheichem* and *lo sisa sheima shav.*[47] The prohibition applies to the litigants as well; they may not try to present their case to a *dayan* in the absence of the other party. It should be noted that ex parte communication might also void the legal enforceability of an arbitration agreement

Rabbinic Arbitrators

Many people bring a Rabbinic arbitrator, or *toen*, to represent them at a *din Torah*. A *toen* is familiar with the *beis din* system and is able to guide the litigants throughout the process. His role includes advising the parties, preparing the case, and helping them present their claims to the *beis din*. While there is certainly a legitimate role for such advocates, one needs to be vigilant before hiring a *toen* to ensure that he is dealing with a reputable person. One should also be aware that engaging a *toen* will generally increase the cost and the length of the *din Torah*.

45. As noted before, the practice of a *zabla beis din* is to allow each party's *borrer* to be in contact with his party.

46. *Choshen Mishpat* 17:5. See *Pischei Teshuvah* 8 for a discussion whether this prohibition is Biblical or Rabbinic, and whether a *dayan* who listens to one party without the other present is disqualified from issuing a *psak*.

47. *Shemos* 23:1.

See *Chofetz Chaim, Pesicha Be'er Mayim Chaim* 2, second explanation that suggests that when a person relates his claim without the opposing party, he will inevitably exaggerate his claim.

Psak — Verdict

Beis din generally issues its verdicts in writing.[48] The verdict need not be a unanimous decision. The *beis din* will issue a ruling based on the opinion of a majority of the judges.[49] However, all of the judges must sign the final verdict.[50]

Beis din generally does not explain the reasons for its *psak*. The judges simply issue a ruling of what the parties' obligations are, and do not explain how they arrived at this conclusion.[51]

Appealing a Psak Din

A *beis din* will typically refuse to reopen a case that was heard and adjudicated by another *beis din*.[52] If one believes that the *beis din* erred in its decision, the only recourse is to ask the original *beis din* to reconsider the case.

If one finds new evidence, he has the right to present the evidence to the *beis din* and have them reconsider the case.[53] If the *beis din* agrees that the evidence may impact the verdict, they will reconvene.

Enforcing the Psak

One is obligated to follow the ruling of *beis din*. If one of the parties does not listen to the *psak*, *beis din* may put them

48. Halachah does not require a written *psak* (*Choshen Mishpat* 19:1). However, in practice, the *psak* will usually be written to ensure that it can be enforced.

49. Ibid. 18:1.

50. *Yerushalmi* (*zeh borrer*, halachah 10); *Avkas Rocheil* 19; *Aruch HaShulchan* 19:2. Although see *Mabit* 1:172, *Shaar Mishpat* 19, *Ketzos* 19(2), *Birkei Yosef* 19:2.

51. Although in halachah the parties may be entitled to additional information regarding the verdict (*Choshen Mishpat* 14:1, 14:4), *batei din* typically include a waiver of this right in the Arbitration Agreement.

52. *Hagahos HaSma* 19:2 (2); *Aruch HaShulchan* 12:3; *Levush* 12:2. See also *Pischei Teshuvah* 19:3 for parameters of this rule.

53. *Choshen Mishpat* 20:1.

in excommunication or *nidui*,[54] and/or allow the other party to confirm the award in a secular court. Although the losing party may ask the court to vacate the *psak*, the courts generally will uphold the *psak* of the *beis din*, provided that appropriate arbitration agreements were signed, and that the proceedings were carried out according to law.

Afterword

Parashas Yisro, the description of the Jewish nation receiving the Ten Commandments, is preceded and followed by a discussion of the laws of Choshen Mishpat. The Midrash[55] *gives the following parable. An aristocratic woman is surrounded and protected by her guards. She is preceded by an armed vanguard and followed by armed servants.*

So too, the Torah, our precious way of life, needs to be surrounded by mishpat. Justice is the "protection" the Torah requires.

Mishpat is not simply the mechanism to safeguard society or to further commerce. It creates the framework and environment within which Torah can flourish.

It is my tefillah that this work should contribute to the knowledge and observance of Choshen Mishpat and be marbeh kevod Shamayim.

54. Ibid. 19:3.

55. *Shemos Rabbah* 30:3.

Appendices

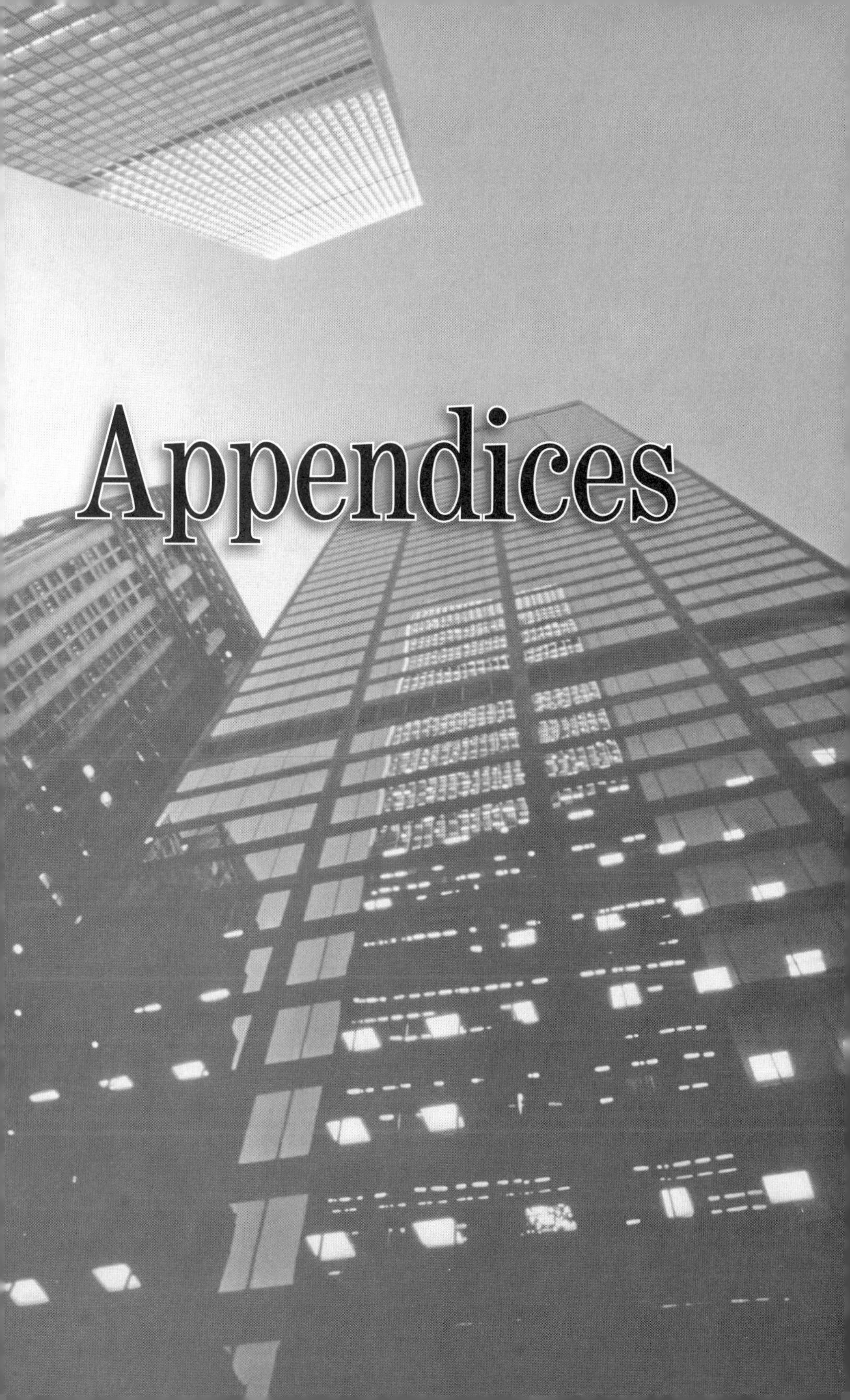

These forms are being presented here as a public service. They may be copied, provided that they are identified as being reprinted with the permission of Beis Din Maysharim and ArtScroll/Mesorah.

Though these documents are, to our understanding, halachically valid and legally binding, a Rav and attorney should be consulted before executing these documents. Beis Din Maysharim, the author, and the publisher accept no liability, nor do they make any representation or warranty with regard to these documents.

RABBINICAL COURT
MAYSHARIM
GUIDED BY RABBI NISSIM KARELITZ
BAIS DIN TZEDEK OF BNEI BRAK

בית דין צדק
מישרים
בהכוונת בית דין צדק - בני ברק
בראשות מרן הגאון **רבי נסים קרליץ** שליט"א

Heter Iska to Attach to Legal Documents

I, ______________ ("Recipient"), have received $_____ from ______________ ("Investing Partner"), for investment in an *iska* partnership, subject to the following terms:

1. Partnership

In exchange for the money received, I hereby assign to the Investing Partner a share (in the value of the money received) in all investments, businesses, and real estate that I own. If I identify a specific investment that I believe will be more profitable, I shall assign to the Investing Partner a share of that investment. The Investing Partner shall pay one dollar for my services during the term of the *iska*.

2. Profits and Losses

(a) All profits, capital gains, or losses arising from this investment shall be shared equally between the Investing Partner and the Recipient.

(b) Any claim regarding the amount of profits generated by this investment shall be verified under solemn oath, administered by an Orthodox Jewish Court of Law.

(c) Any claim of loss must be verified through the testimony of two qualified witnesses before an Orthodox Jewish Court of Law.

(d) It is agreed that if I pay to the Investing Partner the amount equal to the principal, interest, fees, points, penalties, and any other payments or consideration called for by the attached documents, as per the schedule of said documents, as payment for his share of the principal and profits of this *iska*, I will not

Office & Mailing Address: 625 Forest Avenue, Lakewood, N.J. 08701 • **Telephone:** 732.905.3388 • **Fax:** 732.905.5880
Rabbinical Courtrooms: 625 Forest Avenue, Lakewood, N.J. (Rear Entrance) **לשכות הבד"צ:**
2913 Avenue L, Brooklyn, N.Y. (Lower Level)

RABBINICAL COURT
MAYSHARIM
GUIDED BY RABBI NISSIM KARELITZ
BAIS DIN TZEDEK OF BNEI BRAK

בית דין צדק
מישרים
בהכוונת בית דין צדק - בני ברק
בראשות מרן הגאון רבי נסים קרליץ שליט"א

be required to make an oath, nor will I be required to notify the Partner regarding the profits that were realized. Additional profits, if any, shall be my sole property.

3. Miscellaneous

(a) This *iska* shall be returned by the dates specified in the attached documents. In the event any payment is not made by the due date, the money shall be reinvested under the terms of the *iska*.

(b) Additional documents, including but not limited to, a promissory note and a mortgage note, have been executed regarding these funds. Said documents contain additional terms and conditions that are to be interpreted in a manner consistent with the laws of *ribbis* and this *heter iska*. To the extent necessary by halachah, this *heter iska* shall override said documents. Any payments made that are not justified by this *iska* shall reduce the outstanding principal.

4. Dispute Resolution

All disputes that may arise regarding or associated with this Agreement shall be resolved and established exclusively by binding arbitration at the ______________________ (name of mutually agreed-upon *beis din*). Judgment rendered by the aforesaid authority may be entered in any court having jurisdiction thereof. The non-prevailing Party shall be liable to the prevailing Party for all costs and expenses related to any dispute-resolution proceeding, including reasonable attorney's fees.

This Agreement shall follow the guidelines of *heter iska* as explained in *Sefer Bris Yehudah*. This Agreement is intended to be, and is, binding, consistent with the binding nature of all agreements, documents, obligations, and acquisitions that are properly effected in a Jewish Court of Law in accordance with the laws and rules established by Rabbinical authorities. A proper

RABBINICAL COURT
MAYSHARIM
GUIDED BY RABBI NISSIM KARELITZ
BAIS DIN TZEDEK OF BNEI BRAK

בית דין צדק
מישרים
בהכוונת בית דין צדק - בני ברק
בראשות מרן הגאון רבי נסים קרליץ שליט"א

kinyan suddar was executed to create this partnership. This is all valid and in good standing.

We hereby affix our signatures on this ______ day of ________ 20 ___ .

________________ Recipient ________________ Investing Partner

All this was done in front of us, the below signatories, and we signed at the direction of the Parties.

________________ Witness ________________ Witness

RABBINICAL COURT
MAYSHARIM
GUIDED BY RABBI NISSIM KARELITZ
BAIS DIN TZEDEK OF BNEI BRAK

בית דין צדק
מישרים
בהכוונת בית דין צדק - בני ברק
בראשות מרן הגאון **רבי נסים קרליץ** שליט"א

Heter Iska for Funds Used for Personal Use[1]

I, ______________ ("Recipient"), have received $____ from ______________ ("Investing Partner"), for investment in an *iska* partnership, subject to the following terms:

1. Partnership

In exchange for the money received, I hereby assign to the Investing Partner a share (in the value of the money received) in all investments, businesses, and real estate that I own. If I identify a specific investment that I believe will be more profitable, I shall transfer and assign to the Investing Partner a share of that investment. The Investing Partner shall pay one dollar for my services during the term of the *iska.*

2. Profits and Losses

(a) Any profits, capital gains, or losses arising from this investment shall be shared equally between the Investing Partner and the Recipient.

(b) Any claim regarding the amount of profits generated by this investment shall be verified under solemn oath, administered by an Orthodox Jewish Court of Law.

(c) Any claim of loss must be verified through the testimony of two qualified witnesses before an Orthodox Jewish Court of Law.

(d) It is agreed that if I return the principal of this *iska*, and in addition, pay to the Investing Partner the amount equal to a ____ percent annual return as payment for his share of profits, I will not be required to take an oath, nor will I be required to notify the

1. Please note that this may only be used if the recipient has other investments to assign to the Investing Partner, as explained in Chapter 6.

Office & Mailing Address: 625 Forest Avenue, Lakewood, N.J. 08701 • **Telephone:** 732.905.3388 • **Fax:** 732.905.5880

Rabbinical Courtrooms: 625 Forest Avenue, Lakewood, N.J. (Rear Entrance) **:לשכות הבד"צ**
2913 Avenue L, Brooklyn, N.Y. (Lower Level)

Partner regarding the profits that were realized. Additional profits, if any, shall be my sole property.

3. Miscellaneous

(a) This *iska* shall be returned by ______________ (date). In the event any payment is not made by the due date, the money shall be reinvested under the terms of the *iska*.

(b) This agreement supersedes any other agreement between the two Parties in regards to these funds.

4. Dispute Resolution

All disputes that may arise regarding or associated with this Agreement shall be resolved and established exclusively by binding arbitration at the ______________________ (name of mutually agreed-upon *beis din*), or its designee. Judgment rendered by the aforesaid authority may be entered in any court having jurisdiction thereof. The non-prevailing Party shall be liable to the prevailing Party for all costs and expenses related to any dispute resolution proceeding, including reasonable attorney's fees.

This Agreement shall follow the guidelines of *heter iska* as explained in *Sefer Bris Yehudah*. This Agreement is intended to be, and is, binding, consistent with the binding nature of all agreements, documents, obligations, and acquisitions that are properly effected in a Jewish Court of Law in accordance with the laws and rules established by Rabbinical authorities. A proper *kinyan suddar* was executed to create this partnership. This is all valid and in good standing.

We hereby affix our signatures on this ________ day of ____________ 20___ .

________________________ Recipient

________________________ Investing Partner

All this was done in front of us, the below signatories, and we signed at the direction of the Parties.

________________________ Witness

________________________ Witness

RABBINICAL COURT
MAYSHARIM
GUIDED BY RABBI NISSIM KARELITZ
BAIS DIN TZEDEK OF BNEI BRAK

בית דין צדק
מישרים
בהכוונת בית דין צדק - בני ברק
בראשות מרן הגאון **רבי נסים קרליץ** שליט"א

Heter Iska Kulo Pekadon

I, ______________ ("Recipient"), have received $_____ from ______________ ("Investor"), for investment in an *iska* partnership, subject to the following terms:

1. Partnership

In exchange for the money received, I hereby assign to the Investing Partner a share (in the value of the money received) in all investments, businesses, and real estate that I own. If I identify a specific investment that I believe will be more profitable, I shall transfer and assign to the Investing Partner a share of that investment.

2. Profits and Losses

(a) Any profits, capital gains, or losses arising from this investment shall be borne by the Investor. However, Recipient shall receive 5 percent (5%) of profits as a management fee.

(b) Any claim regarding the amount of profits generated by this investment shall be verified under solemn oath, administered by an Orthodox Jewish Court of Law.

(c) Any claim of loss must be verified through the testimony of two qualified witnesses, before an Orthodox Jewish Court of Law.

(d) It is agreed that if I pay to the Investor the sum of $_____ by _______ 20___, as payment for his share of the profits generated, then I will not be required to take an oath, nor will I be required to notify the partner regarding the profits that were realized. Additional profits, if any, shall be my sole property.

3. Miscellaneous

(a) This *iska* shall be returned by ______________ (date). In the

Office & Mailing Address: 625 Forest Avenue, Lakewood, N.J. 08701 • **Telephone:** 732.905.3388 • **Fax:** 732.905.5880

Rabbinical Courtrooms: 625 Forest Avenue, Lakewood, N.J. (Rear Entrance) **לשכות הבד"צ:**
2913 Avenue L, Brooklyn, N.Y. (Lower Level)

RABBINICAL COURT
MAYSHARIM
GUIDED BY RABBI NISSIM KARELITZ
BAIS DIN TZEDEK OF BNEI BRAK

בית דין צדק
מישרים
בהכוונת בית דין צדק - בני ברק
בראשות מרן הגאון רבי נסים קרליץ שליט"א

event any payment is not made by the due date, the money shall be reinvested under the terms of the iska.

(b) This agreement supersedes any other agreement between the two parties in regards to these funds.

4. Dispute Resolution

All disputes that may arise regarding or associated with this Agreement shall be resolved and established exclusively by binding arbitration at the ______________ (name of mutually agreed-upon *beis din*). Judgment rendered by the aforesaid authority may be entered in any court having jurisdiction thereof. The non-prevailing Party shall be liable to the prevailing Party for all costs and expenses related to any dispute resolution proceeding, including reasonable attorney's fees.

This agreement shall follow the guidelines of *heter iska* as explained in *Sefer Bris Yehudah*. This Agreement is intended to be, and is, binding, consistent with the binding nature of all agreements, documents, obligations, and acquisitions that are properly effected in a Jewish Court of Law in accordance with the laws and rules established by Rabbinical authorities. A proper *kinyan suddar* was executed to create this partnership. This is all valid and in good standing.

We hereby affix our signatures on this ______ day of ________ 20 ___ .

______________________ Recipient

______________________ Investor

All this was done in front of us, the below signatories, and we signed at the direction of the Parties.

______________________ Witness

______________________ Witness

RABBINICAL COURT
MAYSHARIM
GUIDED BY RABBI NISSIM KARELITZ
BAIS DIN TZEDEK OF BNEI BRAK

בית דין צדק
מישרים
בהכוונת בית דין צדק - בני ברק
בראשות מרן הגאון **רבי נסים קרליץ** שליט"א

Iska for a Deposit on New Construction

I, ____________________ ("Recipient"), have received $______ from ____________ ("Investor"), for investment in an *iska* partnership, subject to the following terms:

1. Partnership

In exchange for the money received, I hereby assign to the Investing Partner a share (in the value of the money received) in all investments, businesses, and real estate that I own. If I identify a specific investment that I believe will be more profitable, I shall transfer and assign to the Investing Partner a share of that investment.

2. Profits and Losses

(a) Any profits, capital gains, or losses arising from this investment shall be borne by the Investor. However, Recipient shall receive 5 percent (5%) of profits as a management fee.

(b) Any claim regarding the amount of profits generated by this investment shall be verified under solemn oath, administered by an Orthodox Jewish Court of Law.

(c) Any claim of loss must be verified through the testimony of two qualified witnesses, before an Orthodox Jewish Court of Law.

(d) It is agreed that if I sell to the Investor the property and improvements described in the attached document, as per the terms and conditions of said documents, then I will not be required to take an oath, nor will I be required to notify the partner regarding the profits that were realized. Additional profits, if any, shall be my sole property.

Office & Mailing Address: 625 Forest Avenue, Lakewood, N.J. 08701 • **Telephone:** 732.905.3388 • **Fax:** 732.905.5880

Rabbinical Courtrooms: 625 Forest Avenue, Lakewood, N.J. (Rear Entrance) **לשכות הבד"צ:**
2913 Avenue L, Brooklyn, N.Y. (Lower Level)

RABBINICAL COURT
MAYSHARIM
GUIDED BY RABBI NISSIM KARELITZ
BAIS DIN TZEDEK OF BNEI BRAK

בית דין צדק
מישרים
בהכוונת בית דין צדק - בני ברק
בראשות מרן הגאון **רבי נסים קרליץ** שליט"א

3. Miscellaneous

This agreement supersedes any other agreement between the two Parties in regards to these funds.

4. Dispute Resolution

All disputes that may arise regarding or associated with this Agreement shall be resolved and established exclusively by binding arbitration at the ______________________ (name of mutually agreed-upon *beis din*). Judgment rendered by the aforesaid authority may be entered in any court having jurisdiction thereof. The non-prevailing Party shall be liable to the prevailing Party for all costs and expenses related to any dispute-resolution proceeding, including reasonable attorney's fees.

This agreement shall follow the guidelines of *heter iska* as explained in *Sefer Bris Yehudah*. This Agreement is intended to be, and is, binding, consistent with the binding nature of all agreements, documents, obligations, and acquisitions that are properly effected in a Jewish Court of Law in accordance with the laws and rules established by Rabbinical authorities. A proper *kinyan suddar* was executed to create this partnership. This is all valid and in good standing.

We hereby affix our signatures on this ________ day of __________ 20 ___ .

______________________ Recipient

______________________ Investor

All this was done in front of us, the below signatories, and we signed at the direction of the Parties.

______________________ Witness

______________________ Witness

RABBINICAL COURT
MAYSHARIM
GUIDED BY RABBI NISSIM KARELITZ
BAIS DIN TZEDEK OF BNEI BRAK

בית דין צדק
מישרים
בהכוונת בית דין צדק - בני ברק
בראשות מרן הגאון רבי נסים קרליץ שליט"א

Dispute Resolution

All disputes that may arise regarding or associated with this Agreement shall be resolved and established exclusively by binding arbitration at the ______________________ (name of mutually agreed-upon *beis din*) or its designee. Judgment rendered by the aforesaid authority may be entered in any court having jurisdiction thereof.

This Agreement Validation clause is intended to be added as a rider to legal CONTRACTS. An attorney and a *dayan* familiar with the particulars of the courts and the secular laws should be consulted before executing any of these documents.

Agreement Validation

The Parties hereby admit and confess (with the same effect as if verified by the testimony of 100 valid and consistent witnesses) that all of the terms, obligations, and covenants set out in the various agreements, contracts and/or *heter iskas* (collective "AGREEMENT") executed today between the undersigned Parties were effected and finalized concurrently herewith according to Jewish Law by formal *kinyan agav suddar*, and were stated and intended to be effective immediately, all in full accordance with all requisite procedures set out in the Code of Jewish Law (the "Code") and with use of a valid *suddar*. The *kinyan* was made in a duly constituted Orthodox Jewish Court of Law (*beis din chashuv*) in accordance with each of the varying procedures required by all of the various Jewish halachic authorities, so that all Jewish halachic authorities deem the terms, obligations, and covenants valid, without any *asmachta* (as defined in the Code)

Office & Mailing Address: 625 Forest Avenue, Lakewood, N.J. 08701 • **Telephone:** 732.905.3388 • **Fax:** 732.905.5880

Rabbinical Courtrooms: 625 Forest Avenue, Lakewood, N.J. (Rear Entrance) **לשכות הבד"צ:**
2913 Avenue L, Brooklyn, N.Y. (Lower Level)

RABBINICAL COURT
MAYSHARIM
GUIDED BY RABBI NISSIM KARELITZ
BAIS DIN TZEDEK OF BNEI BRAK

בית דין צדק
מישרים
בהכוונת בית דין צדק - בני ברק
בראשות מרן הגאון **רבי נסים קרליץ** שליט"א

claim of invalidation and without any other claim of invalidation. In addition, the conditions referred to in this Agreement are and were all set in the manner used by *Bnei Gad* and *Bnei Reuven* and in accordance with all other requirements that are set out in the Code for the valid and binding setting of conditions.

The Parties specifically acknowledge that although the agreement was drafted in accordance with secular legal terminology, the intent of the Parties was to create immediate and binding monetary obligations. Any terminology describing a *Kinyan Devarim* or *Ein Bo Mamash* is for legal purposes only.

The Parties accept as conclusive and binding the position of any Jewish halachic authority, even if in the minority or otherwise not generally accepted, that most broadly supports the validity and enforceability of this Agreement and its implied intent. The Parties irrevocably and without time limit invalidate and disqualify any witness or judge who testifies or rules, or seeks to testify or rule, that any provision of this Agreement that either Party seeks to enforce is void or unenforceable, in whole or in part, by reason of any defense, counterclaim, or otherwise.

The Parties are agreeing to all provisions of this Agreement knowingly and willingly and without duress or pressure. The Parties, irrevocably and without time limit, void any declaration of disclaimer (including any declaration of disclaimer that purports to disclaim the voiding effect of this paragraph, ad infinitum) that they may ever have made regarding this Agreement, and they represent and warrant that they did not make or purport to make any such declaration of disclaimer. The Parties hereby irrevocably void and waive any defense or counterclaim that could void or impair or in any way limit the validity and enforceability of this Agreement.

This Agreement is intended to be, and is, binding, consistent with the binding nature of all agreements, documents, obligations, and

RABBINICAL COURT
MAYSHARIM
GUIDED BY RABBI NISSIM KARELITZ
BAIS DIN TZEDEK OF BNEI BRAK

בית דין צדק
מישרים
בהכוונת בית דין צדק - בני ברק
בראשות מרן הגאון רבי נסים קרליץ שליט"א

acquisitions that are properly effected in a Jewish Court of Law in accordance with the laws and rules established by Rabbinical authorities. THIS IS ALL VALID AND IN GOOD STANDING.

We hereby affix our signatures on this ______ day of ________ 20 ___ .

______________________ Recipient

______________________ Investor

All this was done in front of us, the below signatories, and we signed at the direction of the Parties.

______________________ Witness

______________________ Witness

RABBINICAL COURT
MAYSHARIM
GUIDED BY RABBI NISSIM KARELITZ
BAIS DIN TZEDEK OF BNEI BRAK

בית דין צדק
מישרים
בהכוונת בית דין צדק - בני ברק
בראשות מרן הגאון רבי נסים קרליץ שליט"א

Agreement to Submit to Arbitration

WE, the undersigned (Parties), hereby agree to submit to binding arbitration all the controversies (claims and counterclaims) between the undersigned Parties, including without limitation:

____

____

WE further agree that the controversy be heard and determined by a panel of any three arbitrators (Arbitrators) of __________________ (Court). It is agreed that all the Court's fees, costs, and expenses, including without limitation the costs of any experts required in reaching a decision, shall be divided evenly amongst the Parties; that partial or final adjudication of the controversy may be withheld if there are any outstanding fees, costs, or expenses owed to the Court; that the Arbitrators may make their award based upon *din Torah*, compromise, settlement, or any other way they wish to reach a decision; that the Arbitrators shall be empowered to issue such intermediate decisions or orders as they deem necessary; that no transcript nor recording of the proceeding need be made; that the Parties waive the right to cross-examination except under the procedures set by the Arbitrators; that the Arbitrators may follow any procedure as they decide; that the Arbitrators may determine evidentiary issues; that the Arbitrators shall be empowered to issue subpoenas for witnesses and the production of documents; that the arbitration may be conducted in whole or in part in a language other than English; that hearings may be held on Sundays and other legal holidays; that it shall be the decision of the Arbitrators as to

Office & Mailing Address: 625 Forest Avenue, Lakewood, N.J. 08701 • **Telephone:** 732.905.3388 • **Fax:** 732.905.5880

Rabbinical Courtrooms: 625 Forest Avenue, Lakewood, N.J. (Rear Entrance) **:לשכות הבד"צ**
2913 Avenue L, Brooklyn, N.Y. (Lower Level)

RABBINICAL COURT
MAYSHARIM
GUIDED BY RABBI NISSIM KARELITZ
BAIS DIN TZEDEK OF BNEI BRAK

בית דין צדק
מישרים
בהכוונת בית דין צדק - בני ברק
בראשות מרן הגאון רבי נסים קרליץ שליט"א

whether a matter is related to the dispute or not; that the award of the Arbitrators shall be in writing and shall be signed by a majority of the Arbitrators and need not be acknowledged or notarized to be confirmed or enforced; that the Arbitrators need not explain to the Parties or to anyone else the reason for their decision; that in the event that one Arbitrator resigns, is incapacitated, or can not continue for any other reason, the remaining two Arbitrators may elect to continue the proceeding and they shall have the same powers and authority.

WE understand that we have the right to be represented by attorneys and/or other advisers in the arbitration at any time, but that any Party may elect to proceed without an attorney, and the Parties shall have the right to argue for themselves before the Arbitrators. The Parties hereby waive formal notice of the time and place of the arbitration proceeding and consent that the arbitration be held and commence with the jurisdiction of the Arbitrators to continue until a final award be made. The Parties agree that the Arbitrators shall have the right to hear testimony and evidence without the presence of a Party if the Party does not attend a scheduled hearing. In the event that a Party is a corporate entity, the undersigned fully warrants that he has full rights and authority to represent said corporate entity and enter into this Agreement on its behalf. In the event that after an award is made, a dispute between the Parties arises as to the interpretation of the award, compliance of the Parties, or if a Party motions for reargument due to a claim of a judicial error or new evidence, etc., the Parties agree that the Arbitrators shall have binding jurisdiction on the matters, and the Parties authorize the Arbitrators to add to, amend, change, or clarify a decision, to the extent permitted by law. In the event that a Party does not abide by and perform any award or decision rendered by the Arbitrators

RABBINICAL COURT
MAYSHARIM
GUIDED BY RABBI NISSIM KARELITZ
BAIS DIN TZEDEK OF BNEI BRAK

בית דין צדק
מישרים
בהכוונת בית דין צדק - בני ברק
בראשות מרן הגאון **רבי נסים קרליץ** שליט"א

or seeks to vacate such decision or award, the Parties authorize the Arbitrators to award additional fees and legal costs.

WE further agree not to subpoena any Member of the Court as witnesses in a hearing held in a secular or religious court concerning this proceeding, not to bring suit against any Member in a secular or religious court, and waive any claims against all Members arising from their conduct of this arbitration. The Parties agree to fully indemnify and hold harmless the Members individually and jointly for any expenses, fees, loss, damage, or outlay, including without limitation all attorney fees and court costs which the Members may at any time sustain, incur, or be exposed to in relation to any subpoenas or suit instituted or threatened against the Members jointly or individually in connection to this controversy.

WE further agree to faithfully abide by and perform any interim or final award or decision rendered by the Arbitrators. The decree of the Arbitrators shall be enforceable in the courts in the State of New Jersey and/or New York. The Arbitrators shall not be required to take an oath or administer an oath to any witness or Party at the hearing. The terms of this agreement are severable, and the illegality or viability of any terms of this agreement shall not affect the remainder of this agreement, which shall remain valid and enforceable. The Parties submit themselves to the personal jurisdiction of the courts of the State of New Jersey and/or New York for any action or proceeding to confirm or enforce a decree of the Arbitrators pursuant to NJSA 2A:24-1 et. seq. and Article 75 of the New York Civil Practice Law and Rules. All notices and service of the Arbitrators' award shall be sufficient if a) personally delivered or b) deposited in the U.S. Mail by regular or certified mail or c) deposited with a reputable private courier service, directed to a Party at his/

RABBINICAL COURT
MAYSHARIM
GUIDED BY RABBI NISSIM KARELITZ
BAIS DIN TZEDEK OF BNEI BRAK

בית דין צדק
מישרים
בהכוונת בית דין צדק - בני ברק
בראשות מרן הגאון רבי נסים קרליץ שליט"א

her last-known address. All notices shall be effective upon such personal delivery, or two (2) business days after being deposited in the U. S. Mail or with private courier service as noted above.

Dated __________ 20 ___ .

Signature	Signature
Print Name	Print Name
Signature	Signature
Print Name	Print Name

RABBINICAL COURT
MAYSHARIM
GUIDED BY RABBI NISSIM KARELITZ
BAIS DIN TZEDEK OF BNEI BRAK

בית דין צדק
מישרים
בהכוונת בית דין צדק - בני ברק
בראשות מרן הגאון רבי נסים קרליץ שליט"א

מ·י·ש·ר·י·ם

Partnership and Lease-to-Own Agreement

THIS PARTNERSHIP and LEASE-TO-OWN AGREEMENT ("Agreement") made and effective today, by and between the following individuals, referred to in this Agreement as the "Parties": ______________ ("Lessor"), and ______________ ("Lessee"), in regard to the real estate property located at ______________ ("Property").

The Parties wish to set forth, in a written Agreement, the terms and conditions by which they will associate themselves in the Partnership.

NOW, THEREFORE, in consideration of the promises contained in this Agreement, the Parties hereby obligate themselves and affirm in writing their association as a Partnership in accordance with the following provisions:

1. Title to Partnership Property

If, for purposes of confidentiality or otherwise, title to Partnership property is taken in the name of any individual Party, the assets shall be considered to be owned by the Partnership and all beneficial interests shall accrue to the Parties in the percentages set forth in this Agreement. The Partnership shall compensate said nominee or individual Party for all costs and consequences, tax or otherwise, relating to his taking title of Property.

Lessor has advanced ____________ (amount) and Lessee has advanced ____________ (amount); each Party has attained ownership of the Property in a percentage proportionate to his investment.

2. Rent and Terms

Lessor hereby demises his portion of Property ______________ ("Lessor's Portion") to Lessee for a ____________ (length of time) term commencing

RABBINICAL COURT
MAYSHARIM
GUIDED BY RABBI NISSIM KARELITZ
BAIS DIN TZEDEK OF BNEI BRAK

בית דין צדק
מישרים
בהכוונת בית דין צדק - בני ברק
בראשות מרן הגאון **רבי נסים קרליץ** שליט"א

on ________ (date). Lessee shall pay to Lessor a monthly rental fee equivalent to the monthly interest amount Lessor is obligated to pay his lender for the mortgage associated with the Property. In addition, as rental for Lessor's Portion, Lessee shall pay all sewer and water charges, taxes, fines, insurance, and other costs associated with the Property. Furthermore, as additional rent, Lessee shall maintain adequate insurance so that Lessor may suffer no loss in case of suit of damage to the Property. Lessee shall maintain Property in good condition at all times and pay for its normal upkeep. Any costs or reduction in Property value which result from Lessee's failure to honor these terms shall be borne by Lessee alone.

3. Purchase

Lessor agrees to sell, and Lessee agrees to purchase, Lessor's Portion over the next _____ years, in monthly increments equivalent to the monthly principal amount Lessor is obligated to pay his lender for the mortgage associated with the Property. The monthly proportionate amount of Lessor's Portion shall be sold to Lessee when each respective payment is made. Lessee may at any time purchase any additional portion of Lessor's Portion. Lessor agrees not to create any lien on the Property without written permission from Lessee. Lessor accepts responsibility for any damage to Property by theft or loss, excluding losses caused by Lessee's failure to obtain appropriate insurance.

4. Default

In the event Lessee fails to make timely monthly payments or otherwise comply with any provision set forth in this Agreement, Lessor may, at Lessor's option, immediately terminate this Agreement, dissolve Partnership, liquidate Property, and/or

RABBINICAL COURT
MAYSHARIM
GUIDED BY RABBI NISSIM KARELITZ
BAIS DIN TZEDEK OF BNEI BRAK

בית דין צדק
מישרים
בהכוונת בית דין צדק · בני ברק
בראשות מרן הגאון **רבי נסים קרליץ** שליט"א

exercise any and all other rights and remedies available to Lessor at law or in equity.

5. Dispute Resolution

All disputes that may arise regarding or associated with this Agreement shall be resolved and established exclusively by binding arbitration at the ______________________ (name of mutually agreed-upon *beis din*) or its designee. Judgment rendered by the aforesaid authority may be entered in any court having jurisdiction thereof. The non-prevailing Party shall be liable to the prevailing Party for all costs and expenses related to any dispute-resolution proceeding, including reasonable attorney fees.

6. General

This Agreement contains the entire agreement of the Parties with respect to the Partnership and lease-to-own arrangement and supersedes any previous oral or written communications, representations, understandings, or agreements between the Parties or any representative thereof; and may be amended only by the written agreement executed and delivered by all of the Parties. This agreement shall follow the guidelines established in *Igros Moshe*, *Yoreh Deah* 2:62.

7. Binding Upon Heirs

This Agreement shall bind each of the Parties and shall inure to the benefit of and be binding upon their respective heirs, executors, administrators, devisees, legatees, successors, and assigns.

8. Agreement Validation

The Parties hereby admit and confess (with the same effect as if verified by the testimony of 100 valid and consistent witnesses) that all of the terms, obligations, and covenants set out in this Agreement were effected and finalized concurrently herewith

RABBINICAL COURT
MAYSHARIM
GUIDED BY RABBI NISSIM KARELITZ
BAIS DIN TZEDEK OF BNEI BRAK

בית דין צדק
מישרים
בהכוונת בית דין צדק - בני ברק
בראשות מרן הגאון **רבי נסים קרליץ** שליט"א

according to Jewish Law by formal *kinyan agav suddar*, and were stated and intended to be effective immediately, all in full accordance with all requisite procedures set out in the Code of Jewish Law (the "Code") and with use of a *valid suddar*. The *kinyan* was made in a duly constituted Orthodox Jewish Court of Law (*beis din chashuv*) in accordance with each of the varying procedures required by all of the various Jewish halachic authorities, so that all Jewish halachic authorities deem the terms, obligations, and covenants valid, without any *asmachta* (as defined in the Code) claim of invalidation and without any other claim of invalidation. In addition, the conditions referred to in this Agreement are and were all set in the manner used by *Bnei Gad* and *Bnei Reuven* and in accordance with all other requirements that are set out in the Code for the valid and binding setting of conditions.

The Parties accept as conclusive and binding the position of any Jewish halachic authority, even if in the minority or otherwise not generally accepted, that most broadly supports the validity and enforceability of this Agreement and its implied intent. The Parties irrevocably and without time limit invalidate and disqualify any witness or judge who testifies or rules, or seeks to testify or rule, that any provision of this Agreement that either party seeks to enforce, is void or unenforceable, in whole or in part, by reason of any defense, counterclaim, or otherwise.

The Parties are agreeing to all provisions of this Agreement knowingly and willingly and without duress or pressure. The Parties, irrevocably and without time limit, void any declaration of disclaimer (including any declaration of disclaimer that purports to disclaim the voiding effect of this paragraph, ad infinitum) that they may ever have made regarding this Agreement, and they represent and warrant that they did not make or purport to make any such declaration of disclaimer. The Parties hereby irrevocably

RABBINICAL COURT
MAYSHARIM
GUIDED BY RABBI NISSIM KARELITZ
BAIS DIN TZEDEK OF BNEI BRAK

בית דין צדק
מישרים
בהכוונת בית דין צדק - בני ברק
בראשות מרן הגאון **רבי נסים קרליץ** שליט"א

void and waive any defense or counterclaim that could void or impair or in any way limit the validity and enforceability of this Agreement.

This Agreement is intended to be, and is, binding, consistent with the binding nature of all agreements, documents, obligations, and acquisitions that are properly effected in a Jewish Court of Law in accordance with the laws and rules established by Rabbinical authorities. THIS IS ALL VALID AND IN GOOD STANDING.

We hereby affix our signatures on this ______ day of ________ 20 __ .

____________________	____________________
Recipient	Investor

All this was done in front of us, the below signatories, and we signed at the direction of the Parties.

____________________	____________________
Witness	Witness

RABBINICAL COURT
MAYSHARIM
GUIDED BY RABBI NISSIM KARELITZ
BAIS DIN TZEDEK OF BNEI BRAK

בית דין צדק
מישרים
בהכוונת בית דין צדק - בני ברק
בראשות מרן הגאון רבי נסים קרליץ שליט"א

Heter Iska Klali

The undersigned, as authorized representatives of ______________ hereby declare and admit that any agreements entered into by the above-mentioned company that would violate any of the laws of *ribbis* shall be structured as an *iska* partnership. The *iska* partnership shall be subject to the following terms.

All profits and losses shall be shared equally between the Investing and Managing Partners. The Managing Partner must verify any claim of loss through the testimony of two halachically acceptable witnesses in an Orthodox Jewish Court of Law. Any claim regarding the amount of profits generated by the joint venture must be verified with a solemn oath, administered by an Orthodox Jewish court of law. In the event that it is halachically preferable, this *iska* shall be structured as *kulo pekadon.*

In the event of a claim of loss, the Investing Partner may demand a full and immediate payment of the remaining balance of this *iska.*

The Managing Partners obligate themselves to manage the *iska* partnership in the manner deemed most beneficial to the Investing partner. All investments owned by the Managing Partners shall be used to create this *iska* partnership, provided that the ventures are halachically permissible. In the event that the Managing Partner identifies a specific investment that he believes will generate greater returns, he shall assign that investment to the Investing Partner. The Managing Partner shall be paid one dollar for his services during the term of the *iska.*

It is agreed that if the Managing Partner pays the amount equal to the principal, fees, points, penalties, interest, plus any other

Office & Mailing Address: 625 Forest Avenue, Lakewood, N.J. 08701 • **Telephone:** 732.905.3388 • **Fax:** 732.905.5880

Rabbinical Courtrooms: 625 Forest Avenue, Lakewood, N.J. (Rear Entrance) **:לשכות הבד"צ**
2913 Avenue L, Brooklyn, N.Y. (Lower Level)

payments called for by a contract signed by the two Parties, as per the payment schedule of said contract, the Investing Partner shall waive his right to demand verification of the results of the investment. These payments include the one-dollar token payment mentioned above. Any additional profits shall belong solely to the Managing Partner.

Any payments made that are not justified by this *iska* agreement shall reduce the principal balance of this *iska*. Any future payments that are made to avoid the above-mentioned verification shall be increased to compensate for any discrepancy.

This document shall override any other agreements, even those that do not reference this document. Any mention of loans or interest shall be interpreted as an *iska* and to payments mentioned above. No agent of the company shall be authorized to enter into any agreements that violate the laws of *ribbis* or this *iska*. This declaration is legally binding and may be enforced in any Jewish or civil court, even in the event that one of the Parties was unaware of its existence.

This document is intended to be, and is, binding, consistent with the binding nature of all agreements, documents, obligations, and acquisitions that are properly effected in a duly constituted Jewish Court of Law in accordance with the laws and rules established by Rabbinical authorities. THIS IS ALL VALID AND IN GOOD STANDING.

We hereby affix our signatures on this ______ day of ________ 20 ___ .

______________________ ______________________

RABBINICAL COURT
MAYSHARIM
GUIDED BY RABBI NISSIM KARELITZ
BAIS DIN TZEDEK OF BNEI BRAK

בית דין צדק
מישרים
בהכוונת בית דין צדק - בני ברק
בראשות מרן הגאון **רבי נסים קרליץ** שליט״א

מ·י·ש·ר·י·ם

שטר בירורין

אנו, בעלי הדינים החתומים מטה, מודים בהודאה גמורה וחתימת ידינו תעיד עלינו יותר ממאה עדים כשרים ונאמנים, שקיבלנו עלינו לסדר כל טענותינו בהדין ודברים שבינינו, כולל כל התביעות וכל התביעות הנגדיות של הצדדים, אצל הרבנים הדיינים, הרה״ג מוהר״ר__________ שליט״א, והרה״ג מוהר״ר__________ שליט״א, והרה״ג מוהר״ר __________ שליט״א, והתחייבנו ומחלנו ככל שיפסקו עלינו הן דין [הן פשר קרוב לדין הן פשר] הן טעות אפילו טעות בדבר משנה, וקיבלנו לציית לפסק דינם בלי שום השמטה וערעור כלל.

והותנה במפורש ונמחל מראש שיכולים הדיינים לדון ולקבל עדות בכל זמן ועת שירצו, אפילו בלילה או בערב שבת וכדומה; [ושיכולים לדון אף אם שמעו דברי בעל דין אחד שלא בפני בעל דין חבירו;] ושאם אחד מבעלי הדין ישתמט מהדין תורה, שאז יכולים הבי״ד להמשיך הדין תורה ולשמוע טענות והוכחות ולקבל עדות ולפסוק הדין תורה אף שלא בפניו; ושסמכות הבי״ד תהא בתקפה עד לסוף ביצוע פסק הדין; ושבידם להכריע בנוגע כל סכסוך בביצוע פסק הדין, או בפירוש פסק הדין, וכן בידם להכריע במקרה שאי מהצדדים יש לו טענות או ראיות לסתור את הדין, וכמו כן אם בפסק הדין לא הכריעו (מאיזה טעם שיהיה) על כל הנושאים שהיו שייכים להדין תורה, יש בידם להכריע ולפסוק ע״ז גם אח״כ; ושההכרעה תהא על דעת רוב הבי״ד, והרוב יוכל להכריע אף אם אחד מהדיינים יסתלק ואף אם אחד מהדיינים יאמר איני יודע; ושלא יהא בידינו לשאול ״מאיזה טעם דנתוני״; ושיש בידם לקבוע המציאות ע״פ אומד דעתם ולפסוק כפי נטיית הכרעתם; ושלא יהא כח לשום בי״ד שבעולם לבטל או לשנות פסק הדין אף אם לפי דעתם טעו הדיינים הנ״ל, ורק אם הדיינים בעצמם יחליטו על פי רוב דעות שהיה טעות בפסקם, אז בידם לחזור או לשנות פסק הדין; ושנמחל כל תביעת ממון או תביעה אחרת שיכולה להיות לנו עליהם. ~~~~~~

ובאם אחד או יותר מהחתומים מטה חותמים בשם חברה או עמותה וכיוצ״ב, מצהיר בזאת החותם כי בסמכותו המלאה מכל בחינה שהיא להתדיין בנושאים האמורים לעיל וכי חתימתו דלמטה מחייבת לכל דבר וענין, ובמידה ויתברר שאינו כן אזי הוא מתחייב ונוטל על עצמו אישית את כל החיובים הנובעים משטר בוררין זה בכפוף להחלטת הבי״ד.

Office & Mailing Address: 625 Forest Avenue, Lakewood, N.J. 08701 • **Telephone:** 732.905.3388 • **Fax:** 732.905.5880

Rabbinical Courtrooms: 625 Forest Avenue, Lakewood, N.J. (Rear Entrance) **:לשכות הבד״צ**
2913 Avenue L, Brooklyn, N.Y. (Lower Level)

RABBINICAL COURT
MAYSHARIM
GUIDED BY RABBI NISSIM KARELITZ
BAIS DIN TZEDEK OF BNEI BRAK

בית דין צדק
מישרים
בהכוונת בית דין צדק - בני ברק
בראשות מרן הגאון **רבי נסים קרליץ** שליט"א

וכל הנ"ל נעשה בקנין גמור אגב סודר במנא דכשר למקניא ביי מעכשיו (ר"ל בזמן הקנין) בפני בי"ד חשוב, בצירוף עוד קניינים וחיזוקים באופן היותר מועיל על פי תוה"ק, ובאופן שאין שום חשש קנין דברים או אסמכתא או שום ריעותא שבעולם, ובביטול כל מיני מודעות שבעולם ובביטול כל מודעי דנפיק מגו מודעי עד עולם, ובפסילת עדים שיעידו לבטל שטר זה מחמת איזה חסרון שבעולם, כחומר קניינין ותנאין העשויים כתקנת חז"ל דלא כאסמכתא ודלא כטופסי דשטרי, הכל שריר וקים.

וע"ז באעה"ח ביום ___ לחודש _____ שנת _____ לפ"ק

בעל דין ____________ מורשה ____________ עפ"י צווי בע"ד הנ"ל
בעל דין ____________ מורשה ____________ עפ"י צווי בע"ד הנ"ל
בעל דין ____________ מורשה ____________ עפ"י צווי בע"ד הנ"ל
בעל דין ____________ מורשה ____________ עפ"י צווי בע"ד הנ"ל
בעל דין ____________ מורשה ____________ עפ"י צווי בע"ד הנ"ל

Appendix II

Glossary of Halachic Business Terms

agav — see *kinyan agav.*

ani ha'mehapech — prohibition regarding interfering with another Jew's business deal.

ani ha'menakef — If a person invested significant effort to obtain an item, one may not preempt him.

areiv — guarantor; a person who guarantees a prospective lender that he will repay the loan should the borrower default

areiv kablan — see *areiv stam.*

areiv stam — a guarantor who is liable to repay a loan only if the borrower defaults on his obligations. The lender must first take appropriate steps to collect from the borrower. Only after he is unable to collect from the borrower does he have the right to collect from the guarantor.

In contrast, the lender may collect from an *areiv kablan* immediately and he has no obligation to first approach the borrower to ask for payment.

Today, virtually every guarantor is an *areiv kablan.*

asmachta — lit. reliance; term used by the Talmud for an agreement based on speculation. In general, an *asmachta* involves one party consenting to surrender to the other a certain sum of money, depending on the performance of a certain act or the outcome of a particular event. In each case, the individual obligating himself enters into the agreement "relying" that the outcome will be favorable and that he will not actually have to pay.

avak ribbis — lit. dust of ribbis, secondary ribbis; a form of interest that is prohibited by Rabbinic law. See *ribbis ketzutzah.*

bal talin — Scripture instructs one to pay his Jewish workers in a timely fashion. Delaying payment is prohibited.

bar metzra — law of a neighbor. The Sages enacted that if someone wishes to sell his property, his neighbor who owns an adjacent property has first option to purchase (providing he is willing to pay the price that a third party would). The law goes so far as to invalidate a sale to a third party; the neighbor can take the property away from the purchaser by paying him the purchase price.

b'yomo titein scharo — commandment to pay a worker on the day the wages are due.

chalifin — see *kinyan chalifin.*

chatzi milveh v'chatzi pekadon — the term for a standard *heter iska.* Half the funds are advanced as a loan (*milveh*) for which the borrower accepts full responsibility and the investor does not receive any profits. The other half of the funds are advanced as a *pekadon* for which the investor bears all the risks and all the profits.

chazakah — (a) legal presumption that conditions remain unchanged unless proven otherwise; (b) one of the methods of acquiring real estate by performing an act of improving the property, such as enclosing it with a fence or plowing it in preparation for planting; (c) "established rights" — uncontested usage of another's property establishes the right to such usage; since the owner registered no protest, acquiescence is assumed; (d) uncontested holding of real property for three years as a basis for claiming acquisition of title from the prior owner.

din areiv — law of guarantor. This law provides that in consideration for a lender transferring his money to another party (i.e., the borrower) on the guarantor's say-so, the guarantor obligates himself to repay the loan if the borrower defaults.

dina d'malchusa dina — the concept that secular law has validity and is accepted.

ein ona'ah lekarka — Sales of real estate are not subject to the regular laws of *ona'ah.*

eino b'reshuso — an item that is not yet in one's possession.

forward contract — an agreement whereby a buyer buys goods to be delivered at a later date, at a price fixed at the time of the agreement.

geneivas daas — deception; misleading or misrepresenting.

gud agud — lit. you set or I will set; a formula for the dissolution of a partnership. A partner proposes "gud or agud," meaning "either you set a price for my share and buy it or I will set a price for your share and buy it."

hagbahah — lifting; one of the methods of acquisition used for movable objects.

hamotzi meichaveiro — The burden of proof lies with the one who seeks to remove something from another's possession.

heter iska — an instrument to provide would-be lenders with a way to receive a return on their money without violating the laws of *ribbis.*

heter iska klali — a document stating that all transactions done shall be in accordance with the terms of a *heter iska.*

late-payment penalty — a penalty for late payment. Such a penalty does not constitute *ribbis* when it is a one-time fee imposed on a sale or lease transaction. A charge that increases over time, or a one-time penalty on a loan, is prohibited.

iska — a joint business venture undertaken by two partners. One partner, the financier, supplies the capital (either money or goods) for the venture. The other partner, the recipient of the capital, is the managing or working partner, and he conducts the business. The profits are shared between the partners and the capital is returned to the financier upon the conclusion of the venture. The usual arrangement is that the profits are divided equally.

In such a venture, the arrangement was that the managing partner had no stake whatsoever in the capital, and the share of the profits he received was simply his wage for managing the enterprise. Therefore, in the event the venture failed, all losses had to be sustained by the financier. However, the

Rabbis enacted that the managing partner sustain a share of the losses, corresponding to his share of the profits. Thus, when he undertakes to manage an *iska* for half the profits he also assumes liability for half the losses.

k'poel batul — the reduced salary that a worker would accept if he would be given time off and not required to work (e.g., taking a sabbatical).

kablan — independent contractor.

karka — real estate, real property.

kinyan [pl. **kinyanim**] — formal act of acquisition. An action that causes an agreement or exchange to be legally binding.

kinyan agav — lit. acquisition by dint of; the term for the acquisition of movable property by means of the acquisition of land. The *kinyan* used for the land serves for the movable property.

kinyan chalifin — lit. acquisition by exchange. (a) Even exchange: an exchange of two items of comparable value, in which each item serves as payment for the other. The acquisition of any of the items automatically effects the acquisition of the other. (b) Uneven exchange: An item of relatively negligible value is given in order to effect the acquisition of the item for sale. A handkerchief or the like is traditionally used.

kinyan chatzeir — the acquisition of movable property by virtue of it being in the premises of the person acquiring it.

kinyan chazakah — see *chazakah* (b).

kinyan devarim — A *kinyan* that does not attempt to create a monetary obligation. Such *kinyanim* are not valid in halachah.

kinyan kesef — acquisition through money or an item of value.

kinyan odiysah — acquisition by dint of admission that the object belongs to someone else.

kinyan shtar — acquisition by means of a legal document.

kinyan situmta — lit. acquisition by [making] a mark; an act recognized by custom as a legal mode of acquisition.

kinyan suddar — a mode of transaction in which movable

objects are exchanged to pay for each other. As opposed to the *chalifin* mode, which is a simple barter, here the objects are seen as representing monetary value and are exchanged on that basis. However, unlike a regular cash transaction, this transaction is irrevocably effected upon mere exchange. See also *kinyan chalifin* (b).

kinyan yad — acquisition by holding in one's hand.

kulo pekadon — a *heter iska* form that designates the entire advance as a *pekadon,* for which the investor bears all losses and receives all profits.

lifnei eivar — "Do not place a stumbling block before a blind person." This refers to (a) giving bad advice to someone who is "blind in the matter"; (b) enabling one to violate a prohibition.

lo ba l'olam — something that does not yet exist or is not yet in the seller's possession. (The classic example is an egg that has not yet been laid.)

maruphia — prohibition against pursuing or luring away someone's steady client.

mashkanta — a pledged property. The pledged property is land that a borrower placed in the possession of a lender as security for a debt. Being in possession of the property, the lender has the right to use it and to take its crops. However, such benefits often constitute *ribbis* on the loan. Therefore, the lender has to arrange to reduce the debt periodically in view of the benefit he derives from the pledged property.

mechusar amana — one who reneges on a verbal agreement.

mekach ta'us — a mistaken sale. When a seller delivers to the buyer a defective item, it is deemed a mistaken sale and is invalid.

merei kama — the original owner.

meshichah — pulling, or otherwise causing an object to more; one of the methods of acquisition used for movable property.

mi shepara — lit. the One Who exacted retribution. It is a formal censure issued by *beis din* to a party who retracts from an agreement after payment was made, but before the transaction has been consummated with the appropriate *kinyan.*

migo — lit. since; a rule of procedure. If one makes a claim that seems improbable, it nonetheless must be accepted, "since" had he wished to tell an untruth he would have chosen a more probable claim that is certainly acceptable to the court.

minhag — custom.

minhag hamakom — lit. the custom of the place, i.e., the prevailing norm.

mitaltelin — movable objects.

muchzak — one who has the assumed legal possession of an object.

neshech — lit. a bite. Interest on loans is called *neshech* since it "bites at the borrower."

odiysah — see *kinyan odiysah.*

ona'ah — wronging or cheating. This refers to price fraud — overpaying or underpaying relative to the market value of the item. In general, if the discrepancy between the market price and that paid is one-sixth, the cheated party is entitled to full payment of the discrepancy from the other party. If it is more than a sixth, the sale may be voided.

ona'as devarim — harmful words.

pekadon — an object deposited with a custodian for safekeeping.

poel — salaried worker.

ribbis — a Talmudic term for interest (see *neshech* and *tarbis*).

ribbis ketzutzah — prearranged interest. This is a charge of interest arranged at the time of the loan. This type of interest is prohibited by Biblical law.

sadeh ha'asuyah lita — appropriate (albeit unauthorized) improvements.

sadeh she'ein asuyah lita — atypical improvements. See *sadeh ha'asuyah lita.*

shtar [pl. **shtaros**] — legal document(s).

tarbis — type of interest. The term is often used when referring to interest realized from trading in goods.

tarsha — a sale on credit when a higher price is quoted for delayed payment. Generally, such surcharges are prohibited because they constitute "reward for waiting."

tenai — an explicit conditional clause.

trei tarie — change in price.

tzon barzel — This is a form of *iska* where one partner consigns goods to another with which to engage in business, and the profits are to be shared. However, all losses must be borne by the recipient partner. The value of the goods is assessed at the time of delivery and the recipient partner is fully responsible for that amount, irrespective of whether the venture succeeds or fails. Thus, the financier stands only to gain, not to lose.

yesh lo — lit. he has. Advance payment on a forward contract is generally permitted when the seller has the goods in stock at the time of payment. This condition is known as *yesh lo.*

yored shelo bershus — These laws govern the amount of compensation a worker is entitled to for unauthorized work.

This volume is part of
THE ARTSCROLL SERIES®
an ongoing project of
translations, commentaries and expositions
on Scripture, Mishnah, Talmud, Halachah,
liturgy, history, the classic Rabbinic writings,
biographies and thought.

For a brochure of current publications
visit your local Hebrew bookseller
or contact the publisher:

Mesorah Publications, ltd
4401 Second Avenue
Brooklyn, New York 11232
(718) 921-9000
www.artscroll.com